Frommer's

Banff &
Canadia_____ ___es
day BY day®

4th Edition

by Christie Pashby

FrommerMedia LLC

Contents

Published by:

Frommer Media LLC

Copyright © 2020 by Frommer Media LLC. All rights reserved. No part of this publication may be reproduced, stored in a retrieval system, or transmitted in any form or by any means, electronic, mechanical, photocopying, recording, scanning or otherwise, except as permitted under Sections 107 or 108 of the 1976 United States Copyright Act, without the prior written permission of the Publisher. Requests to the Publisher for permission should be addressed to Support@FrommerMedia.com.

Frommer's is a registered trademark of Arthur Frommer. Frommer Media LLC is not associated with any product or vendor mentioned in this book.

ISBN: 978-1-628-87495-2 (paper); 978-1-628-87496-9 (ebk)

Editorial Director: Pauline Frommer
Editor: Alexis Lipsitz Flippin
Production Editor: Heather Wilcox
Photo Editor: Meghan Lamb
Photo Assistants: Liz Ford and Jill Sakowitz
Cartographer: Roberta Stockwell
Indexer: Maro Riofrancos

Front cover photos, left to right: Panithi Utamachant/Shutterstock.com, Galyna Andrushko/Shutterstock.com, Chris Kolaczan/Shutterstock.com

Back cover photo: Jeff Whyte/Shutterstock.com

For information on our other products or services, see www.frommers.com.

Frommer Media LLC also publishes its books in a variety of electronic formats. Some content that appears in print may not be available in electronic formats.

Manufactured in China

5   4   3   2   1

About This Guide

Organizing your time. That's what this guide is all about.

Other guides give you long lists of things to see and do and then expect you to fit the pieces together. The Day by Day guides are different. These guides tell you the best of everything, and then they show you how to see it in the smartest, most time-efficient way. Our authors have designed detailed itineraries organized by time, neighborhood, or special interest. And each tour comes with a bulleted map that takes you from stop to stop.

Hoping to hike to a lookout above a glacier, ride horseback to a high alpine lake, or give rock-climbing a try? Planning to spend a few days exploring the fresh powder snow on some of the world's finest ski slopes, take a horse-drawn carriage ride under the winter stars, or mush with dog sleds across a frozen meadow? Whatever your interest or schedule, the Day by Day guides give you the smartest routes to follow. Not only do we take you to the top attractions, hotels, and restaurants, but we also help you access those special moments that locals get to experience—those "finds" that turn tourists into travelers.

The Day by Days are also your top choice if you're looking for one complete guide for all your travel needs. The best hotels and restaurants for every budget, the greatest shopping values, the wildest nightlife—it's all here.

Why should you trust our judgment? Because our authors personally visit each place they write about. They're an independent lot who say what they think and would never include places they wouldn't recommend to their best friends. They're also open to suggestions from readers. If you'd like to contact them, please send your comments our way at feedback@frommers.com, and we'll pass them on.

Enjoy your Day by Day guide—the most helpful travel companion you can buy. And have the trip of a lifetime.

About the Author

Christie Pashby, author of this edition and the many previous editions of Frommer's guidebooks to the Canadian Rockies, has lived in the beautiful Canadian Rockies of Alberta, Canada, for 20 years. She holds a BA from McGill University and a Bachelor of Journalism degree from the University of King's College. In addition to writing countless travel guides to South America and Canada for Frommer's and working as a freelance writer and content creator, Christie now explores the far corners of the world with her favorite travel buddy, her young daughter, Manuela.

An Additional Note

Please be advised that travel information is subject to change at any time—and this is especially true of prices. We therefore suggest that you write or call ahead for confirmation when making your travel plans. The authors, editors, and publisher cannot be held responsible for the experiences of readers while traveling. Your safety is important to us, however, so we encourage you to stay alert and be aware of your surroundings.

Star Ratings, Icons & Abbreviations

Every hotel, restaurant, and attraction listing in this guide has been ranked for quality, value, service, amenities, and special features using a **star-rating system.** Hotels, restaurants, attractions, shopping, and nightlife are rated on a scale of zero stars (recommended) to three stars (exceptional). In addition to the star-rating system, we also use a **kids icon** to point out the best bets for families. Within each tour, we recommend cafes, bars, or restaurants where you can take a break. Each of these stops appears in a shaded box marked with a coffee-cup-shaped bullet 🍵.

Frommers.com

Now that you have this guidebook to help you plan a great trip, visit our website at **www.frommers.com** for additional travel information on more than 4,000 destinations. We update features regularly to give you instant access to the most current trip-planning information available. At Frommers.com, you'll find scoops on the best airfares, lodging rates, and car rental bargains. You can even book your travel online through our reliable travel booking partners. Other popular features include:

- Online updates of our most popular guidebooks

- Vacation sweepstakes and contest giveaways

- Newsletters highlighting the hottest travel trends

- Online travel message boards with featured travel discussions

A Note on Prices

In the "Take a Break" (🍵) and "Best Bets" sections of this book, we have used a system of dollar signs to show a range of costs for 1 night in a hotel (the price of a double-occupancy room) or the cost of an entree at a restaurant. Use the following table to decipher the dollar signs:

Cost	Hotels	Restaurants
$	under $100	under $10
$$	$100–$200	$10–$20
$$$	$200–$300	$20–$30
$$$$	$300–$400	$30–$40
$$$$$	over $400	over $40

How to Contact Us

In researching this book, we discovered many wonderful places—hotels, restaurants, shops, and more. We're sure you'll find others. Please tell us about them, so we can share the information with your fellow travelers in upcoming editions. If you were disappointed with a recommendation, we'd love to know that, too. Please write to: Support@FrommerMedia.com.

18 Favorite
Moments

18 Favorite Moments

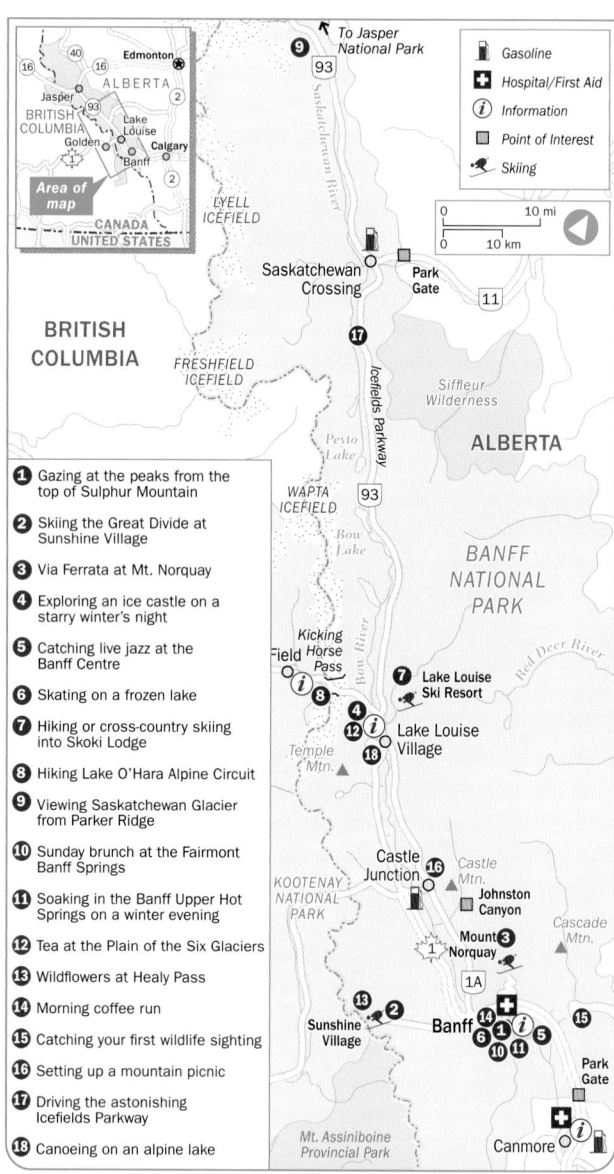

1 Gazing at the peaks from the top of Sulphur Mountain

2 Skiing the Great Divide at Sunshine Village

3 Via Ferrata at Mt. Norquay

4 Exploring an ice castle on a starry winter's night

5 Catching live jazz at the Banff Centre

6 Skating on a frozen lake

7 Hiking or cross-country skiing into Skoki Lodge

8 Hiking Lake O'Hara Alpine Circuit

9 Viewing Saskatchewan Glacier from Parker Ridge

10 Sunday brunch at the Fairmont Banff Springs

11 Soaking in the Banff Upper Hot Springs on a winter evening

12 Tea at the Plain of the Six Glaciers

13 Wildflowers at Healy Pass

14 Morning coffee run

15 Catching your first wildlife sighting

16 Setting up a mountain picnic

17 Driving the astonishing Icefields Parkway

18 Canoeing on an alpine lake

Previous page: Canoes on Moraine Lake.

Banff has been drawing visitors to the Canadian Rocky Mountains for more than a century. They're drawn primarily to nature and the stunning landscapes. It's not necessarily hip (although Banff has trendy restaurants), and it's certainly nothing new. Banff is dependable yet surprising, a place to stretch yourself physically and reward yourself mentally. The following are some of my favorite experiences in Canada's premier mountain wilderness.

❶ Gazing at the peaks from the top of Sulphur Mountain. It's the easiest summit in the Canadian Rockies. Take the 8-minute gondola ride to the top of Sulphur Mountain, then walk the elevated 1km (⅔-mile) boardwalk to Sanson Peak, a truly jaw-dropping lookout. Six mountain ranges are arrayed beneath you. There's a great restaurant and impressive interpretive displays at the top. Hardcore hikers can hike up the 5.3km (3.3-mile) switchback trail and then reward their knees by riding the gondola down. See p 13, ❸.

❷ Skiing the Great Divide at Sunshine Village. On a perfect winter day, catch the Continental Divide chair up to the top of Lookout Mountain, crossing from Alberta into British Columbia en route. The view of Mt. Assiniboine, the "Matterhorn of the Rockies," is magnificent, and when the powder is fresh and the sun is shining, your ski back down will be even more thrilling. See p 43, ❿.

❸ Via Ferrata at Norquay. Banff now has its own amazing Via Ferrata, an assisted climbing experience that involves a series of ladders, hanging bridges, and out-of-this-world views, all with an expert to lead the way. If you want some adrenaline, this is the best place to find it! See p 152.

❹ Exploring an ice castle on a starry winter's night. Late January brings the annual Ice Magic event to the frozen shores of Lake Louise. Under the dark sky and beneath the icy glaciers of Mt. Victoria, carvers from around the world craft magical creations, culminating with a frozen castle that stays on the lake as long as the lake is frozen. Rent some skates at the Fairmont

Sulphur Mountain offers the easiest summit in the Canadian Rockies.

The Via Ferrata is a protected climbing route that can accommodate climbers of varying abilities.

Chateau Lake Louise, snuggle by the outdoor fire, and sip hot chocolate—the ingredients of a midwinter's dream come true. See p 162.

5 Catching live jazz at the Banff Centre. Year-round concerts at this globally renowned arts and cultural center bring in some of the sharpest musicians from around the world. During the summer, many shows go outside at a beautiful amphitheater. An inspiring way to spend the evening! See p 55, ⑮.

6 Skating on a frozen lake. Clear as glass on a crisp winter day, the shallow Vermillion Lakes, close to the Town of Banff, make for a magical ice rink. The mountain views and glimpses of fish wintering below the ice add to the icy drama. What could be more Canadian? Just be sure to check ice thickness with Parks Canada first. In Jasper, try Pyramid Lake. See p 42, ❸.

7 Hiking or cross-country skiing into Skoki Lodge. This historic cabin tucked in the woods behind Lake Louise Ski Resort may be the place that defines rustic mountain charm. The 11km (6.8-mile) trail leads to a wooden cabin with private rooms, home cooking, endless trails—and no electricity or running water. It's like stepping back in time to a pure and unspoiled mountain retreat. See p 81.

8 Hiking the Lake O'Hara Alpine Circuit. Just the word "O'Hara" brings oohs and aahs from veteran hikers. Across the British Columbia border behind Lake Louise, in Yoho National Park, this is an exquisite hiking destination, dotted with meadows, lookouts, ridge-walks, turquoise lakes, and meticulously chiseled stone trails. Choose from a half-dozen superb hikes, but the Alpine Circuit highlights the best of the best. Remember to book your bus ride up to the lake well in advance. See p 26, Day 9.

9 Viewing the Saskatchewan Glacier from Parker Ridge. Hike for just over an hour for views even more stunning than those you can see from your car on the Icefields Parkway. The trail starts steeply but soon plateaus out into the subalpine zone, offering gorgeous views of the Saskatchewan Glacier and Mt. Athabasca. Don't forget to look down and around you too—you may see fossils, rosy finches, mountain goats, and maybe even a grizzly bear. For solitude and spectacular vistas, few short hikes in the world can compare. See p 46, ❼.

⑩ Sunday brunch at the Fairmont Banff Springs. In the stately Vermillion Room inside this legendary hotel, you can sample a stellar array of gourmet Canadiana, from smoked Wild Pacific salmon and free-range eggs Benedict to roasted Alberta beef and maple brownies. Ask for a window table for views of Fairholme Range and Bow River and bring your appetite. Reservations recommended. *See p 13,* ❷.

⑪ Soaking in the Banff Upper Hot Springs on a winter evening. If it's cold and you've been skiing all day, you're in the right town—just head to the historic bathhouse to relax in the natural hot pools (ranging from 99°–104°F/37°–40°C), open until 10pm weeknights in winter and 11pm on winter weekends. Other hot springs in the mountain parks worth visiting include Miette Hot Springs in Jasper National Park and the Radium Hot Springs in Kootenay National Park. *See p 14,* ❼.

⑫ Tea at the Plain of the Six Glaciers. Drawing hikers since 1924, this historic tea house is a rustic cabin nestled in a gorgeous location at the back of Lake Louise. It's a 2-hour hike to get here—surely

The crystal-clear surface of Lake O'Hara.

you deserve a piece of chocolate cake or banana loaf? Take your pot of tea and sit outside to marvel at the six glaciers that cling to Aberdeen, Lefroy, Victoria, and Popes Peak. *See p 146.*

⑬ Wildflowers at Healy Pass. In the high alpine zone, hardy wildflowers like moss campion, purple saxifrage, glacier lilies, and alpine forget-me-nots bloom into gorgeous colors from mid-July to mid-August. This pass just beside Sunshine Village ski area is one of the finest areas for these brilliant

Ice skating and hot chocolate at Fairmont Lake Louise.

displays. Hike the 12km (7.5-mile) trail up to alpine meadows or cheat by taking the Sunshine Meadows shuttle up most of the way. In Jasper, head to Mt. Edith Cavell. *See p 100,* ❼.

⓮ **Morning coffee run.** Early morning is the quietest time of the day on the otherwise-bustling main strip of Banff Avenue. Before 9am, it's the peaceful terrain of locals. Join them for a cafe latte and some homemade granola (served with berry compote and yogurt) at the Wild Flour Bakery. As the workers head off, relish your vacation time with a stroll along the Bow River. In Jasper, do the same at the Bear's Paw Bakery. *See p 127.*

⓯ **Catching your first wildlife sighting.** Whether it's an elk munching on lawn grass or a grizzly bear crossing an avalanche path, each glimpse of a wild animal in Banff is a gift. There are no guarantees, but it's a good bet that you'll see bighorn sheep at Lake Minnewanka at dusk or dawn. Some animals, of course, require more caution than others. Visit the Parks Canada Visitor Centres for more information. *See p 13,* ❶.

⓰ **Setting up a mountain picnic.** Quieter than the Trans-Canada

Canoeing on a serene alpine lake.

Highway, the Bow Valley Parkway's best picnic spot is at the Storm Mountain Lookout, just north of Castle Junction, for great views and photo ops. Pick up supplies for a picnic at Nester's Market in Banff or at Laggan's in Lake Louise.

⓱ **Driving the astonishing Icefields Parkway.** For 230km (143 miles), drive a road that feels like it's been carved inside the earth, with massive mountains clinging to the Continental Divide, ancient glaciers, and ragged peaks. At the middle are the Columbia Icefields, the liquid heart from which the waters of the nation pump. Oh, and there are mountain goats and grizzly bears too! *See p 64.*

⓲ **Canoeing on an alpine lake.** Emerald, Maligne, Moraine . . . their names simply invite you to grab a paddle and launch a canoe upon their sublime shores. Out alone (or with a friend) on a placid alpine lake, with your reflection blending with that of giant rocky peaks on the ripples beside you, you'll find you're living inside your own postcard from paradise. Moraine Lake is next to Lake Louise and is less visited but still easy to access, making it my top choice. *See p 63,* ❽. ●

1

Strategies for Seeing Banff & the Canadian Rockies

Banff & the Canadian Rockies

Previous page: Lake Moraine.

The beautiful Canadian Rockies are a vast area with much to see and do. You need to plan according to the seasons, the length of your visit, and your goals and tastes. Don't try to do it all—the magic in Banff is in the quietest moments. In this chapter, I offer tips to help you make the most of your time.

Rule #1: Get out of town!

While the Town of Banff holds most of the lodgings and restaurants, not to mention shops and nightlife, it's the rest of the park that will most astound you. Those interested in solitude should head to a nearby national park—Jasper in the north or Kootenay and Yoho to the west—or to one of the many backcountry lodges dotted throughout the park. Even day trips in a car or a short hike counts toward spreading your wings here.

Rule #2: Go to the experts.

The Parks Canada Visitor Centres should be your first stop, whether it's in the Town of Banff, at Lake Louise, or in Jasper. Pick up maps and permits and take in interpretive exhibits that will greatly enhance your experience in the Canadian Rockies. The friendly staff members have the latest trail, road, avalanche, and wildlife reports.

Rule #3: Don't overschedule.

Jam-packing your days from an early-morning bird-watching trip to a late-night stargazing excursion will only leave you exhausted. The loveliest moments in Banff are those that surprise you—spotting a wolf on a quiet road or having a leisurely picnic by the river. Give yourself time for spontaneous adventure and explorations.

Rule #4: Allow plenty of travel time.

Not only are the distances great; you'll find lots of mountains along the way that provide twists and turns—there are few straight lines in the Canadian Rockies. And along the way from A to B, there'll likely be dozens of photo opportunities and maybe even wildlife sightings. Plan to get out of the car often and take your time while driving.

Rule #5: Come in the shoulder season.

Not only will you save money; you'll avoid the crowds. June is considered off-season, and September (my favorite month in Banff) is great for hiking. For winter travelers, try pre-Christmas December for good deals and April for spring skiing.

The Lake Louise Visitor Centre provides maps, permits, and park information.

Mountain biking with Banff Adventures.

Rule #6: Be prepared for weather.

In the Rockies, it's common to see all four seasons in a single day, any time of the year. Bring appropriate clothing and never hit the trail without a good jacket, hat, sunscreen, and a bottle of water.

Rule #7: Try something new.

Banff is a great place to do something you've never done. Hiking isn't just for the superfit, and horseback riding ain't only for cowboys.

Sleigh ride.

In wintertime, take a snowboard lesson or try ice skating. Vacations are for breaking free!

Rule #8: Pick a central activity each day & plan around it.

For days when you plan to head out for a hike or to hit the slopes, get prepared the evening before. Pack food, get your gear ready, and check the latest conditions. And get a good night's sleep! Be logical so that you don't have to back-track.

Rule #9: Think outside the park.

Save cash by staying in a hotel just outside Banff. The Town of Canmore, just 20km (12 miles)—a 15-minute drive—east of Banff, is a lovely mountain town with an impressive list of affordable hotel options and fabulous restaurants.

Rule #10: Use this book as a reference, not a concrete plan.

Don't worry; I won't be hurt if you don't follow every single tour I lay out here. Read through the options I present, pick the ones that most appeal to you, and adapt them to your personal preferences. ●

Banff in Three Days

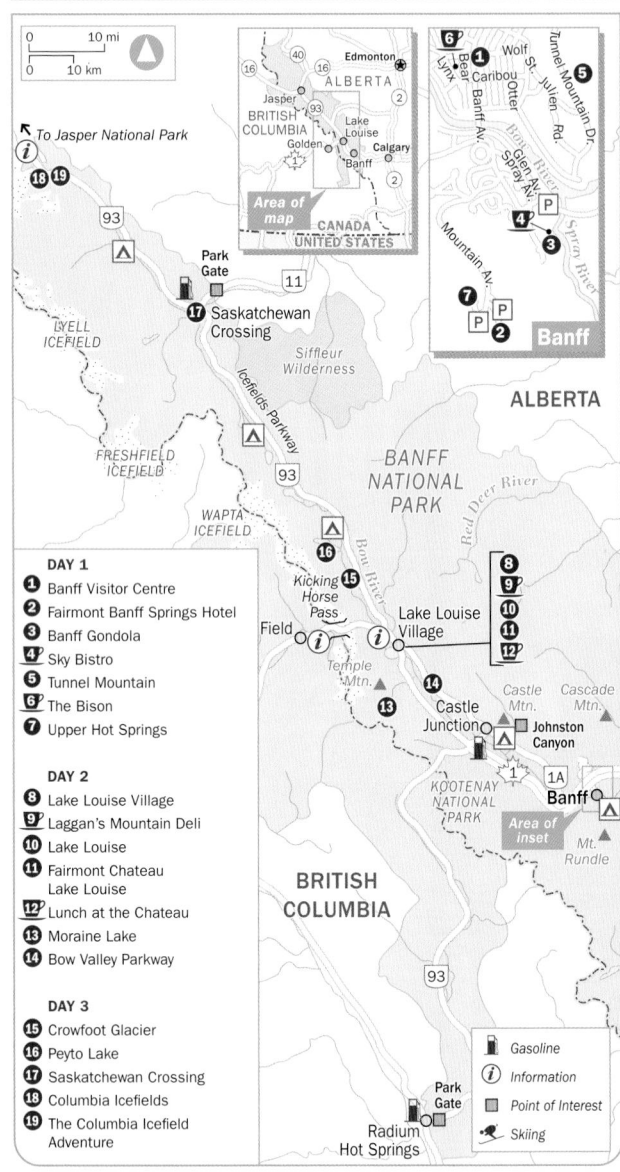

DAY 1

1. Banff Visitor Centre
2. Fairmont Banff Springs Hotel
3. Banff Gondola
4. Sky Bistro
5. Tunnel Mountain
6. The Bison
7. Upper Hot Springs

DAY 2

8. Lake Louise Village
9. Laggan's Mountain Deli
10. Lake Louise
11. Fairmont Chateau Lake Louise
12. Lunch at the Chateau
13. Moraine Lake
14. Bow Valley Parkway

DAY 3

15. Crowfoot Glacier
16. Peyto Lake
17. Saskatchewan Crossing
18. Columbia Icefields
19. The Columbia Icefield Adventure

Gasoline

(i) Information

Point of Interest

Skiing

Previous page: Shopping in downtown Banff.

▌ocated at the confluence of the Spray and Bow rivers, and on the lower slopes of Tunnel and Sulphur mountains, the Town of Banff is rich in culture and history, with adventure at your doorstep.

Travel Tip

Avoid parking hassles by using the ROAM bus system, which runs down all the routes mentioned below and well beyond. An unlimited day pass costs $5. For more information, call ☎ 403/762-0606 or go to www.roamtransit.com. Days 2 and 3 require your own vehicle.

Day 1

❶ ★★ Banff Visitor Centre. No visit to Banff should start anywhere else. Stock up on maps and free self-guided tour brochures and get helpful advice from the friendly, knowledgeable staff of the Parks Canada, Banff/Lake Louise Tourism Bureau, and Friends of Banff desks. ⓦ 30 min. 224 Banff Ave. www. banfflakelouise.com. ☎ 403/762-1550. Oct 9–Mar daily 9am–5pm; May 18–Oct 8 9am–8pm. Closed Dec 25.

Hop on the ROAM bus 2 or drive up Banff Ave. over the Bow River Bridge. Take a left after the bridge onto Spray Ave. Continue to:

❷ ★★ Fairmont Banff Springs Hotel. You can't miss the unmistakable stone towers and green roof of this national landmark. Ostentatious and oozing with amenities, it's an expensive place to stay (p 79) but a marvelous building and certainly a must-see on any trip to Banff. Nonguests are welcome to grab a meal, visit the spa, or take a short tour of the hotel. ⓦ 45 min. 405 Spray Ave. www.fairmont.com/banff. ☎ 403/762-2211.

From the Banff Springs, head back down Spray Ave., then left on Mountain Ave. to the end.

❸ ★ kids Banff Gondola. A quick 8-minute gondola ride takes you to the top of the 2,285m (7,496 ft.) Sulphur Mountain. Walk the elevated boardwalk to Sanson Peak. Bring at least a sweater! ⓦ 70 min. At the end of Mountain Rd., 2.5km (1½ miles) from Banff Ave. www. banffjaspercollection.com. ☎ 403/762-6700. Rates depend on availability. Adults from $53, kids 6 & up $29 (ages 6–13 free before 10am). Kids under 6 free. Mid-Oct to mid-May 10am–8pm; mid-May to June 30 8am–9:30pm; July 1–Sept 5 8am–10:30pm; Sept 6 to mid-Oct 8am–9:30pm.

Nonguests can enjoy the spa at the Fairmont Banff Springs Hotel.

Sulphur Mountain Summit of the Banff Gondola.

4️⃣ Sky Bistro. Not only is this the most buzzed-about restaurant in Banff; the views are truly stunning. For a lunch to remember, book at Sky Bistro before you come to the Gondola. And if you're on a budget, try the slightly more accessible Northern Lights Café, also at the Gondola's Upper Terminal. *See p 74. At the Banff Gondola's Upper Terminal. www.banffjaspercollection. ca.* ☎ 403/762-7486. $$.

Head back into the Town of Banff & then walk up Wolf St. toward the Banff Centre, keeping an eye out for the trail head for:

5️⃣ ★★ Tunnel Mountain Hike. Work off lunch by hiking this classic Banff trail that heads right out of

Enjoy stunning views while you dine at the Sky Bistro.

the heart of town. It's a 2.3km (1.4-mile) hike that takes you 300m (984 ft.) up to the summit. One of the oldest trails in the park, this is very popular with Banff locals. ⏱ *2½ hr. Trail head is at St. Julien Rd., 300m (984 ft.) uphill from the Wolf St. junction.*

Head back into town on Wolf St., turning left on Bear St. Half a block down, you'll find:

6️⃣ The Bison. Hit the sunny patio here for some of the best views in town, overlooking Bear Street and Mt. Rundle. Upscale cheese and meat trays make great appetizers, and there's a long wine-by-the-glass menu and local beers on tap. *See p 71. 211 Bear St. www. thebison.ca.* ☎ 403/762-5550. $$.

After a leisurely meal, hop back on the ROAM bus 1 or drive up Mountain Rd. toward:

7️⃣ ★★ Upper Hot Springs. For more than a century, visitors have come to Banff to "take the waters." Evenings are the best time to visit these historic pools. ⏱ *60 min. At the end of Mountain Rd., 2.5km (1½ miles) from downtown Banff.* ☎ *403/762-1515. Oct 31–May 14 Sun–Thurs 10am–10pm, Fri–Sat 10am–11pm; mid-May to mid-Oct 9am–11pm. Adults $8.50, seniors & children (3–17) $7.50.*

Day 2

Your day begins with a delightful 45-minute drive to Lake Louise. Head straight there from Banff—you'll have time later in the afternoon to look around the Bow Valley. Your goal is to beat the crowds to the lake and secure the best light for photographing.

⑧ ★ Lake Louise Village. A small hamlet just off the Trans-Canada Highway, this collection of hotels, restaurants, gas stations, and shops is centered at the Samson Mall. Pick up a snack or grab a new fleece if the weather has soured. The Parks Canada Information Centre is just behind the shopping plaza, worth a visit for trail and wildlife updates. ⏱ *40 min. 58km (36 miles) west of Town of Banff on Trans-Canada Hwy. 1.*

⑨ Laggan's Mountain Deli. This unpretentious coffee and sandwich shop is popular with hikers, bikers, skiers, and anybody on the move. It's in the middle of Samson Mall. Tip: Beat the crowds by entering the alternative door on the left side and heading for the second cashier. *101 Lake Louise Dr., in Samson Mall.* ☎ *403/522-2017. $.*

Relaxing in Banff Upper Hot Springs.

It's hard to take a bad photo of lovely Lake Louise.

Drive out of the Samson Mall parking lot onto Village Rd., turning left at Lake Louise Dr. Head up the hill until you reach:

⑩ ★★★ Lake Louise. Perhaps the most photographed lake in Canada, this stunner draws thousands of visitors weekly from every corner of the globe. At the back of the lake, Mt. Victoria and the Victoria Glacier make an imposing backdrop. Aim to be here by 9am. Take an hour to stroll to the back of the lake. Find a quiet spot to soak it all in.

It's impossible to miss the massive building to your right:

⑪ ★★ Fairmont Chateau Lake Louise. This landmark hotel is known as "'the diamond in the wilderness." For more than 125 years, mountaineers, artists, and lovers of the outdoors have been drawn to the sublime landscape and this gracious hotel. ⏱ *30 min. 111 Lake Louise Dr. www.fairmont.com/lake-louise.* ☎ *403/522-1818.*

⑫ Lunch at the Chateau. If you're not a guest, you can experience the refined elegance of the famed Fairmont hotel by reserving a table for a stunning lunch in the Lakeview Lounge. By reservation only. *111 Lake Louise Dr.* ☎ *403/522-1818. $$$.*

The lookout onto Peyto Lake is a short hike away from the Icefields Parkway.

Drive out of the parking lot & take the first right on Moraine Lake Rd., which leads you to:

⑬ ★★★ Moraine Lake. Some say Louise's less-visited sister lake is even more beautiful. Wild and dramatic, Moraine Lake is surrounded by 10 spirelike peaks. A great interpretive trail leads to the Moraine Lake Rockpile. ⏱ *45 min. 13km (8 miles) south of Lake Louise on Moraine Lake Rd.*

Bid farewell to the Lake Louise area, driving back down to the village. Drive over the Trans-Canada Hwy., taking the next right on to:

⑭ Bow Valley Parkway 1A. Built in 1920, the first road connecting Banff and Lake Louise still feels more like a mountain road than an expressway. Compared to the Trans-Canada Highway, the parkway is quieter and gives you a much better chance of wildlife sightings.

The day ends as you drive back on Bow Valley Pkwy. 1A & then finally on the Trans-Canada Hwy. into the Town of Banff.

Day 3
One of the most beautiful drives in the entire world, a day on the Icefields is not to be missed.

Continuing north on the Icefields Parkway (also known as Hwy. 93) from Lake Louise, the road steadily climbs higher and higher, and the views become more and more dramatic as you make your way through three river valleys and pass beneath towering glacier-topped peaks. Get an early start, as the first stop is over an hour from Banff. *Note:* You must have a valid Park Pass to drive on this highway.

Travel Tip

Food options are next-to-nonexistent between Lake Louise and the Columbia Icefield (which has good restaurants), so pick up a picnic there or in Banff. See p 59.

⑮ ★ Crowfoot Glacier. The first of a long lineup of glaciers once resembled the foot of a crow (hence the name) but has shrunk significantly. Interpretive signs are posted at the roadside viewpoint. ⏱ *10 min. 32km (20 miles) from Lake Louise on Hwy. 93, the Icefields Pkwy.*

Continue north on the Icefields Pkwy. to:

⑯ ★★ Peyto Lake. There is a short interpretive trail to this beautifully turquoise gem, named for pioneer guide Bill Peyto, who was also a warden in Banff National Park. ⏲ *20 min. 42km (26 miles) from Lake Louise on Hwy. 93, the Icefields Pkwy.*

Continue north on the Icefields Pkwy. to:

⓱ Saskatchewan Crossing.

This is the only place with any kind of services between Lake Louise and the Icefield Centre. Besides lovely views of the Mistaya, Howse, and North Saskatchewan river valleys, it has a warden station, gas station, snack bar, and gift shop. ⏲ *10 min. 50km (31 miles) from Lake Louise on Hwy. 93, the Icefields Pkwy.*

Continue north on the Icefields Pkwy. to:

⓲ ★★★ Columbia Icefield.

Just north of the Banff-Jasper park border, this is an area of glacial ice and snow measuring 190 sq. km (73 sq. miles) and up to 350m (1,148 ft.) deep in places. It'll give you an idea what the northern part of North America may have looked like during Earth's last ice age. Six main glaciers flow from the Columbia Icefield. Park at the **Icefield Centre,** the main building in the area. This is where you need to go to sign up for a tour on the

Columbia Icefield's giant snocoach. ⏲ *2–3 hr. total. 125km (78 miles) from Lake Louise on Hwy. 93, the Icefield Pkwy.* ☎ *780/852-6288. May 1 to late Sept 10am–5pm. Closed late Sept to Apr 30.*

Directly across the highway is:

⓳ ★★ kids The Columbia Icefield Adventure. Take a giant

snocoach onto the Athabasca Glacier, which drops you off in the middle of the ice, where you can stroll around. Then, walk out on a glass-floored platform overlooking the Sunwapta Valley at the Skywalk. Book ahead of time online, or you'll have to wait for availability in tours, especially in July and August. Come early or late for shorter wait times. Tours leave every 15 minutes or so. ⏲ *2 hr. 125km (78 miles) from Lake Louise on Hwy. 93, the Icefields Pkwy. www.banffjaspercollection. com.* ☎ *403/762-6735. Kids under 5 free. Rate includes Icefield Adventure & Skywalk. Adults $109, kids 6–15 $49. Apr 29–June 2 & Sept 2–30 10am–5pm; June 3–July 14 9am– 6pm; July 15–Sept 1 10am–5pm; Oct 1–20 10am–4pm.*

The day ends with you retracing your steps back to Banff on Hwy. 93 and then on Trans-Canada Hwy. 1.

Tour of the Columbia Icefield.

Best in One Week

1 Town of Banff
2 Horseback riding at the Spray River
3 Lake Louise
4 Icefields Parkway
5 Hiking at Lake Louise
6 Yoho National Park
   6a Spiral Tunnels
   6b Takakkaw Falls
   6c Field
   6d Siding General Store and Café
   6e Emerald Lake
   6f Cilantro on the Lake
7 Biking at Lake Louise

H aving a few extra days allows you time to explore the backcountry of Banff National Park and visit the historically—and geographically—fascinating Yoho National Park, next door to Banff. You can blend active adventures, such as hiking and horseback riding, with traditional touring and sightseeing.

Day 1
Follows the Town of Banff tour from Day 1, above.

Day 2
Saddle up today to head into the mountains. Follow in the steps of cowboys, pack guides, and wilderness explorers near Banff. **Banff Trail Riders,** who have run trail rides in Banff for nearly 50 years, has a full-day trip that heads up the Spray River and includes a barbecue lunch (p 155). *138 Banff Ave.* ☎ *800/661-8352 or 403/762-4551.*

Day 3
Today follows Day 2 of "Banff in 3 Days" with one difference: Drive up to Lake Louise on the Bow Valley Parkway, stopping at Johnston Canyon and Muleshoe en route (p 59, ❷ and ❸), and plan on spending the next few nights based out of Lake Louise after visiting the area.
Trail riding with Banff Trail Riders.

Climbing the frozen Upper Falls in Johnston Canyon.

Day 4
Today follows Day 3 of "Banff in Three Days," taking in all the highlights of the spectacular Icefields Parkway and returning to Lake Louise in the evening.

Day 5
Lake Louise hiking: In a land of superlatives, you have many outstanding hiking options to choose from. The classic Lake Louise hike, the **Highline Trail,** connects Lake Agnes with the Plain of the Six Glaciers, two historic teahouses, massive glaciers, and a lovely, gentle downhill finish. *Tip:* Pick up lunch supplies at **Laggan's** in Samson Mall and be sure to bring plenty of water! *See chapter 6 for trail descriptions.*

Day 6

Yoho National Park: "Yoho" is an expression of awe and wonder in the Cree language, and that's just what you'll experience in this park, located just over the provincial border from Banff in British Columbia. Yoho showcases the western slopes of the Rockies with dozens of spectacular waterfalls and the Kicking Horse River. It's also an interesting spot for history buffs.

Take Trans-Canada Hwy. 1 west from Lake Louise 9.2km (5¾ miles) to the border between Alberta & British Columbia.

Approximately 8.7km (5½ miles) west of the border, turn off into the roadside interpretive display at:

6A ★ Spiral Tunnels. Steep as it is, the CPR (Canadian Pacific Railway) in the 1880s selected the Kicking Horse Pass as the easiest way over the Rockies. But it was still very, very steep, and soon enough trains were crashing down the so-called Big Hill. The Spiral Tunnels were designed more than 100 years ago to take trains through two loops dug inside Cathedral Mountain, easing the grade. View the Spiral Tunnels from the side of Trans-Canada Highway 1 just up the hill from Field; there are excellent interpretive signs, and if your timing's good, you'll actually catch a train going through the tunnels (on an average day, 25 to 30 trains pass through the tunnels, although not on a regular schedule).

Continue down the hill on Trans-Canada Hwy. 1 another 3.7km (2¼ miles), turning right at Yoho Valley Rd. for:

6B ★★ Takakkaw Falls. Reach the fourth-highest waterfall in Canada by driving up the Kicking Horse River on Yoho Valley Road (not recommended for large RVs or trailers). If you love waterfalls, you've come to the right place. Hike another hour along the Yoho Valley trail past Staircase Falls and Point Lace Falls to see Laughing Falls and then on to beautiful Twin Falls.

Drive back out to Trans-Canada Hwy. 1, continuing 1.8km (1 mile) west to the Field turnoff.

6C ★ Field. With a population of only 200 souls, the tiny Town of Field, BC, has a gorgeous setting beside the Kicking Horse River and beneath Mt. Stephen. It has a few charming shops, including the **Velvet Antler Pottery** (314 Stephen Ave., next to Siding Café; http://velvetantlerpottery.com; ☎ 250/343-6456). ⏲ *30 min. 27km (17 miles) from Lake Louise.*

Takakkaw Falls in Yoho National Park.

Cilantro on the Lake provides stunning alpine views in summertime.

Head through tiny Field, turning right on Kicking Horse Ave. Make a quick U-turn at Stephen Ave. to find:

6D ★ **Siding General Store and Café.** A cozy deli in historic Field is a good stop any time of day: Come prehike for a breakfast sandwich or to get a "designer" sandwich to go. Or drop by posthike for a date square, brownie, and cup of tea. It's even open for dinner, with salads, pastas, and a great veggie chili. *Open summers only. 318 Stephen Ave., at the corner of Kicking Horse Ave. www.thesidingcafe.ca.* ☎ 250/343-6002. $$.

Back out on Trans-Canada Hwy. 1, turn left (west) & continue 2km (1¼ miles) to the turnoff for Emerald Lake Rd. Drive 8km (5 miles) until you reach:

6E ★★ **Emerald Lake.** Move past the crowded parking lot and hike the lovely 5km (3.1-mile) trail around this marvelous alpine lake. With just a little bit of up and down, this wide trail is rich and delightful, circling the pristine Emerald Lake and almost easy enough to be considered a stroll. Legendary local guide Tom Wilson is credited for having discovered this natural marvel in 1882 as part

of a route-scouting for the Canadian Pacific Railroad. This is a great family outing or leg-stretcher; it showcases a gem of a lake, and the interpretive signs are informative.

6F ★ **Cilantro on the Lake.** Open only during the summer, this pretty mountain bistro at Emerald Lake Lodge offers wood-fired flat-bread pizzas, gourmet burgers, and micro-brewed beer in a sublimely beautiful setting. Sit on the lovely, sunny patio overlooking Emerald Lake or inside the spectacular timber-frame lodge. *On Emerald Lake Rd., 8km (5 miles) off Trans-Canada Hwy. 1, at a turnoff 2km (1¼ miles) south of Field. www.crmr.com/emerald.* ☎ 250/343-6321. $$.

Day 7
Your final day is for some morning adventure. Rent a mountain bike from **Wilson Mountain Sports** in Samson Mall (from $39/day; www.wmsll.com; ☎ **866/929-3636** or 403/522-3636) and ride the 9km (5.6-mile) return classic **Tramline Trail.** Families will prefer the gentle Bow River Loop or the Great Divide Bike Path, which is better suited to a road bike. Then give yourself plenty of time to say goodbye to the Rockies and head out.

Best in Two Weeks

DAY 1
1 Town of Banff

DAY 2
2 Horseback Riding on the Spray River

DAY 3
3 Sunshine Meadows

DAY 4
4 Kootenay National Park

DAY 5
5 Lake Louise

DAY 6
6 Hiking in Paradise Valley/ Larch Valley

DAY 7
7 Yoho National Park

DAY 8
8 Camping at Lake O'Hara

DAY 9
9 Hiking at Lake O'Hara

DAY 10
10 Icefields Parkway

DAY 11
11 Tour of Jasper Townsite and Area

DAY 12
12 Maligne Valley

DAY 13
13 Rafting the Athabasca River

DAY 14
14 Breakfast at Bear's Paw

ucky are those with time to linger in the Canadian Rockies. After all, there are nearly 23,000 sq. km (8,880 sq. ft.) of mountain wilderness to explore, and that takes time. Blending sightseeing with active adventures and allowing you to roam from Banff up to Jasper, this is perhaps the ultimate 2-week vacation in this inimitable setting. Just be sure to book ahead of time, particularly your night at Yoho National Park's Lake O'Hara—either the campground or the historic and peerless Lake O'Hara Lodge. For more details, see p 137.

Day 1
See Day 1 from the "Banff in Three Days" tour, p 12.

Day 2
Aim to hit the trail today on horseback. See Day 2 of "Best in One Week," p 19.

Day 3
★★ kids **Sunshine Meadows.**
When the snow melts at the world-famous Sunshine Village ski area, the alpine meadows blossom into a multicolored dreamland hugging the Continental Divide, great for moderate hiking amid more than 340 species of wildflowers. The Garden Path Trail is breathtaking in late July and August. To the south, you can see Mount Assiniboine, the "Matterhorn of the Rockies."

Enjoying the views in Sunshine Meadows.

Take a bus from the parking lot or right from the Town of Banff and skip the arduous uphill hike. *Tip:* Book the morning buses ahead of time and don't forget to bring a lunch and bear spray, drink water, and use plenty of sunscreen. *8km (5 miles) west of Banff on the Sunshine Rd. www.sunshinemeadows. com.* ☎ *403/762-7889. $45 adults, $23 children 6–15. June 28–Sept 8 8am–6pm.*

Day 4
★★ kids **Kootenay National Park.** Less visited and wonderfully expansive, Kootenay is an off-the-beaten-path destination that makes a great day trip from Banff. This park is particularly friendly to families, with lots of kids in strollers and some great picnic spots.

Drive Trans-Canada Hwy. 1 west to Castle Junction & take Hwy. 93 south. Length: 132km (82 miles) each way.

Travel Tip

Driving Hwy. 93 at dusk is prime wildlife-viewing time, so keep an eye out and drive safely.

❶ ★ kids Fireweed Trail. A 20-minute loop explains why natural forest fires are healthy and good for the environment. As you continue through Kootenay, you may be driving through a number of fire sites, so getting the lowdown here will help you understand and appreciate the burned landscapes. ◷ *15 min. 95km (59 miles) from Radium, on the Alberta–British Columbia (& Banff–Kootenay) border.*

Continue southwest of Hwy. 93.

❷ ★★ Stanley Glacier. One of my favorite shorter hikes in the Rockies, this trail takes you from fire (a lightning-provoked burn from 1968) to ice (the Stanley Glacier) in just 2.5km (1.5 miles). Most of the 395m (1,296 ft.) to be climbed are at the beginning, leaving you time to amble amid a hanging valley with awesome views. Great for families. ◷ *3 hr. Trail head is 3.2km (2 miles) west of the Alberta–British Columbia (& Banff–Kootenay national parks) border on the south side of the highway.*

❸ Marble Canyon. A narrow trail of limestone carved by two retreating glaciers, this is a cool, shady spot on a hot day. Kids will find this short hike intriguing, but keep a sharp eye on them because the trail can get very slippery. ◷ *30 min. 89km (55 miles) from Radium, 7km (4⅓ miles) from Alberta–British Columbia (& Banff–Kootenay national parks) border on the north side of the highway.*

❹ ★ Paint Pots. Natives came together at these remote cold springs to gather ocher, an iron-based mineral that was baked, crushed, mixed with grease, and used as a paint for teepees, pictographs, and personal adornment. There's an excellent wheelchair-accessible and stroller-friendly 30-minute interpretive trail. ◷ *40 min. 85km (53 miles) from Radium, 10km (6¼ miles) from Alberta–British Columbia (& Banff–Kootenay national parks) border on the north side of the highway.*

❺ ★★ Radium Hot Springs Pool. Nestled in a canyon rich with oxide, these "sacred mountain waters" are surrounded by an orange-sunset vibe. The pools are more spacious than those in Banff, and there are often bighorn sheep milling about. ◷ *2 hr. See p 115, ❻.*

Natives once used the colorful minerals from these cold springs to make paints.

take you all day. *See p 145,* ⓫*.*
*Trail head: Paradise Valley parking
lot 2.5km (1½ miles) south from Lake
Louise Rd.*

Day 7
Visit Yoho National Park, as
described in Day 6 of "Best in One
Week," p 20.

Day 8
Camping at Lake O'Hara. Just
the mention of Yoho National
Park's Lake O'Hara makes diehard
hikers get misty. It's also a great
first-camping outing, since you
access the backcountry campground via a Parks Canada–run
bus—meaning you don't have to
carry a heavy load and you can
camp in comfort. But you must
book a campsite well ahead of
time. The bus departs daily from a
parking lot just off Trans-Canada
Highway at 8:30am, 10:30am,
3:30pm, and 5:30pm, and you must
have a reservation. Once you've set
up your tent and settled in, hike
around the namesake lake for orientation and then head past
Schäffer Lake to beautiful Lake
McArthur, a great 2- to 3-hour hike.
See p 108.

*Sinclair Canyon marks the striking exit
out of Kootenay.*

*The soothing mineral waters of the
Radium Hot Springs Pool.*

❻ **Sinclair Canyon.** With this
stunning farewell, Kootenay closes
with a bang just shy of the village
of Radium Hot Springs. Your car
barely sneaks through iron-rich cliffs
that are part of the Redwall Fault
and form a dramatic entrance to
the Columbia Valley. There's a
small roadside pull-off just west of
the canyon where you can get out
of the car to walk through the giant
walls and take photos—it's especially gorgeous at sunset. Watch for
bighorn sheep on the roadside.
🕐 *10 min. 1.5km (1 mile) from
Radium & 131km (81 miles) from
Alberta–British Columbia (& Banff–
Kootenay national parks) border in
the middle of the highway.*

Day 5
Travel from Banff to Lake Louise,
following Day 3 of "Best in One
Week," p 19.

Day 6
Hiking Paradise Valley. Rewarding and challenging, this hike starts
in Paradise Valley, just south of
Lake Louise. You'll take in a long
list of highlights, such as the
"Giant's Staircase," Lake Annette,
and gorgeous views of Mt. Temple.
It's a 22km (13.6-mile) hike that will

Northern Lights over the Jasper National Park Information Centre.

Day 9

Hiking at Lake O'Hara. Few places in the world can rival the stunning scenery, historic trail system, varied landscape, and special charm of this tiny area tucked beneath the Continental Divide. Spend your day on the Lake O'Hara Alpine Circuit, one of the best hikes in the entire world. It'll lead you past such glorious sites as the Opabin Plateau, the Yukness Ledges, and Lake Oesa. After taking the bus from just outside Le Relais Day Shelter back to the parking lot (the last bus of the day leaves at 6:30pm), head back to Lake Louise. *See p 108.*

Day 10

Today follows Day 3 of "Banff in Three Days" (p 16) but continues past the Columbia Icefield to the Town of Jasper. Follow Highway 93, the Icefields Parkway, north 105km (65 miles) to Jasper townsite. You should have time to squeeze in the outstanding hike to **Wilcox Pass** as well, for a jaw-dropping lookout over the Columbia Icefield. *See p 149,* ⑲.

Day 11

Tour of Jasper Townsite & Area. Located in an expansive valley on the west bank of the Athabasca River, Jasper has an off-season population that hovers around 5,000 but blossoms to more than 20,000 in the summer. That's when university students from across Canada head here for summer jobs and to mingle with the thousands of travelers passing through, turning the somewhat sleepy mountain town into a vibrant destination. The town itself is quite large, but most visitors stick to the two main drags, Connaught Drive and Patricia Street. That's where you'll find the good restaurants, shops, and outfitters.

❶ ★ **Jasper National Park Information Centre.** Stop here to get permits, maps, and brochures and to have the friendly staff help you make the most of your day. ⏱ *20 min. 500 Connaught Dr.* ☎ *780/852-6176.*

Head west across Connaught Dr. (also known as Hwy. 93), continuing through the lights at the junction with Hwy. 16. Take the first right on Whistlers Rd., continuing uphill until you reach:

❷ ★ **Jasper Skytram.** Your quickest and easiest way to the high alpine terrain, this 7-minute gondola ride takes you up 973m

(3,192 ft.), just short of the summit of Whistlers Mountain. From the top, the views of the Athabasca and Miette valleys are stunning. There's a well-marked, although quite steep, 45-minute self-guided trail to the summit of the mountain. Watch for hoary marmots and white-tailed ptarmigan. Lineups can be intense, so try to head there in the morning. ⏱ *90 min. 3km (1¾ miles) south of Jasper on Hwy. 93, turn left/west on Whistler Mountain Rd. for another 4km (2½ miles). www.jasperskytram.com.* ☎ *866/850-8726 & 780/852-3093. Adults $49, kids 6–15 $26. Mar 22– May 16 & Sept 2–Oct 27 10am–5pm; May 17–June 20 9am–8pm; June 21– Sept 2 8am–9pm.*

Return to Hwy. 93 & head south 21km (13 miles) to the junction with Hwy. 93A, which heads north. Just past the turnoff is:

❸ **Athabasca Falls.** Known more for its force than its height, this is one of the most impressive waterfalls in the Rockies, where the Athabasca River (the same one born at the Columbia Icefield and the most important river in Jasper National Park) thunders over a layer of hard quartzite and through a narrow limestone gorge. ⏱ *20 min. 25km (15 miles) south of Jasper.*

Continue north on scenic Hwy. 93A 18km (11 miles) to Cavell Rd., a narrow & winding mountain road that requires much attention from drivers. At 15km (9⅓ miles), you'll arrive at the parking lot beneath:

❹ ★★ **Mt. Edith Cavell.** This is the highest and arguably the most scenic mountain in all of Jasper, named for a World War I British nurse. The Angel Glacier saddles the northeastern slope and sends a tongue of ice off the cliffside into a milky blue lake. The Path of the Glacier Trail takes you over boulders, shrubbery, pebbles, and sand through a landscape that, less than a century ago, was covered by a glacier. ⏱ *45 min. Follow Hwy. 93A to Cavell Rd. Continue another 12km (7½ miles) to the parking lot.*

Take Cavell Rd. back to Hwy. 93A. Turn left & continue 5.2km (3¼ miles) to the junction with Hwy. 93. Turn left & drive north into the Town of Jasper. Park your car next to the Heritage Railway Station. Cross Connaught Dr. & walk up Miette Ave. to Patricia St.

Jasper Skytram.

5 ★ **Coco's Café.** Where laid-back locals come to grab lunch, this busy little joint on Patricia Street has yummy wraps, curries, and soups that make superb lunches. There's also great cappuccino, latte, and espresso. The cafe is small and can be cramped; expect to literally rub elbows with your neighbors. *608 Patricia St. www. cocoscafe.ca.* ☎ *780/852-4550. $.*

6 ★ **Patricia Street.** Now that you've seen the major highlights south and west of town, spend the afternoon strolling the charming shops of Jasper's main streets. Focus on Patricia Street between Hazel Avenue and Cedar Street and then loop back along Connaught Drive. Slow down, enjoy the expansive views, and pick up a souvenir or two. **Counter Clockwise Emporium** (616 Patricia St.; ☎ 780/852-3152) has everything from books and jewelry to soaps and furniture.

Walking back toward your car, cross Connaught Dr. at Miette Ave. & pop into the:

7 **Heritage Railway Station.** You can almost picture Victorian ladies with their parasols and

Maligne Lake cruise.

elaborate dresses mixing with rough 'n' tumble gold diggers at this old frontier outpost. Trains heading east and west across Canada, including the VIA Rail passenger trains, stop here daily. Now housing the park administration offices, the train station is still a travel hub. ⏱ *10 min. On Connaught Dr. across from Whistlers Hotel.*

8 **Old Fort Point.** Jutting out into the Athabasca River, the point offers great views that take in Jasper townsite, Lac Beauvert, and the Fairmont Jasper Park Lodge. From here you can also catch sight of Mts. Kerkeslin and Hardisty to the southeast and the snowy triangle of Mt. Edith Cavell, shining above all others, to the south. It's a 2-hour hike atop a glacier-carved knoll to complete the loop via the lookout. Hike counterclockwise for a gentler climb. ⏱ *2 hr. To access Old Fort Point, drive 5 min. south of Jasper townsite via Hwy. 93A & Old Fort Point Rd. See p 105,* **5**.

Day 12
The Maligne Valley is a classic glacier-carved hanging valley and a natural wonderland. Have your camera ready—it's also a prime wildlife-viewing spot. Watch for moose, bighorn sheep, bears, and caribou!

Jasper Raft Tours with views of Mt. Edith Cavell.

Take Connaught Dr. east out of town until it joins with Hwy. 16, the Yellowhead Hwy. Continue 4km (2½ miles) east to the bridge over the Athabasca River. Turn right. This is the beginning of the Maligne Valley Rd.

❶ ★★ Maligne Canyon. A waterfall in slow motion, this limestone canyon is at the lip of the Maligne Valley as it meets the much lower Athabasca Valley. A lovely series of bridges and walkways bring you close to the largest underground drainage system known in Canada. At some points, it's only 2m (6.5 ft.) across and 50m (164 ft.) deep! Follow the bridges down, keep right at all the intersections on the self-guided trail, and then loop back up. An updated restaurant has dine-in and takeout meals all day long. ⏱ *30 min. At km 7 (mile 4⅓) on Maligne Valley Rd.*

Continue south on Maligne Valley Rd. until you reach:

❷ Medicine Lake. This could be called Mystery Lake—with no visible drainage, it seems to evaporate into nothing. The early Natives believed this mysterious lake had healing powers—hence the name. ⏱ *10 min. At km 21 (mile 13) on Maligne Valley Rd.*

Continue south on Maligne Valley Rd. until you reach:

❸ ★★ kids Maligne Lake Cruise to Spirit Island. A 90-minute cruise to a tiny, precious island, dotted with a handful of skinny pines and tucked in a placid corner of this glorious lake (the largest lake in Jasper National Park and the second largest glacial lake in the world), is a great outing for families. The island itself is shrouded in mystery and legends, which the guides explain en route. From the deck, watch for eagles, mountain goats, and even the odd avalanche, if it's the right time of year. ⏱ *90 min. At km 45 (mile 28) on Maligne Valley Rd. www.banff jaspercollection.com.* ☎ *800/625-4463. Adults $72, kids ages 5–14 $36. Daily departures hourly from boat docks: thaw date June 7 10am–3pm; June 8–June 27 & Sept 3–Oct 6 8:45am–3:45pm; June 28–Sept 2 9:30am–5:45pm.*

❹ Lunch with a View. With glass panels protecting it, the View Restaurant soaks up the incredible setting at Maligne Lake with a fresh, locally inspired menu. Book ahead! *Inside main lodge at Maligne Lake Cruise. Maligne Lake Rd.* ☎ *780/852-3370. $$*

Return north on Maligne Valley Rd. Just before the Athabasca River bridge, turn left on Old Lodge Rd. You'll pass Lakes Annette & Edith before arriving at:

❺ ★★ Fairmont Jasper Park Lodge.

The largest commercial property in the Canadian Rocky Mountain National Parks, this classic wilderness lodge attracts tourists and dignitaries from around the world. Hike the hour-long walk around Lac Beauvert, rent a canoe for a paddle on the lake, enjoy a meal at one of the hotel's six restaurants, or play a round on the award-winning golf course. ⏲ *60 min. 3.2km (2 miles) west of Maligne Valley Rd. on Old Lodge Rd. www.fairmont.com/jasper.* ☎ *780/852-3301.*

Day 13

📷 Rafting the Athabasca River. Choose between a family-friendly scenic float trip on the Athabasca River or Class III on the Sunwapta River. ("Sunwapta" is a Stoney Indian word meaning "turbulent river.") The big rapid is known as "the Whopper." *Jasper Raft Tours: 611 Patricia St. www.jasperrafttours.com.* ☎ *780/852-2665. Tours depart for the river daily at noon from its office on Patricia St. Adults $75; kids ages 15–17 $25, ages 5–14 $10, ages 4 & under $5.*

If rafting isn't up your alley, book a round at the **Fairmont Jasper Park Lodge's 18-hole course.** (4km/2½ miles east of Jasper townsite on Hwy. 16, then south on Maligne Lake Rd. and a quick left/west after the bridge, follow 3.2km/2 miles to end; www.fairmont.com/jasper/golf; ☎ 780/852-6090; $149–$209; tee times daily 7am–6pm).

Day 14

Grab breakfast at **Bear's Paw** (p 127; 610 Connaught Dr; the original is still at 4 Cedar Ave.; www.bearspawbakery.com; ☎ **780/852-3233**). If you are heading back to Banff, drive south along the Icefields Parkway, retracing your steps. It's 287km (178 miles) or 3½ hours if you don't stop, but you'll likely discover the drive equally intriguing and beautiful in a southerly direction. Plan to stop for some photographing and leg-stretching. If you are heading to Edmonton, which is 370km (230 miles) and about 4 hours east, plan to stop for a soak at the Miette Hot Springs en route. See p 102. ●

The kitchen at Bear's Paw Bakery.

Banff **for Photographers**

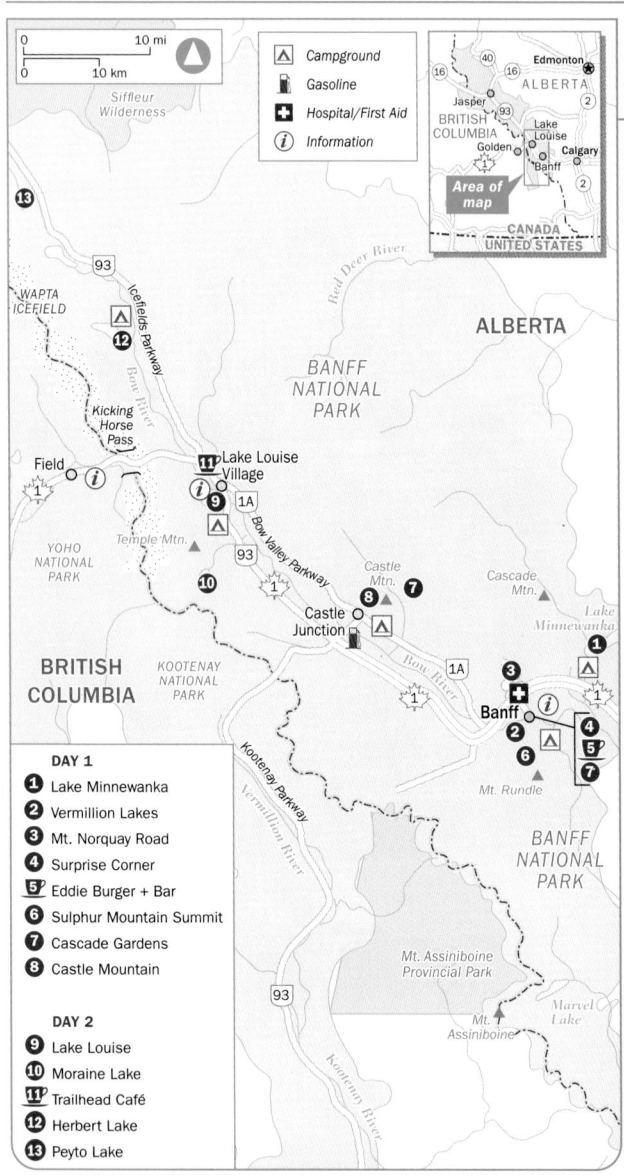

△	Campground
⛽	Gasoline
✚	Hospital/First Aid
(i)	Information

DAY 1

❶ Lake Minnewanka
❷ Vermillion Lakes
❸ Mt. Norquay Road
❹ Surprise Corner
❺ Eddie Burger + Bar
❻ Sulphur Mountain Summit
❼ Cascade Gardens
❽ Castle Mountain

DAY 2

❾ Lake Louise
❿ Moraine Lake
⓫ Trailhead Café
⓬ Herbert Lake
⓭ Peyto Lake

Previous page: Dog sledding on Lake Louise.

Banff National Park is one of the most photographed places in the entire world. It's a delight for expert and amateur shutterbugs alike, where each turn brings another postcard-worthy view. Focusing in on the ultimate photo ops involves timing, patience, and flexibility. But if you get up early and follow these steps, you'll surely gather a series of award-winners.

Day 1

Head out of Banff on Banff Ave., going northeast toward Cascade Mountain. Cross under Trans-Canada Hwy. 1 & continue on:

❶ Minnewanka Road. The easiest place for morning wildlife sightings is this drive just northeast of Banff. Watch for bighorn sheep near Two Jack Lake. A photo of Lake Minnewanka in a storm can be extremely dramatic.

Continue to Trans-Canada Hwy. & take the westbound ramp. Continue to the second Banff exit. Turn right (west) on Vermillion Lakes Rd. & continue to where the road ends.

❷ Mt. Rundle from Vermillion Lakes. The stillness of the morning on these shallow lakes often brings birdlife and moose. Evening offers alpine glow on the ridges of Rundle, that unforgettable peak that may be the most famous in all of Banff. In the summer, you can paddle into the middle of the lake for an undisturbed shot—or skate out on the frozen lakes in the winter for an icy masterpiece.

Take a left at Mt. Norquay Rd.

❸ Mt. Norquay Road. For a great shot that takes in the entire Town of Banff as well as its scenic surroundings, head up the switchbacks of the Norquay Road to the turnoff.

Drive back into Banff along Mt. Norquay Rd., which turns into Gopher St. & then becomes Lynx St. Turn left at Buffalo St. & continue past Banff Ave. After the housing ends, the forest thickens. At the next main switchback, park & get out of the car.

❹ Surprise Corner. At an elbow bend on the edge of Tunnel Mountain, this is the classic viewpoint for admiring the Fairmont Banff Springs Hotel in all its glory. Sulphur Mountain forms the backdrop, and the majestic Bow Falls rumbles beneath. Keep an eye out for fellow photographers crossing the street!

Mt. Rundle may be the most famous peak in Banff.

View of Fairmont Banff from Surprise Corner.

Head back into town on Buffalo St. & turn left at Banff Ave. Continue up Mountain Dr.

5 Lunch at Eddie Burger + Bar. You're hungry and on a tight schedule. For a quick, hearty lunch, you can't beat the homemade burgers at this small joint on Caribou. *(See p 71.) 137C Banff Ave. (on Caribou St.).* ☎ *403/762-2230. $$*

Follow Banff Ave. over the Bow River Bridge. Take a left at the end of the bridge & a quick right into the parking lot.

6 Sulphur Mountain Summit. After lunch, walk the boardwalk along the high alpine ridge that leads to the historic Cosmic Ray Station. The Town of Banff lies below you, and peaks stretch in every single direction. Talk about epic!

Return down Mountain Rd. & turn right before the first streetlight to:

7 Cascade Gardens. At the far end of Banff Avenue, these landscaped gardens provide a great perspective on the hustle and bustle, not to mention the stunning background, of Banff's main drag. Cascade Mountain rises like a pyramid in the distance. Walk from the parking lot to a lookout across the Bow River Bridge. The gardens are open all day June through September and are free to visit.

Drive back out of town, take the Mt. Norquay Rd. & then turn left (west) at Trans-Canada Hwy. 1. The views begin from about 10km (6¼ miles) west of Banff.

8 Castle Mountain. There are plenty of wonderful angles for capturing the many fine details of this beast of a mountain, between Banff and Lake Louise. With the Bow River in your foreground, you'll see a dazzling riot of colors. Catch the late afternoon light from the west

Few Banff visitors leave without a breathtaking photograph of Lake Louise.

Photographing Wildlife

Depending on the time of year and your luck, you'll see a wide range of wildlife while roaming Banff National Park with your camera. June is ideal for black bears; late fall is good for bull elks and moose. It's important, though, to respect park rules and always maintain a safe viewing distance from the animals. Usually, this means at least 30m (98 ft.), but for big animals like moose and bear, keep at least 100m (328 ft.) away.

side of the Vermillion Pass, towards the British Columbia border from Castle Junction.

Turn west on Hwy. 93 toward Radium Hot Springs.

Day 2
From the Town of Banff, head west on Trans-Canada Hwy. 1 58km (36 miles) to Lake Louise. Turn off the highway & head up Lake Louise Rd. to the famous lake.

9 Lake Louise. Beautifully framed by tall peaks, with a shimmering surface and a glacier at the back, this is the most photographed lake in Canada. Come here mid-morning for the best light. In winter, that means between 10am and noon. In summer, aim for an 8:30am start for a shot including the boat docks.

Head down 2.5km (1½ miles) on Lake Louise Rd., turning right on Moraine Lake Rd. & following it for 13km (8 miles).

10 Moraine Lake. I've seen the image of this pristine lake on everything from the former C$10 bill to a beer advertisement. The Valley of the Ten Peaks in the background oozes with drama. Come before noon.

Retrace your route & turn right on Lake Louise Rd., returning to Lake Louise village.

11 Trailhead Café. Pick up lunch to go at this busy little cafe in Samson Mall. Grab a fresh wrap—there are more than a dozen to choose from, but I love the tropical wrap with chicken and mango salsa or the veggie wrap with provolone and basil pesto. They pack up nice and clean for a picnic later on. *In Samson Mall.* ☎ *403/522-2006. $.*

Head west on Trans-Canada Hwy. & then north on Icefields Pkwy. toward Jasper to 2.5km (1½ miles) north of the Icefield Pkwy. gate.

12 Herbert Lake. Because this lake is small and sheltered by the tall peaks around it, it provides glasslike reflection in the morning, with the sun shining on the Bow Range in front as well as Mt. Bosworth to the north or Mt. Temple and the peaks of Lake Louise to the south.

Continue north on Icefields Pkwy. another 39km (24 miles).

13 Peyto Lake. With a blue deeper than the waters of the Caribbean and steep edges of mountain all around, Peyto Lake is a must-stop on the Icefields Parkway. In July and August, wildflowers are blooming. It's well worth the short stroll to the lookout.

Banff with Kids

Campground

Gasoline

(i) **Information**

P **Parking**

Point of Interest

DAY 1

❶ Banff Gondola

❷ Banff Park Museum

❸ Sushi House

❹ Biking on the Sundance Trail or Golf Course Loop

❺ Fairmont Banff Springs Hotel

❻ Grizzly House

❼ Evening Interpretive Theatre

DAY 2

❽ Hiking to Boom Lake

DAY 3

❾ Lake Louise Sightseeing Gondola

❿ Bill Peyto's Café

⓫ Columbia Icefield Adventure

Families flock to Banff for adventure, nature, and quality time surrounded by inspiring fresh air. Lifelong mountain lovers are born here every day—just ask the locals, most of whom first fell for these peaks on a family vacation. The keys to keeping kids engaged include getting out of the car a lot, following your nose with a sense of adventure and discovery, and keeping track of all that you see and learn. Be sure to pick up Parks Canada's excellent "Xplorers" workbook for kids, which is full of fun activities and ways to discover the park. It's available at all Visitor Information Centres.

Thousands of wildlife species are on display at the Banff Park Museum.

Day 1
Drive south on Banff Ave., over the Bow River Bridge. Turn left & then right quickly on to Mountain Rd. Follow until it ends at:

1 Banff Gondola. This may be your child's first summit, and the thrill won't soon be forgotten. After the 8-minute gondola ride drops you on top of the world, hike the 700 steps, across a secure boardwalk, to the top of Samson's Peak. ⏱ *90 min. See p 13,* **3**.

Head back down Mountain Ave., turning left onto Spray Rd. & right over the Bow River Bridge. Take a

quick left onto Buffalo St. & then turn left into the parking lots between Central Park &:

2 Banff Park Museum National Historic Site. Kids will like the discovery room inside this natural history museum, which is inside a log building built in 1903. With more than 5,000 species of birds, insects, and wildlife on display, it's a one-stop shop for learning about the Rockies. Great on a rainy day. ⏱ *45 min. See p 52,* **4**.

You can leave your car parked next to the museum. Walk up Banff Ave., turning right at Caribou St. Half a block later on your left-hand side is:

3 Sushi House. Family-friendly restaurants are a dime a dozen in Banff. But adventurous kids will love choosing sushi off a model train at the tiny Sushi House. Each dish is priced according to the color of the plate—and just ask the sushi master inside the tracks you'd like something special. The food is fresh, and the atmosphere is fun. *304 Caribou St.* ☎ *403/762-4353. $.*

Walk to the west end of Caribou St., turning left on Bear St. to the shop for:

4 Biking. Rent a bike in Banff and head up the Sundance Trail toward Sundance Canyon. The 3.7km (2.3-mile) trail has little elevation gain

At Sushi House, diners select dishes that arrive via a model railroad.

and is paved the entire way. Another option good for families is the 15km (9⅓-mile) Golf Course Loop. It's peaceful and pretty. **Banff Adventures** (211 Bear St.; www.banffadventures.com; ☎ **403/762-4554**) rents kids' bikes, trailers, and strollers.

After dropping off your bikes, return to your car. Drive back over the Bow River Bridge, taking a left onto Spray Rd. Follow it until it ends at:

⑤ The "Castle in the Rockies." Little girls will love to dress up and explore inside the utterly distinctive Fairmont Banff Springs Hotel. Before you settle in for an English-style tea, roam medieval corridors and wander through luxurious ballrooms. ⏱ *90 min. 405 Spray Ave. www.fairmont.com/banff.* ☎ *403/762-6860. Tea in the Rundle Lounge C$42 adults, C$18 kids ages 6–12.*

From Banff Ave., turn east or right on Wolf St. & then northeast or left on Tunnel Mountain Rd. Drive 4km (2½ miles) to the entrance to Tunnel Mountain Campground:

⑥ Grizzly House. A mashup of Gilligan's Island and Heidi's alpine shack, Grizzly House has loads of personality. It's noisy and raucous,

great for energetic families. The specialties are cheese or beef fondues, but the exotic version has you hot-dipping shark, alligator, rattlesnake, ostrich, and frogs' legs. *207 Banff Ave. www.banffgrizzlyhouse. com.* ☎ *403/762-4055. $$.*

⑦ Evening Interpretive Theater. Nature interpreters from Banff National Park offer of evening activities at the Tunnel Mountain Theatre, inside the Tunnel Mountain Campground. Throughout the summer, daily programs at 7:30pm, range from a historical rendition of Banff's legendary characters to stories of adventure in the peaks. They're fun, participatory, and a great learning experience. Best of all, they're free! ⏱ *45 min. Contact Parks Canada for schedules at* ☎ *403/762-1550.*

Day 2
Grab a picnic lunch, bear spray, water, sunscreen, and rain gear and hit the trails. Drive west from Banff on Trans-Canada Hwy. 1 28km (17 miles) to Castle Junction. Turn west onto Hwy. 93A S.

⑧ Hiking to Boom Lake. Scores of life-long hikers have had their first thrills on the trail here in Banff. There are many kid-friendly hikes to choose from. The relatively gentle climb to Boom Lake, is surrounded by a massive limestone wall and has a real sense of discovery to it. Bring a picnic—it's a 10km (6.2-mile) return trip that will take you 4 hours or so. *Trail head is off Hwy. 93 S., 7km (4 miles) west of Castle Junction.*

Day 3
Head out of Banff, west on Trans-Canada Hwy. 1 (58km/36 miles) to the turnoff for Lake Louise. Turn right, heading up the hill to:

9 Lake Louise Sightseeing Gondola.
Kids are intrigued by grizzly bears, and this is a superb place to learn more about the often-misunderstood beast that rules the Banff backcountry. Interpretive guides explain how the "grizz" makes its home. 🕐 *2 hr. See p 63, 9.*

Drive down the hill, over Trans-Canada Hwy. 1. At the main intersection, turn right on Village Rd. past Samson Mall. Past the Post Hotel, take a left into the entrance for:

10 Bill Peyto's Café.
Inside the Lake Louise Hostel and Alpine Centre, this cafe serves healthy, creative food priced for most budgets. The timber-framed room with stone fireplace makes for a relaxed, friendly atmosphere. Try the bison burgers, the Alberta beef chili, or the Alpine club sandwich. *In the Lake Louise*

Teatime at the "Castle in the Rockies."

Hostel & Alpine Centre. 203 Village Rd. www.hihostels.ca; search for "Bill Peyto's." ☎ 403/522-2200. $.

Exit Lake Louise, turning west or left onto Trans-Canada Hwy. 1. Turn north on Hwy. 93, the Icefields Pkwy., continuing for 130km (81 miles) until you reach:

11 Columbia Icefield Adventure.
Hop on a giant tractorlike bus with sky-high wheels called a "snocoach," drive onto a frozen tongue of ice, and then hike out on the ice—not your average day in the park. Tours can be combined with a visit to the Glacier Skywalk glass-bottomed platform. It's best to visit the icefield in the morning or late afternoon to avoid the throngs of tourists arriving by bus. *Tour lasts* 🕐 *90 min. See p 99, 2.*

Enjoying a family-friendly bike route.

Banff in Wintertime

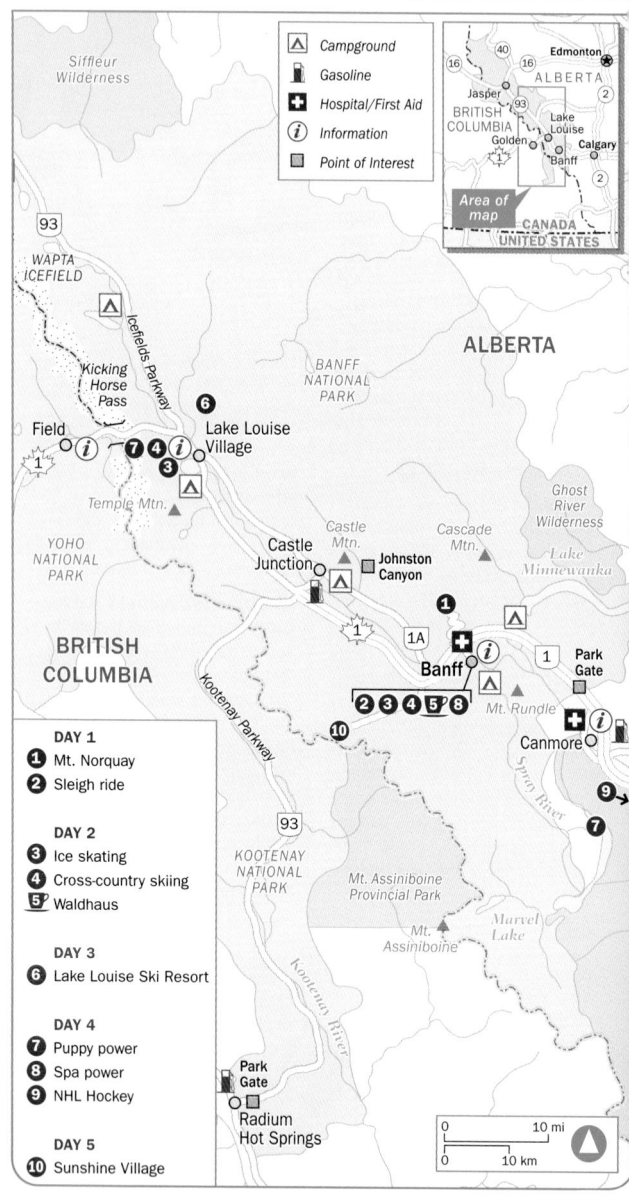

△	Campground
⛽	Gasoline
✚	Hospital/First Aid
ⓘ	Information
▢	Point of Interest

DAY 1
❶ Mt. Norquay
❷ Sleigh ride

DAY 2
❸ Ice skating
❹ Cross-country skiing
5 Waldhaus

DAY 3
❻ Lake Louise Ski Resort

DAY 4
❼ Puppy power
❽ Spa power
❾ NHL Hockey

DAY 5
❿ Sunshine Village

Banff becomes a winter wonderland from late November through early April. Famous for its crisp blue skies, winter in the Canadian Rockies is just as beautiful as summer. In fact, many people swear that winter is an even better time to visit. For those not hindered by the cold, skiing in Banff is a one-of-a-kind experience. And don't forget all those snowmen and -women waiting to be built and evening strolls waiting to be taken under star-studded skies, often active with the stunning *aurora borealis* ("northern lights").

Skiiing Mt. Norquay.

Day 1
❶ Alpine Skiing at Mt. Norquay. A week is just barely enough time to sample the best the area has to offer. Together, the three ski resorts in Banff—Mt. Norquay, Sunshine Village, and Ski Louise—make this one of the great ski destinations in North America. I recommend visiting them each for at least a day. For Day 6, you could return to whichever you liked best (and that's an endless debate that rages on in Banff and will give you plenty to chat with folks about on the chairlift!). The **SkiBig 3** partnership sells a package to all three (www.skibig3.com; ☎ **877/754-7080** or 403/762-4561). Guided experiences include ski coaching, insider terrain, and passes to all three resorts. Mt. Norquay is a locals' favorite because it's intimate and less than 15 minutes from Banff Avenue. It has plenty of intermediate runs and makes a good half-day. Economical ski-by-the-hour deals are good for lighter days. *www.banffnorquay.com.* ☎ *403/762-4421. See p 157.*

Evening 1
❷ Sleigh Ride. For a romantic winter evening, snuggle up under a cozy wool blanket with someone special, join your cowboy guide,

Sleigh ride with Banff Trail Riders.

Ice skating and the Ice Castle at the Fairmont Chateau Lake Louise.

and head out for a one-horse open-sleigh ride with **Banff Trail Riders.** *132 Banff Ave. www.horseback.com.* ☎ *403/762-4551. C$32 adults, C$27 kids ages 4–12.*

Day 2

❸ **Ice Skating.** There are a number of places where you can skate outdoors under the winter sky. It's an exhilarating activity that's popular with families. Try the Vermillion Lakes, just outside the Town of Banff, in the early winter before the snow starts to pile up. Take Mt. Norquay Road out of town, turning left on Vermillion Lakes Drive just before Trans-Canada Hwy. 1. You can rent skates in Banff at **Snowtips** (225 Bear St.; www.snowtips-bactrax.com; ☎ **403/762-8177;** from C$14/day). At the Fairmont Chateau Lake Louise, there is an outdoor rink on the lake with a spectacular ice castle built right on top. It's a very scenic and romantic place to skate. *At the top of Lake Louise Dr. Rent skates at Chateau Mountain Sports inside the hotel. www.chateaumountainsports.com.* ☎ *403/522-3837. From C$13 for 2 hr. or C$16/day.*

❹ **Cross-country Skiing.** A wonderful way to explore the park in winter, cross-country (or "Nordic") skiing promises great exercise, views—and solitude, if you're seeking it. There are more than 80km (50 miles) of managed trails in Banff National Park, many of them within a half-hour drive of Banff townsite. The cross-country ski season runs from December to March. Try the Spray River Loop, which departs from the parking lot at Bow Falls, and the Shoreline Trail at Lake Louise, which starts just in front of the Chateau Lake Louise. See p 158 for ski-rental information.

You Are in Avalanche Country

The Canadian Rockies is avalanche country. An extremely powerful wave of snow and ice that cracks off a mountain slope, an avalanche can destroy everything in its path. It's extremely challenging to predict when an avalanche might occur and even more challenging to escape if you are caught in one. Drivers should avoid stopping in areas where Parks Canada has posted an AVALANCHE ZONE sign. Parks Canada updates avalanche forecasts regularly throughout the winter. In Banff, call ☎ **403/762-1460.**

5 **Waldhaus.** On a crisp winter night, your cheeks aglow from a day in the mountains, what could be more divine than a steaming pot of Alpine-inspired fondue? The best fondue in Banff is at this Bavarian-style cottage in the woods beneath the Fairmont Banff Springs Hotel. *405 Spray Ave. www.fairmont.com/banff.* ☎ *403/762-6860. See p 79. $$$.*

Day 3

6 **Ski Lake Louise.** For jaw-dropping views, coupled with an incredibly varied terrain, head to the legendary **Lake Louise Ski Resort** across the valley from its famed namesake lake. Be sure to drop by cozy Temple Lodge for lunch. Nonskiers can go snowshoeing or on a guided wildlife tour. ☎ *800/258-7669 or 403/522-3555. See p 157.*

Day 4

7 **Puppy Power.** It's one of the oldest forms of transportation in the world. Dog sledding is offered just outside Banff in Kananaskis Country. Drive the dogs or just ride along as you mush your way across a frozen lake. *Book through Snowy Owl Sled Dog Tours. www.snowyowltours.com.* ☎ *403/678-4369. 104-602 Bow Valley Pkwy., Canmore. Starting at C$226 per person.*

8 **Spa Power.** Work out all those après-ski kinks with a visit to the private and decadent **Willow Stream Spa** at the Fairmont Banff Hot Springs. After soaking in the mineral pools, indulge in a deep-tissue or mountain hot-stone massage. *405 Spray Ave. www.fairmont.com/banff-springs/willow-stream/.* ☎ *800/404-1772 or 403/762-2211. From C$209 for 60 min.*

Dog sledding with the Powder Hound Express dog team at Snowy Owl Tours.

Evening 3 or 4

9 **NHL Hockey.** Hockey is a fast-paced game, and you'll catch some of the world's best ice hockey players in action at the Calgary Saddledome, as you cheer on the NHL's Calgary Flames. Pure Canadiana! *Book through Banff Adventures (www.banffadventures.com;* (☎ *403/762-4554; from C$250/person), which has shuttles from Banff for all Flames home games.*

Day 5

10 **Sunshine Village.** Tucked along the Continental Divide, beautiful Sunshine Village generally has the best snow, lots of good intermediate runs, and the notoriously extreme Delirium Dive, for experts only. Sunshine also has the best terrain park in the area and magnificent views of Mt. Assiniboine. Even better, spend the night at **Sunshine Mountain Lodge** and get first turns in the morning. *www.skibanff.com.* ☎ *800/661-1676 or 403/762-6500. See p 157.*

Glaciers & Wildlife

GLACIERS

1. Mt. Temple
2. Mt. Victoria
3. Bath Glacier
4. Crowfoot Glacier
5. Bow Glacier
6. Snowbird Glacier
7. Saskatchewan Glacier
8. Columbia Icefield
9. Athabasca Glacier
10. Snow Dome

WILDLIFE

11. Urban elk in town of Banff
12. Minnewanka Loop
13. Muleshoe
14. Bourgeau Wildlife Overpass
15. Helen Lake
16. Bow Summit
17. Waterfowl Lakes
18. Mt. Coleman

Studying the cycles of nature in the incredible mountain wilderness of the Canadian Rockies is enlightening, astounding, and inspiring. There are more than 1,000 glaciers in Banff, and all of them are retreating. Scientists say the glaciers of Banff lost 25% of their mass during the 20th century. Most can't be seen from the convenience of the major highways. There is, however, an easy-to-access and varied selection you can spot from the roadside, ranging from almost-hidden glaciers like the Snowbird to the most famous glacier in North America, the Athabasca.

Travel Tip

Most of these glaciers are northeast-facing, so the light is better for seeing them in the first half of the day.

Glaciers in Banff National Park

1 Mt. Temple. This may be my favorite peak in Banff. With a giant pyramid-like shape and a beautiful glacier below its summit, Mt. Temple dominates the horizon south of Lake Louise. *6km (3¾ miles) east of Lake Louise on Trans-Canada Hwy. 1.*

2 Mt. Victoria. One of the most photographed mountains in the world, this wide peak provides the scenic backdrop to Lake Louise. Always snow-covered, it's best appreciated from the 5.3km (3.3-mile) hike to the Plain of the Six Glaciers, where the Aberdeen, Upper Lefroy, Lower Lefroy, Upper Victoria, Lower Victoria, and Pope's glaciers (as seen left to right or southeast to southwest) are all visible. It's a 4-hour round-trip that departs on the shore of Lake Louise just past the Fairmont Chateau Lake Louise, heading to the right around the lake. *See p 145, ⑨.*

3 Bath Glacier. Part of the mighty Waputik Icefield, the Bath Glacier hugs the mid-ridge of Mt. Daly. It can be seen at Mt. Hector, just north of Lake Louise. *17km (11 miles) north of Lake Louise on Hwy. 93.*

4 Crowfoot Glacier. Years ago, the three toelike extensions of this glacier clung to the side of a cliff. The lowest "toe" has retreated completely, leaving a rare two-toed crow. *32km (20 miles) north of Lake Louise on Hwy. 93.*

5 Bow Glacier. Visible at the back of the valley behind Num-Ti-Jah Lodge, the Bow Glacier is the same glacier that originally carved

Train through Bow Valley.

Hiking to Saskatchewan Glacier.

out the entire Bow Valley (which you've driven through as you came northwest from Banff) 10,000 years ago. For a closer view, hike the 4.6km (2.9-mile) trail to Bow Glacier Falls, which starts just behind Num-Ti-Jah Lodge. *36km (22 miles) north of Lake Louise on Hwy. 93.*

⑥ Snowbird Glacier. Clinging to the east face of Mt. Patterson, just north of Bow Pass, the beautiful Snowbird Glacier drapes over a cliff, with wings that are limited in size by the width of each ledge. Only the left wing is visible from the highway, best seen 3.1km (2 miles) north of the Silverhorn Creek Bridge, on the west side of the highway at the bottom of the hill past Bow Summit. *48km (30 miles) north of Lake Louise on Hwy. 93.*

The frozen river of Athabasca Glacier.

⑦ Saskatchewan Glacier. The longest tongue of ice flowing off the Columbia Icefield, this is a classic outlet valley glacier. The best view is from Parker Ridge, a superb 2.7km (1.7-mile) hike up the ridge from the highway. *117km (73 miles) north of Lake Louise on Hwy. 93. See p 148,* **⑰**.

⑧ Columbia Icefield. The largest frozen ice mass south of the Arctic Circle, this icefield measures 325 sq. km (125 sq. miles). It includes six glaciers: Athabasca, Saskatchewan, Dome, Columbia, Castleguard, and Stutfield. *125km (78 miles) north of Lake Louise on Hwy. 93. See p 99,* **❶**, *for more information on experiencing the Icefield.*

⑨ Athabasca Glacier. The most famous glacier in North America is in Jasper National Park. It's also the easiest glacier to access—more than 10,000 people visit this frozen river of ice each busy summer day. *125km (78 miles) north of Lake Louise on Hwy. 93. See p 67,* **⑩**.

⑩ Snow Dome. Also in Jasper National Park, this peak is a hydrological apex, one of only two in the world. Here water flows in three directions: north to the Arctic Ocean, east to the Atlantic Ocean, and west to the Pacific Ocean. The Dome Glacier can be seen on Snowdome's north side as you approach the Columbia Icefield from the north on Hwy. 93.

Banff is no zoo! Here, animals roam free, and the natural rhythms of the wilderness are maintained. There are 53 species of wild mammals in Banff, 13 of which are on Parks Canada's "Species at Risk" list. Count yourself lucky if you catch any wildlife sightings in Banff. But if you follow this list, your chances will be higher. Dawn and dusk are the best times of day for spotting wildlife. Be sure to keep track and report all wildlife sightings to Parks Canada at ☎ **403/762-1470.**

Wildlife in Banff National Park

⓫ Urban Elk in the Town of Banff. During certain times of the year (mainly spring and summer), elk make their way into the heart of the Town of Banff. The drive around the Banff Springs Golf Course is a prime area for spotting these magnificent mammals. *At the end of Golf Course Dr. past Bow Falls.*

Bighorn sheep in Banff.

⓬ Minnewanka Loop. Just northeast of the Town of Banff, the drive along Minnewanka Road is particularly good for seeing bighorn sheep, which often gather near Two Jack Lake, 12km (7½ miles) from the Town of Banff on Minnewanka Loop. *Take Banff Ave. to the northeast out of town. It turns into Minnewanka Loop after going under Trans-Canada Hwy.*

An aerial of a Banff National Park Wildlife Overpass.

⓭ Muleshoe. An open pasture off Bow Valley Parkway (Hwy. 1A), this is a good spot for coyotes, elk, and mule deer. Birders also come here to spot Western Tanagers and Hammond's flycatchers. *Take Trans-Canada Hwy. 15.5km (3½ miles) west of Banff to Bow Valley Pkwy. (Hwy. 1A). Continue for 5.5km (3½ miles) to the Muleshoe Picnic Area.*

⓮ Bourgeau Wildlife Overpass. This is one of six specially designed tree-covered bridges that go over Trans-Canada Hwy. 1 west of Banff and allow wildlife like bears, elk, coyotes, wolves, cougars, and moose to roam freely in their natural habitat. The bridges are aimed at reducing the large number of mammals (and humans) that were being killed by vehicles, and they've been extremely successful. There are also 38 underpasses between Banff and Lake Louise. A small but smart interpretive display can be visited at the Hwy. 1 Castle viewpoint rest area located just 1.5km (0.9 miles) west of the Redearth Creek trail head,

Bear Jams: Keep Moving, People!

Everybody's thrilled to catch a glimpse of a bear in the wild. In the Canadian Rockies, there are more "bear jams" than "traffic jams" as tourists pile up in their vehicles to snap photos of grizzlies or black bears, creating chaos on the roads. Whistling, yelling, running about . . . tourists behave strangely in the presence of these magnificent mammals, causing problems that can turn fatal for the bears and for other drivers. If you see a bear and want a closer look, slow down safely, but do not stop. Give the bear space. The moment one car stops, everybody stops. No matter the circumstances, stay in your vehicle and do not approach the bear. Once alerted to the sighting of a bear, Parks Canada staff and often the police will appear at the scene to urge travelers to keep moving. Remember to call in a bear sighting to ☎ **403/762-1470.**

another 9.5km (6 miles) past the Bourgeau Overpass. *11km (6¾ miles) northwest of Banff on Trans-Canada Hwy. 1.*

⑮ **Helen Lake.** From the high alpine environment of this hiking trail near the Crowfoot Glacier, you'll be tramping through prime grizzly bear habitat. You may also spot white-tailed ptarmigan, grouse, and golden eagles. *33km (21 miles) north of Lake Louise on Icefields Pkwy. See p 147,* ⑮.

⑯ **Bow Summit.** Following the short interpretive trail to the Peyto Lake and on to the Bow Summit lookout, you may be able to see cute little mammals, such as pikas (which look like miniature rabbits) and hoary marmots. *41km (25 miles) north of Lake Louise on Icefields Pkwy.*

⑰ **Waterfowl Lakes.** You won't be surprised to see mallard ducks and loons on these lakes. What may well surprise you, however, is

Pika eating grass in Banff.

spotting a moose. Summer evenings are the best time. *58km (36 miles) north of Lake Louise on Icefields Pkwy.*

⑱ **Mt. Coleman.** From the picnic area at its base, mountain goats can be spotted clinging precariously to the cliff of this peak. *100km (62 miles) north of Lake Louise on Icefields Pkwy.* ●

The Town of Banff

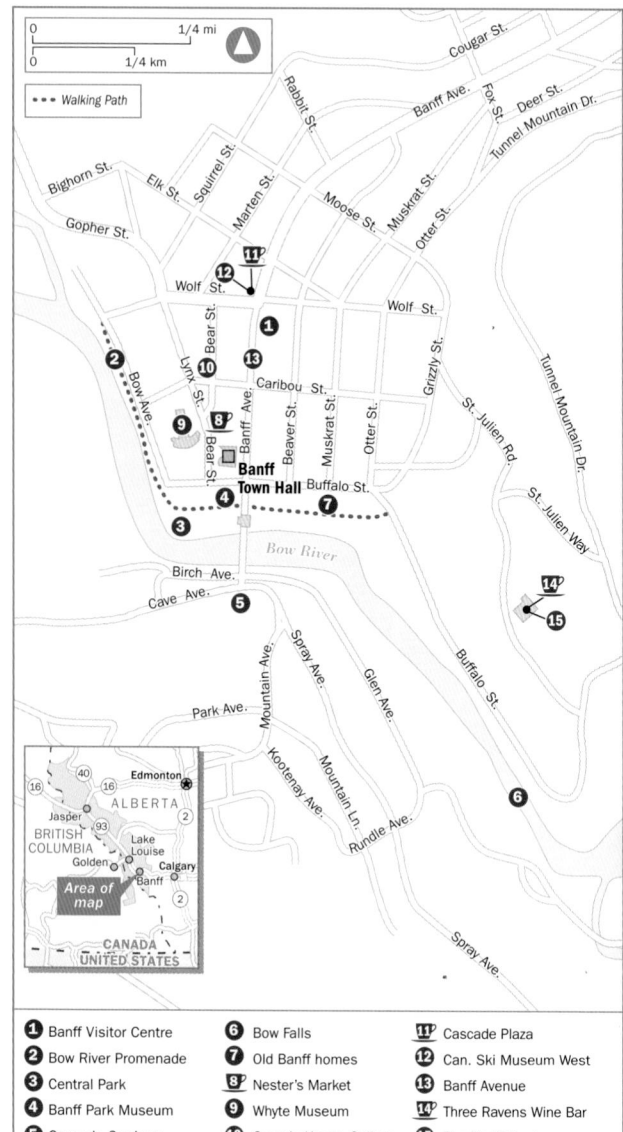

1 Banff Visitor Centre
2 Bow River Promenade
3 Central Park
4 Banff Park Museum
5 Cascade Gardens
6 Bow Falls
7 Old Banff homes
8 Nester's Market
9 Whyte Museum
10 Canada House Gallery
11 Cascade Plaza
12 Can. Ski Museum West
13 Banff Avenue
14 Three Ravens Wine Bar
15 The Banff Centre

Previous page: Banff Avenue.

The Town of Banff is the beating heart of Canada's first and most important national park. Planned and organized as a resort town from the beginning, the focus here remains on pleasing visitors. You'll find historic and natural highlights dotted around the outskirts of town, but the center of all things is bustling Banff Avenue, the main drag. Here, tourists speaking dozens of languages nip in and out of shops, pop into a pub for a pint, get their skis and bikes tuned up, and enjoy some truly fabulous cuisine.

❶ ★★ Banff Visitor Centre.
This is a must for your first stop of the day. Located in the heritage building in the heart of "downtown" Banff, it's a great orientation center, with helpful desks staffed by the friendly folks at Parks Canada and the Banff–Lake Louise Tourism Bureau. It has maps, brochures, and trail updates, and staff can help you decide what to do when. At the back, a short video will help you get your bearings and understand just why this place is so important. ⏱ *20 min. 224 Banff Ave. www. banfflakelouise.com.* ☎ *403/762-1550. Mid-May to Sept 8am–8pm; Oct to mid-May 9am–5pm. Closed Dec 25. See p 13,* ❶*.*

Exit the Information Centre and cross Banff Ave. at the lights at the corner of Wolf St. Continue down Wolf St. 3 blocks, crossing Bear and Lynx sts., until you reach:

❷ Bow River Promenade.
The canoe docks mark the beginning of a gentle, paved trail that follows one of Canada's most important rivers. The beautiful Bow River is the longest river in Banff National Park. From its headwaters at Bow Lake, 90km (56 miles) north of the Town of Banff, it flows south and east, passing through Banff, Canmore, and Calgary. It joins the South Saskatchewan River and eventually drains into Hudson Bay and the Atlantic Ocean, on Canada's east coast. This promenade makes for a good stroll full of wonderful views.

Follow the trail downriver, around the bend to:

❸ Central Park.
Site of Canada Day markets, weddings, picnics, and Frisbee-tossing, this is Banff's main outdoor meeting space. During the summer, Parks Canada's

A couple enjoys a walk along the Bow River.

Banff's Cascade Gardens.

"Roving Interpreters" often set up shop at one of the picnic tables (you'll spot them in their red and green uniforms). Sometimes you'll see elk feeding here too! ⏱ *15 min. Along the north shore of the Bow River btw. Banff Ave. & Bow Ave., parallel to Buffalo St.*

Next to the park, on the east side between the park and Banff Ave., is:

❹ ★★ kids **Banff Park Museum.** A beautiful building dating to 1903 and reflecting early Rocky Mountain architecture, this is the oldest natural history museum in Western Canada. It houses an incredibly complete collection of wildlife. It's also a superb rainy-day option. Come for a good look at beaver's teeth or an elk's antler. Daily tours start at 3pm. ⏱ *30 min. 91 Banff Ave.* ☎ *403/762-1558. Adults C$4, seniors C$3, free for kids ages 17 & under. Mid-May to mid-Oct Wed–Sun 9:30am–5pm; Mid-Oct to mid-May Sat–Sun 11am–5pm.*

Walk over the Bow River Bridge. Cross Mountain Rd. & head through the iron gate for a visit to:

❺ **Cascade Gardens.** Inspired by the geological history of the Rockies, this lovely garden includes a series of fountains, or "cascades," that are an essential part of appreciating the architecture and design of the Banff Administration Building. During summer, the local Siksika First Nation erects a traditional tepee here with an interesting cultural exhibit. Turn to face Cascade Mountain and Banff Avenue for that timeless photo opportunity. ⏱ *30 min. At the T-intersection where Spray and Cave aves. meet Banff Ave., just over the Bow River Bridge. Free admission. Daily 24 hr.*

One of Banff's original heritage homes.

Some of the cheeses available at Nester's Market.

Back across Mountain Rd., turn right (east) before crossing the bridge, following the trail 1.2km (0.8 miles) to:

⑥ ★ Bow Falls. Tucked beneath the Fairmont Banff Springs Hotel, Bow Falls lets you escape the hustle and bustle of the busy Banff townsite. The 10m (33-ft.) falls, eroding between two rock formations, roar and wash away any tension you may have picked up. The rock on the left bank of the river is 245 million years old, while the one on the right bank is some 320 million years old. Downstream from the falls, the Banff Springs Golf Course dominates the southern side of the valley.

Walk back upriver. At the Bow River Bridge, take the east (or downriver) sidewalk & begin exploring the historic neighborhoods of "old Banff," along Beaver and Muskrat sts.

⑦ Old Banff Homes. Along Buffalo Street, backing onto the Bow River, are some of the most spectacular homes in Western Canada. Remember, Banff has a "need to reside" rule—only people with jobs or businesses in Banff can live here.

At 313 Buffalo St. is a home dating to 1920 that was once the park superintendent's residence. At the corner of Buffalo and Muskrat streets, you'll find the historic Grant-Hemming home, built in 1921 from local materials (note the Rundlestone steps and riverstone chimney). Next door are legendary naturalist and climatologist Norman Sanson's home and the summer residence of Senator Amedée Forget.

⑧ Nester's Market. If you were drawn to one of the riverside picnic tables along the Bow River, stop in here. With a deli, bakery, and plenty of fresh produce, you can put together a superb lunch to go. *122 Bear St. www.nestersmarket. com/banff.* ☎ *403/762-3663. Daily 8am–11pm. $.*

Walk back to the Bow River trail at the end of Muskrat St. & continue along the river, passing Central Park. On Lynx St., turn right to:

⑨ ★★ Whyte Museum of the Canadian Rockies. This museum houses excellent exhibits on the human history of Banff and holds a

Banff's Whyte Museum.

tremendously wealthy archive of memoirs, sketches, photographs, and personal artifacts of Rocky Mountain pioneers, visionaries, and artists. Changing exhibits shine light on how the mountains have inspired generations; the newest is "Gateway to the Rockies," which looks at local history with interactive displays. Another excellent rainy-day activity. ⏱ *90 min. 111 Bear St. www.whyte.org.* ☎ *403/762-2291. C$10 adults, C$5 students, free for kids under 12. Daily 10am–5pm.*

Cross Lynx St. & head down the lovely Bear St. On the left-hand side, a few shops down, you'll find:

⑩ ★ Canada House Gallery.

Even if you aren't a dedicated art collector, it's worth taking time to explore this fine arts shop and gallery featuring exclusively Canadian art. The focus is on landscape, contemporary, and Native styles. It's not hard to understand how the Rockies inspire these artists. There are often opening receptions for the public on Saturday afternoons. ⏱ *20 min. 201 Bear St. www.canada house.com.* ☎ *403/762-3757. Sun–Thurs 9:30am–6pm; Fri–Sat 9:30am–7pm.*

Follow Bear St. to its terminus at Wolf St. & head into:

⑪ Cascade Plaza. For a quick and affordable pick-me-up, jump into the food court at the basement of Banff's biggest mall. You'll find a dozen different counters serving everything from sushi and pizza to curries. You can buy lunch for under C$12. *317 Banff Ave. www.cascade shops.com.* ☎ *403/762-8484. $.*

The Rockies inspire much of the art at Canada House Gallery.

time to walk the scene and eavesdrop on dozens of languages. A massive redevelopment project in 2007 widened the sidewalks, making street life more pleasant.

Head up Wolf St. & turn right on St. Julien Rd. Follow the curving road until you enter the campus of the Banff Centre.

Downtown Banff.

Before riding the escalators up, start at the bottom-floor display for:

⑫ Canadian Ski Museum West.
From early wooden telemark skis to the latest World Cup victories, the history of Banff's favorite sport is told in displays throughout the three-story Cascade Mall. Start at the first floor and work your way up to follow in chronological order. You may even bump into a real ski legend or two while roaming about Banff. ⏱ *20 min. 317 Banff Ave.* ☎ *403/762-8484. Free admission. Mon–Thurs 10am–8pm; Fri–Sat 10am–9pm; Sun 10am–6pm.*

Exit the mall and turn right to stroll:

⑬ Banff Avenue.
This is one of Canada's iconic main drags, home to great shops, cafes, restaurants, historic buildings, and a general hustle-and-bustle ambience. Take

⑭ ★ Three Ravens Wine Bar.
For a quick preconcert bite to eat, a cocktail, or a postevent glass of wine and dessert, you can't beat this scenic restaurant above the Sally Borden Building in the Banff Centre. It wins for the best restaurant view in Banff, by far. Try a glass of pinot noir from the Okanagan with Spanish paprika beef rolls. *At the Banff Centre on St. Julien Rd. www.banffcentre.ca.* ☎ *403/762-6300. Daily 4pm–midnight. $$.*

⑮ The Banff Centre.
Part of the town's fabric for nearly a century, this world-renowned arts, culture, and educational institution hosts celebrated musicians, writers, and other artists from around the world on a regular basis. The Centre's **Summer Arts Festival** showcases the best in a variety of artistic areas—from costume design and creative writing, to drama and opera, to jazz and classical music. It's another place where the mountains truly awaken inspiration and creativity. Don't miss the chance to take in an inspiring performance, often in the outdoors, during your visit to Banff. *St. Julien Rd. www.banffcentre.ca.* ☎ *403/762-6100.*

Lake Minnewanka

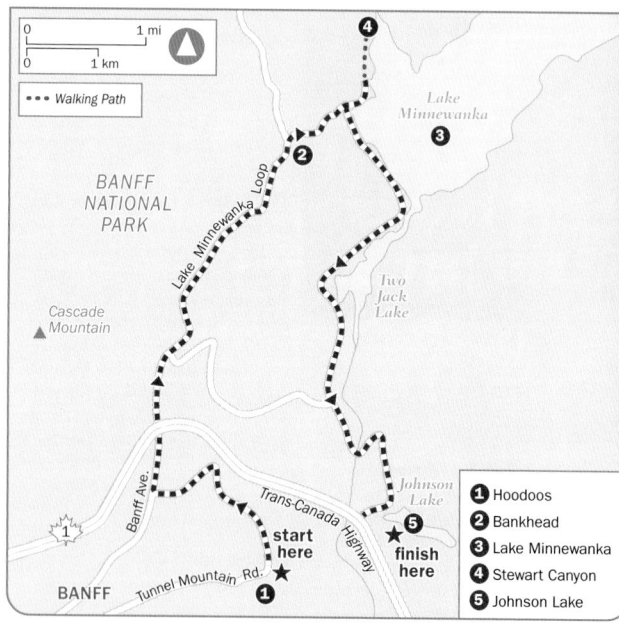

0 1 mi	
0 1 km	

••• Walking Path

BANFF
NATIONAL
PARK

Lake
Minnewanka

Lake Minnewanka Loop

Cascade
▲ Mountain

Two
Jack
Lake

Banff Ave.

Trans-Canada Highway

Johnson
Lake

start
here ★

finish
here ★

Tunnel Mountain Rd.

BANFF

❶ Hoodoos
❷ Bankhead
❸ Lake Minnewanka
❹ Stewart Canyon
❺ Johnson Lake

Some call it a giant bathtub, but Lake Minnewanka does offer unique activities and a chance for open skies. It's the biggest lake in Banff National Park, created by nature and later expanded by humanity. The Minnewanka Loop makes a nice tour from the Town of Banff and can be done in a leisurely 2 or 3 hours. To extend it, add the hike to C-Level Cirque or another of the hikes listed in chapter 6. Watch for bighorn sheep on the road near Two Jack Lake—and remember not to feed them.

❶ **Hoodoos.** The mysterious pillars look like they've been dropped from outer space. In fact, they are freestanding posts made of silt, gravel, and rocks cemented together by dissolved limestone. The uncemented particles were slowly eroded and washed away. A paved, stroller-friendly 500m (1,640-ft.) trail leads to a nice viewpoint that also offers lovely views of Mt. Rundle and the Bow River. *Just off Tunnel Mountain*

Rd. past the entrance to Tunnel Mountain Campground Village I, 4km (2½ miles) east of Banff.

Tunnel Mountain Rd. continues to loop around until it meets up with Lake Minnewanka Rd. again, which passes under Trans-Canada Hwy. 1 and goes northeast along the side of Cascade Mountain. Pull off Lake Minnewanka Rd. after 3km (1¾ miles).

2 Bankhead. Once the working center of Banff, Bankhead was a small settlement that boomed in the early 20th century. Old machinery and foundations are still in place, such as the entranceway to the former church and the transformer building, which features a display about coal mining. A short 10-minute walk about the area, following interpretive displays, helps bring the history to life.

Continue down the road another 2.6km (1½ miles) and pull into the large parking lot just before:

3 Lake Minnewanka. This lake used to be called "the Lake of the Water Spirits" by the Stoney Nation, who apparently feared these spirits and refused to swim in or boat on the lake. Early Europeans took a likewise timid view, calling it "Devil's Lake." Although the water is too cold for a dip, boaters today have no fear. This is the only lake in Banff where motorboats are allowed. From May through October, you can take an enclosed boat trip to the end of the lake. ⏱ *60 min. www.banffjasper collection.com.* ☎ *403/762-3473. Adults C$64, kids ages 6–15 C$32, free for kids 5 & under.*

To the north of the parking lot is a day-use area with picnic tables & shelters. Continue through to reach the trail for Stewart Canyon.

Mt. Rundle, the Bow River, and the hoodoos from the Hoodoo Trail Overlook.

4 ★ Stewart Canyon. A nice 30-minute round-trip walk along the lakeshore takes you to this canyon, named for the first superintendent of Banff National Park. Much of the canyon has lain underwater since Minnewanka was dammed, first in 1895 and again in 1912 and 1941. The highlight is the giant wooden truss bridge. The trail is very accessible (even to wheelchairs).

Returning to the parking lot, head across the causeway, past Two Jack Lake. At 2.4km (1½ miles) from Minnewanka, turn left to:

5 Johnson Lake. Not to be confused with Johnston Canyon, which is farther west, this man-made lake is the best place in Banff for a swim on a hot day. A flat 3.5km (2.1-mile) trail circles the lake; walk counterclockwise to take in views of Cascade Mountain.

Lake Minnewanka used to be known as "the Lake of the Water Spirits."

Bow Valley Parkway

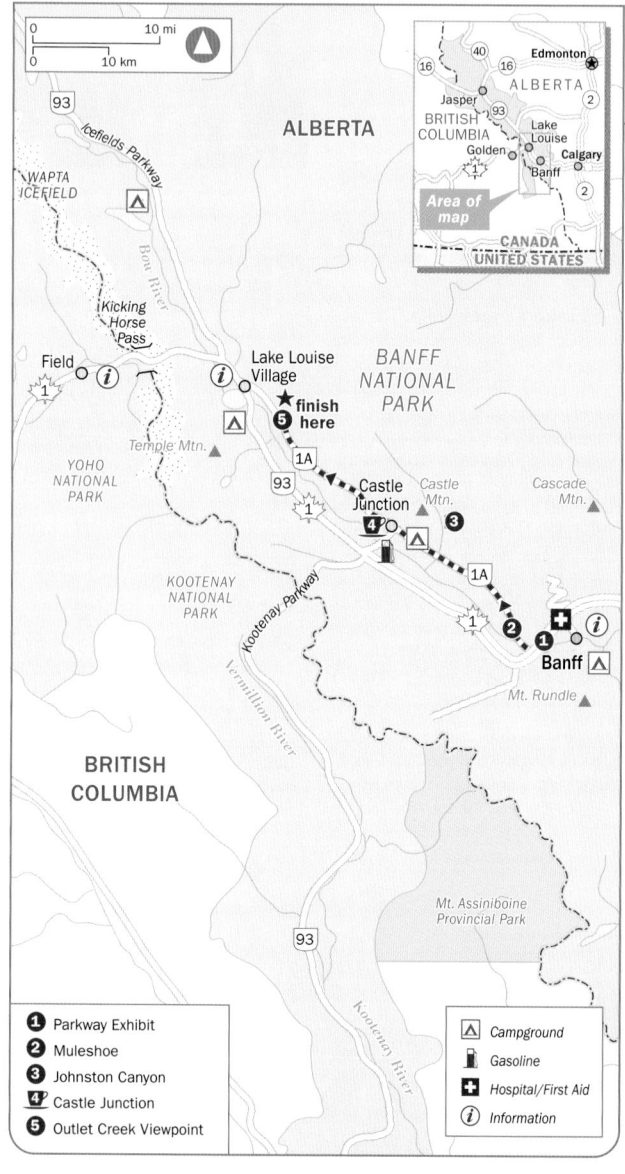

1 Parkway Exhibit
2 Muleshoe
3 Johnston Canyon
4 Castle Junction
5 Outlet Creek Viewpoint

▲ Campground
▐ Gasoline
✚ Hospital/First Aid
ⓘ Information

Bow Valley Parkway (Hwy. 1A) is less congested than Trans-Canada Hwy. 1, although the two roads run parallel along the Bow River. Built in 1920—the first road connecting Banff and Lake Louise—this 51km (32-mile) route still feels more like a mountain road than an expressway. Each of the 13 interpretive stops along the way is worthwhile, but I've selected the best of the bunch. The drive will take about 3 hours, including stops.

Head left (north) on Mt. Norquay Rd. out of the townsite & turn left (west) onto Trans-Canada Hwy. You'll meet up with Bow Valley Pkwy. about 5km (3 miles) from town.

① Parkway Exhibit. Westbound travelers can make a quick stop at this turnoff to orient themselves to the route ahead. There is a good map and a refresher on the etiquette of wildlife encounters. *0.9km (½ mile) from the start of Bow Valley Pkwy.*

② ★ Muleshoe. A short 1km (0.6-mile) trail starts across the highway

The 98-foot-high upper falls of Johnston Canyon.

from the picnic area and explores the remnants of the 1993 pre-scribed fire. *5.5km (3½ miles) from the start of Bow Valley Pkwy.*

③ ★ Johnston Canyon. A walkway leads up this canyon, past two large waterfalls carved through limestone bedrock. The first part of the trail is on a paved surface and is a very gentle climb that ends at the first waterfall, called the Lower Falls. There are interpretive signs on the way up to the Upper Falls, almost twice the height of the Lower Falls and an additional 1.6km (1 mile). *18km (11 miles) west of Banff townsite.*

④ Castle Junction. Three important roads meet here: Bow Valley Parkway, Hwy. 93, and Trans-Canada Hwy. 1. There's a gas station, a small convenience store, and cozy cabins. If you haven't already done so in the Banff townsite, this is a good place to pick up basic picnic supplies. *28km (17 miles) from the Town of Banff.* ☎ 403/522-2783. $.

⑤ Outlet Creek Viewpoint. Here you'll find a grand view of towering Mt. Temple, the third-highest peak in Banff National Park. Known as Morant's Curve, the S-bend in the Canadian Pacific Railway tracks below here offers a classic photo when eastbound trains motor through the valley. *46km (29 miles) from the start of Bow Valley Pkwy.*

Lake Louise

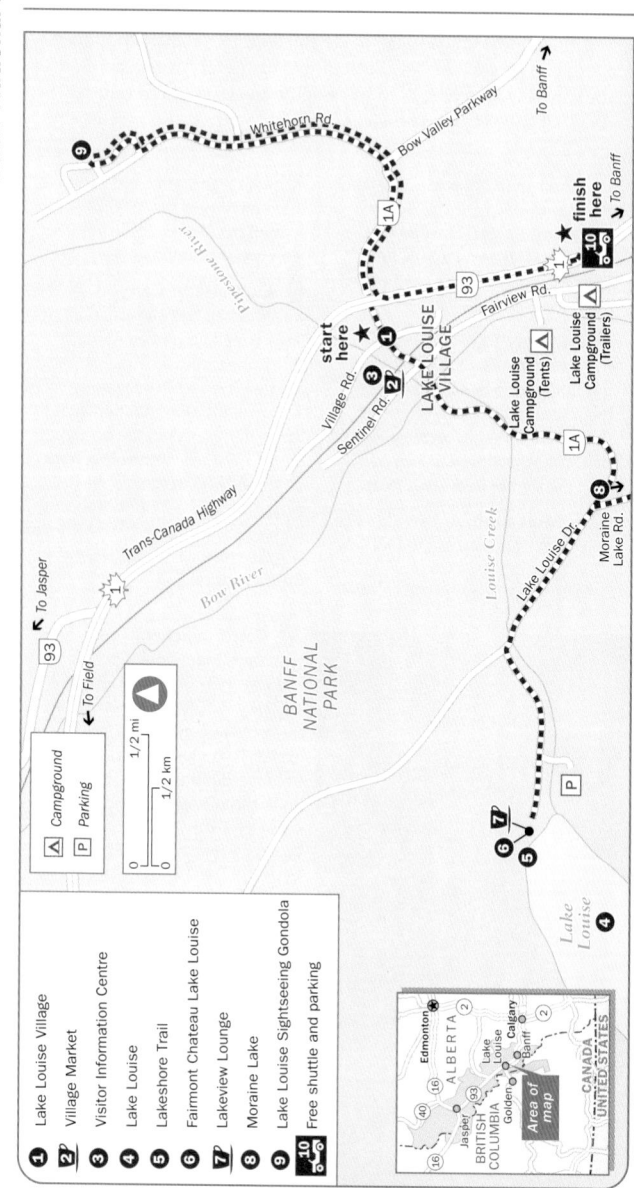

1. Lake Louise Village
2. Village Market
3. Visitor Information Centre
4. Lake Louise
5. Lakeshore Trail
6. Fairmont Chateau Lake Louise
7. Lakeview Lounge
8. Moraine Lake
9. Lake Louise Sightseeing Gondola
10. Free shuttle and parking

You can't come to Banff and not see beautiful and incredibly popular Lake Louise. Situated 56km (35 miles) northwest of the Town of Banff, Lake Louise is perhaps the most photographed lake in the country, one that people from all over the world associate with their image of Canada. It's also the name of the small village just below the lake. While many people drive out just to snap a photo and then return to their hotel, Lake Louise deserves a full day, with at least a short hike and time for tea. Parking has become a big problem; see tips below.

Travel Tip

Leave your car at the parking lot off the highway and board the shuttle up to Lake Louise or Moraine Lake to maximize your time. Or better yet, take the bus right from the Town of Banff. See p 13. If you feel you must drive your own car, be sure to start this day's itinerary well before 8am, or you'll be turned back by full parking lots.

❶ **Lake Louise Village.** Consisting of the key elements of a small village (or "hamlet," as Parks Canada refers to it), here you'll find gas stations, a grocery and liquor store, a post office, an ATM, and an outdoor equipment store. *See p 76 for Lake Louise hotels.*

❷ **Village Market.** Amid the trail maps and souvenirs, pop into this grocery store for picnic supplies. Although it's not as well-stocked as the grocery stores in Banff, you can get dips, veggies, simple sandwiches, snacks, and drinks to fill your backpack. *101 Lake Louise Dr.* ☎ *403/522-3894. $.*

❸ ★ **Visitor Information Centre.** Housed behind Samson Mall, Parks Canada's main outpost in Lake Louise has a ton of information, including exhibits and a theater presenting the geological history of the Canadian Rockies. You can also pick up permits and maps as well as trail, weather, and road reports. *101 Lake Louise Dr.* ☎ *403/522-3833.*

Inside a Samson Mall shop in Lake Louise Village.

The History of the Chateau

The Chateau Lake Louise had humble beginnings, in the form of a cabin built on the site in 1890 by the CPR (Canadian Pacific Railway). By 1917, the cabin had burned to the ground, and a hotel with all the modern amenities of the day was erected in its place. While the Banff Springs Hotel, also run by the CPR, was to be luxurious, the CPR marketed the Chateau Lake Louise as a destination for outdoor adventurers. Mountaineers, artists, and horseback riders flooded in, giving the Chateau a level of popularity and character that the Springs is still striving for. In a hotel with a feel akin to the Swiss Alps, mountain culture is alive and well.

June 1–Sept 30 8:30am–7pm; Oct 1–May 31 9am–5pm.

Follow Lake Louise Dr. through the four-way stop & pass beneath the railway overpass. Continue about 8km (5 miles) or a 5-minute drive from the village up to the lake itself and the often-crowded parking lot.

❹ ★★★ **Lake Louise.** In summer, thousands of people empty out of bus tours in front of the lake each day to have their picture taken and then jump back on to the bus and head off to the next tour stop. It's quite crowded. But the lake is so beautiful and pristine, you should go anyway. Fed by glacial meltwater, Lake Louise is 2.4km (1½ miles) long, 500m (1,640 ft.) wide, and 90m (295 ft.) deep. Behind it is **Mt. Victoria**, at an elevation of 3,464m (11,365 ft.), with the thick **Victoria Glacier** on its front ridge. The lake was named after Princess Louise Caroline Alberta (1849–1939), the fourth daughter of Queen Victoria and later the wife of the governor-general of Canada.

❺ ★ **Lakeshore Trail.** This 2km (1.2-mile) path (each way) runs from the Chateau along the lake's north shore to the western end of the lake. At the back of the lake, quartzite crags are popular with rock climbers. It's open to walkers May through October, depending on snow, and to skiers the rest of the year.

Marvelous views accompany the meals at the Fairmont Chateau Lake Louise.

Hiking Lake Louise.

6 ★ Fairmont Chateau Lake Louise. Often called a "diamond in the wilderness," this impressive and important hotel is rich in history and obviously blessed with an incredible setting. If you aren't a guest, you are welcome to come in for a meal, some shopping or tea, or just roaming and wondering at the fantastic ambience. *See p 79.*

7 Lakeview Lounge. It's all quite civilized inside this superb place for an afternoon tea at the Chateau Lake Louise. The view, stretching across the lake, is divine. Traditional afternoon tea service includes sandwiches, scones, sweets, and polished silver. *www.fairmont.com/lake-louise.* ☎ *403/522-1818. Tea served daily noon–4pm. $$$.*

There is a winding road (open only May–Oct) that takes you the 13km (8 miles) from Lake Louise to Moraine Lake. At the often-crowded parking lot are a lodge, a picnic area, and some interpretive exhibits.

8 ★★★ Moraine Lake. Just south of Lake Louise is another stunning alpine lake, situated in front of the Valley of the Ten Peaks.

Wild and dramatic, Moraine Lake is also very popular. You can rent canoes here for C$40 per hour or walk an excellent interpretive trail to the Moraine Lake Rockpile for the view that used to be on the Canadian C$20 bill. Moraine Lake is also the trail head for a number of the best hikes in Banff National Park (see chapter 6). Again, park in the village and take the shuttle up!

Head back to Lake Louise Rd., down to the village, over Trans-Canada Hwy. 1 & up Whitehorn Rd. to:

9 ★★ kids Lake Louise Sightseeing Gondola. In the summer, take a gondola to the summit of Whitehorn Mountain for excellent views of the Bow Valley, Lake Louise, and the Continental Divide. Naturalists lead guided hikes that are great interactive learning experiences. Grizzly bears have been known to hang out here in the summer, so going with a guide is a wise idea. *At the top of Whitehorn Rd. www.lakelouisegondola.com.* ☎ *403/522-3555. Adults C$38, kids ages 6–15 C$17, kids 5 & under free. Mid-May to mid-June 9am–4pm; mid-June to July 31 8am–5:30pm; Aug 1–Sept 2 8am–6pm; Sept 3–Oct 13 8am–5pm.*

The Icefields Parkway

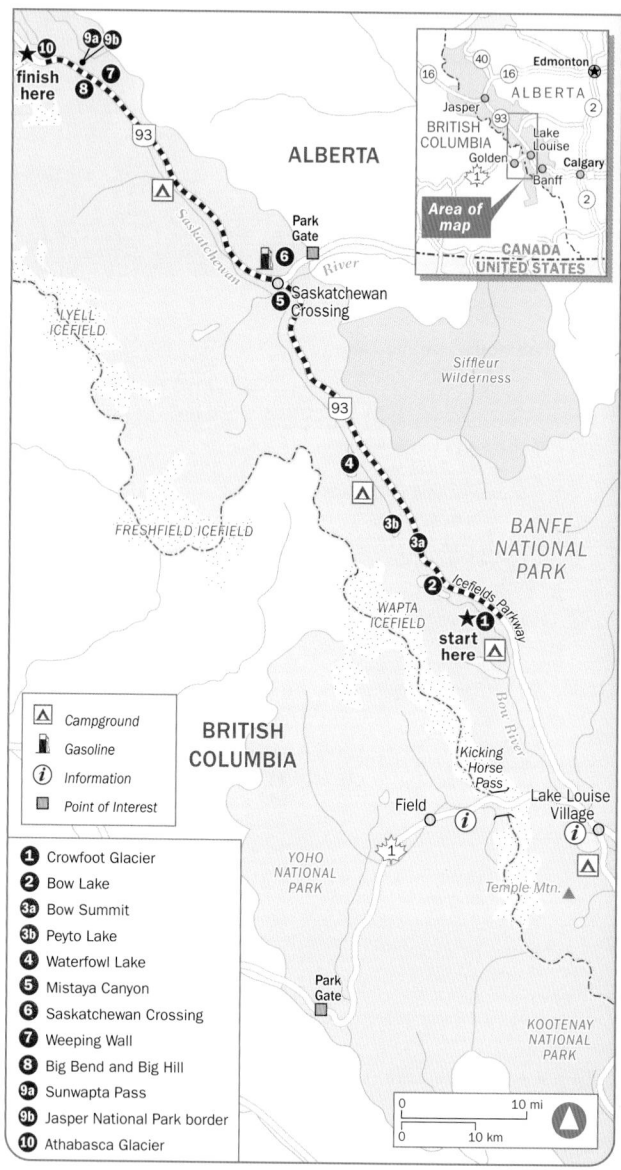

ALBERTA

Park Gate

Saskatchewan Crossing

LYELL ICEFIELD

Siffleur Wilderness

FRESHFIELD ICEFIELD

BANFF NATIONAL PARK

WAPTA ICEFIELD

Icefields Parkway

start here

Bow River

Kicking Horse Pass

BRITISH COLUMBIA

Field

Lake Louise Village

YOHO NATIONAL PARK

Temple Mtn.

Park Gate

KOOTENAY NATIONAL PARK

Legend

- △ Campground
- ⛽ Gasoline
- ⓘ Information
- ▪ Point of Interest

1. Crowfoot Glacier
2. Bow Lake
3a. Bow Summit
3b. Peyto Lake
4. Waterfowl Lake
5. Mistaya Canyon
6. Saskatchewan Crossing
7. Weeping Wall
8. Big Bend and Big Hill
9a. Sunwapta Pass
9b. Jasper National Park border
10. Athabasca Glacier

finish here

Inset map:
Edmonton
ALBERTA
Jasper
BRITISH COLUMBIA
Golden
Lake Louise
Calgary
Banff
Area of map
CANADA
UNITED STATES

0 — 10 mi
0 — 10 km

The landscape you see on the spectacular Icefields Parkway is the kind that used to dominate western North America. Hwy. 93 (Icefields Parkway) connects Banff and Jasper National Parks, and along the way you'll be wowed by raging rivers, turquoise lakes, glacier-clad summits, and massive icefields. The hiking trails and the wildlife viewing are outstanding. Plan to get out of your car often! This tour only covers the highway as far as the Icefields Centre. For information on continuing to Jasper, see p 98.

Travel Tip

If you haven't already got one, pick up a detailed map and guide to Icefields Parkway from the Lake Louise Visitors Centre, in Lake Louise's Samson Mall (101 Lake Louise Dr.; ☎ 403/522-3833).

As you continue north on Icefields Pkwy., the road steadily climbs higher & higher & the views become more & more dramatic as you make your way through three river valleys & pass beneath towering glacier-topped peaks.

❶ Crowfoot Glacier. It's the first of a long lineup of glaciers you'll see. There are interpretive signs posted at the roadside viewpoint. It's a good spot to contemplate the shrinking of the world's glaciers and the impact of climate change. *33km (21 miles) north of the Trans-Canada Hwy. 1 junction at Lake Louise.*

❷ ★ Bow Lake. This ice-blue lake is the third largest in Banff National Park. Almost all of its water is glacier-fed; you can just see the Bow Glacier at the back of the lake. It's a nice place for a picnic. The red-roofed inn on the lake's northeast shore is **Num-Ti-Jah Lodge** (p 81). *34km (21 miles) north of the Trans-Canada Hwy. 1 junction at Lake Louise.*

❸ ★★ Bow Summit and Peyto Lake. At an elevation of 2,069m (6,788 ft.), you're at the highest point in Canada that can be crossed by a highway year-round. Walk the short interpretive trail at Bow Summit to see this beautiful

Sunrise at Crowfoot Mountain and Crowfoot Glacier.

turquoise lake set far below the lookout in a deep glacial valley. It's named for pioneer guide "Wild" Bill Peyto, who was a warden in Banff National Park. Continue along a short extension of the trail, going left and up the hill, for views of the glacier that feeds the lake. *40km (25 miles) north of the Trans-Canada Hwy. 1 junction at Lake Louise.*

As you head north past Peyto Lake, the landscape becomes more barren and beautiful.

④ Waterfowl Lake. Stop at the pullout next to this serene lake to view some of the mighty peaks along the Continental Divide. In fact, all the mountains on the west side of Icefields Parkway form part of the backbone of the continent. From here, you can see Howse Peak and Mt. Chephren, a classically horned peak resembling a pyramid. *56km (35 miles) north of the Trans-Canada Hwy. 1 junction at Lake Louise.*

⑤ ★ Mistaya Canyon. The beauty of this deep canyon is in its sublimely curvy walls, the fierce roar of the water, and the quiet trail, much quieter than at the other famous canyons in the Rockies. The Mistaya River drops off Bow Summit and has carved out a series of potholes along the canyon's walls.

The Mistaya River descends through Mistaya Canyon.

A steep but short 0.5km (0.3-mile) trail leads from the north end of a parking lot on the west side of Icefields Parkway down into to the canyon. *71km (44 miles) north of the Trans-Canada Hwy. 1 junction at Lake Louise.*

⑥ Saskatchewan River Crossing. On the banks of the Saskatchewan River, this crossing is a good place to stretch your legs or have a bite to eat. A roadside resort complex, **The Crossing** (www. thecrossingresort.com), has 66 rooms, dining room, cafeteria, pub, general store, gas station, and gift shop. *77km (48 miles) north of the Trans-Canada Hwy. 1 junction with the start of Icefields Pkwy. 93.*

Bow Lake, the third largest in Banff National Park.

Icewalk Guided Tours

Adventurous folk will want to join a certified mountain guide on an interpretive hike on the ice. Guides with **Athabasca Glacier Icewalks** (www.icewalks.com; ☎ **800/565-7547**) leave daily from the Toe-of-the-Glacier parking lot. Hikes for 3 to 4 hours cost C$110 for adults and C$60 for kids ages 7 to 16 (kids ages 6 and under not allowed). More strenuous and more exploratory 6-hour hikes cost C$175 for adults, C$90 for kids ages 7 to 16.

Pull over on the west side of the highway to get a look at:

7 The Weeping Wall. In the summer you may see only a few drops of water wetting the ridge on the east side of the highway, but in the winter these drips and drops freeze to create a huge frozen waterfall draped in layer upon layer of ice. This is a hot spot for the technical sport of ice climbing. *106km (66 miles) north of the Trans-Canada Hwy. 1 junction at Lake Louise.*

8 Big Bend & Big Hill. A famous hairpin turn is followed by a steep hill, both of which are excruciatingly difficult for cyclists. A pull-out at the top of the hill offers a nice view of Bridal View Falls. *111km (69 miles) north of the Trans-Canada Hwy. 1 junction at Lake Louise.*

9 Sunwapta Pass & Jasper National Park. At 2,023m (6,637 ft.), this is the second-highest point on Icefields Parkway and forms the border between Banff and Jasper National Parks. It's also the border between the two watersheds: The North Saskatchewan River drains from here to Lake Winnipeg, Hudson Bay, and the Atlantic Ocean, while on the other side of the pass, the Sunwapta River eventually makes its way to the Arctic Ocean. It's all downhill from here—108km (67 miles) north on Icefields Parkway to Jasper townsite. *122km (76 miles) north of the Trans-Canada Hwy. 1 junction at Lake Louise.*

10 ★★ Athabasca Glacier. With its tongue almost touching the highway, this is the most accessible of the six principal glaciers that make up the Columbia Icefield, and it's also the most visited glacier in North America. It's receding 2m to 3m (6½–9¾ ft.) each year. Park your car at the Toe-of-the-Glacier trail head (which was covered by ice in the 1950s) and walk down through the lunarlike landscape to the ice. Don't venture onto the ice without a guide (see below). For information on the Athabasca glacier tours, see p 17, **19**. *127km (79 miles) north of the Trans-Canada Hwy. 1 junction at Lake Louise.*

The Crossing Resort at Saskatchewan River Crossing.

Dining in **Banff National Park**

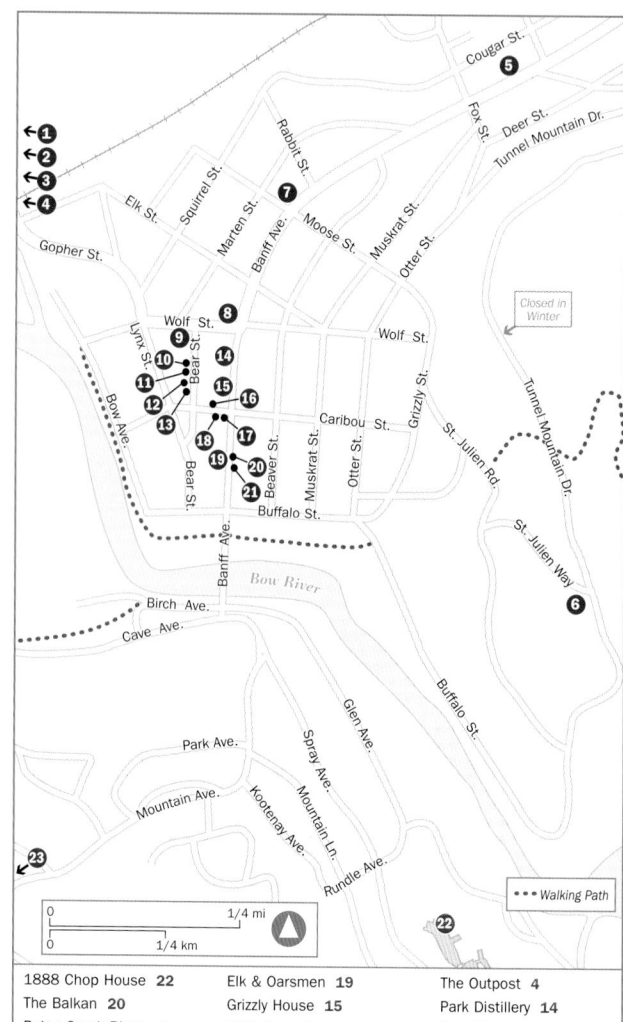

Closed in Winter

Bow River

• • • *Walking Path*

1888 Chop House **22**	Elk & Oarsmen **19**	The Outpost **4**
The Balkan **20**	Grizzly House **15**	Park Distillery **14**
Baker Creek Bistro **1**	JK Bakery **9**	Post Hotel **3**
Bear Street Tavern **12**	Juniper Bistro **2**	Sky Bistro **23**
The Bison **11**	The Keg at Caribou Lodge **5**	Three Ravens **6**
Chaya **21**	Maple Leaf Grill **17**	The Vermillion Room **22**
Coyotes Grill **16**	Nourish **10**	Whitebark Café **7**
Eddie Burger + Bar **18**	Old Spaghetti Factory **8**	Wild Flour **13**

Dining Best Bets

Best **for Adventurous Kids**
Grizzly House $$ 207 Banff Ave.
(p 72)

Best **Bakery**
★ Wild Flour Bakery $ 211 Bear St.
(p 75)

Best **Breakfast**
★★ Coyotes Grill $$ 206 Caribou
St. (p 71)

Best **Brunch**
★★ Vermillion Room $$ In the
Fairmont Banff Springs Hotel, 405
Spray Ave. (p 75)

Best **Burger**
★ Eddie Burger + Bar $ 137C Banff
Ave. (p 71)

Best **Canadiana Cool**
★★ Maple Leaf Grill $$ 137 Banff
Ave. (p 73)

Best **Cheap Bowl of Hot Soup**
Chaya $ 118 Banff Ave. (p 71)

Best **Coffee**
★★ Whitebark Café $ 401 Banff
Ave. (p 75)

Best **for Eating Family-Style**
★ Park Distillery $$ 219 Banff Ave.
(p 74)

Best **for Locavores**
★★ The Bison $$$ 211 Bear St. (p
71)

Best **Mediterranean**
The Balkan $$ 120 Banff Ave. (p. 70)

Best **for Parents with No
Babysitter**
Old Spaghetti Factory $ Cascade
Plaza, 317 Banff Ave., second floor
(p 73)

Best **Patio**
Juniper Bistro $ In the Juniper
Hotel, bottom of Mt. Norquay Rd.
(p 72)

*Wagyu meatball pasta from the Maple
Leaf Grille.*

Best **Pizza**
★★ Bear Street Tavern $$ 211
Bear St. (p 70)

Best **Pub Food**
★ Elk & Oarsmen $$ Upstairs, 119
Banff Ave. (p 72)

Best **Sandwiches-to-Go**
JK Bakery $ 229 Bear St. (p 72)

Best **Splurge**
★★ 1888 Chop House $$$ In the
Fairmont Banff Springs Hotel, 405
Spray Ave. (p 70)

Best **View**
★★ Sky Bistro $$ At the Banff
Gondola, Mountain Rd. (p 74)

Best **Wine Cellar**
★★★ Post Hotel $$$ 200 Pipe-
stone Rd. (p 74)

Best **Place Worth the Drive
from Banff**
★★★ Post Hotel $$ 200 Pipestone
Rd., Lake Louise (p 74)

Best **for Vegans**
Nourish $$ 215 Banff Ave., second
floor (p 73)

Restaurants A to Z

★★ 1888 Chop House BANFF
STEAKHOUSE The newest restaurant at the Fairmont Banff Springs Hotel is definitely worth a visit. The menu is focused on high-end cuts of Alberta beef. Order a dry-aged rib-eye or porterhouse, with thyme-roasted yams and maple carrots on the side. It's decadent and all very delicious. Everything, from the butter to the cocktail garnishes, is made in-house. *In the Fairmont Banff Springs Hotel, 405 Spray Ave. www.1888chophouse.com.* ☎ *403/762-6860. Entrees C$46–C$62. Tues–Sat 6–9pm. Map p 68.*

kids The Balkan BANFF
GREEK The recipes at this family-owned Banff landmark come from the old country—souvlaki, moussaka, arni psito, and donair pitas (just right for lunch). This is a great place for sharing. The new decor oozes Mediterranean sunshine. On Tuesdays and most Thursdays, the place comes alive with belly-dancing and plate-smashing. *120 Banff Ave. www.banffbalkan.ca.* ☎ *403/762-3454. Entrees C$17–C$37. Daily 11am–11pm. Map p 68.*

★ Baker Creek Bistro LAKE
LOUISE *REGIONAL* Fresh, modern food is served by warm and friendly folks inside a heritage cabin just south of Lake Louise. It makes a great pit stop on your way to Lake Louise or Icefields Parkway. *11km (6¾ miles) southeast of Lake Louise & 14km (8¾ miles) north of Castle Junction on Bow Valley Pkwy. (Hwy. 1A). www.bakercreekbistro. com.* ☎ *403/522-2182. Entrees C$28–C$52. Daily noon–3pm & 5–9pm. Map p 68.*

★★ Bear Street Tavern BANFF
PIZZA For a bite and a pint with friends after skiing or biking, this happening spot is my first choice in town. The thin-crust pizza is superbly good—try the Wheeler Hut with wild mushrooms, pine nuts, truffle oil, and pesto. They also have gluten-free pizza. For something truly hearty, try the pork belly macaroni and cheese. There are local beers on tap and daily cocktail specials. *211 Bear St., main floor. www.bear streettavern.ca.* ☎ *403/762-2021. Entrees C$15–C$24. Daily 11:30am–midnight. Map p 68.*

The Balkan is a great place to share Mediterranean specialities.

Pizza and a pint from the Bear Street Tavern.

★★ The Bison BANFF

REGIONAL   Regional and seasonal "Rocky Mountain comfort food" is perfectly suited for Banff. The classic dish is grilled bison rib steak. Everything except the pickles and mayonnaise is made from scratch. The outdoor patio is the nicest in town, and it has a lovely, mellow Sunday brunch. *211 Bear St., upstairs. www.thebison.ca.* ☎ *403/762-5550. Entrees C$24–C$66. Daily 5–11pm; Sun brunch 10am–2pm. Map p 68.*

Chaya BANFF ASIAN   After

you've spent a few hours in the fresh air, the big bowls of steaming Asian soups at Chaya hit the spot. This small spot next to McDonald's is as popular with Banff's quite large Japanese Canadian population as it is with tourists. Try the Udon noodles or teriyaki rice bowls. The miso ramen bowl comes with ground pork and has a nice, spicy kick. It's very small inside, and it can be tough to get a table in peak hours. *118 Banff Ave.* ☎ *403/760-0882. Entrees C$10–C$16. Daily 11:30am–8pm. Map p 68.*

★★ Coyotes Grill BANFF

SOUTHWESTERN   Fresh, healthy, relaxed, and very popular with locals, Santa Fe comes to the Rockies here with corn and chile

peppers on enchiladas, in soups, and even on pizzas. It also serves a superb breakfast. *206 Caribou St. www.coyotesbanff.com.* ☎ *403/762-3963. Entrees C$17–C$33. Daily 7:30am–11pm. Map p 68.*

★ Eddie Burger + Bar BANFF

BURGERS   Build your own gourmet burgers well into the evening at this fun and funky bar. The bison burger comes with sautéed mushrooms, double-smoked bacon, and roasted garlic aioli on an English muffin. Add sweet potato fries and a milkshake. *137C Banff Ave. (on Caribou St.). www.eddieburgerbar. ca.* ☎ *403/762-2230. Entrees C$18–C$22. Daily 11:30am–3am. Map p 68.*

The Bison is home to Rocky Mountain comfort food.

★ Elk & Oarsmen BANFF

PUB Settle in with some locals to watch the game and dig into the best pub food in Banff. Recommended choices are the Black Angus steaks or a burger (you have elk, bison, beef, salmon, or chorizo to choose from!). It has a great patio on the rooftop, regular happy-hour specials, and big-screen TVs. *119 Banff Ave., second floor. www.elkandoarsman.com.* ☎ *403/762-4616. Entrees C$16–C$30. Daily 11am–11pm (pub stays open later). Map p 68.*

Grizzly House BANFF FON-

DUE Fondue has never gone out of style at this over-the-top alcove on Banff Avenue. Veggies, chicken, prawn, beef, even buffalo get dropped into the pot. There's plenty of retro-shtick here to temper the steaming pots of fondue and the smoking-hot plates. Things can get rowdy and noisy, though. *207 Banff Ave. www.banffgrizzly house.com.* ☎ *403/762-4055. Entrees C$21–C$52. Daily 11:30am–midnight. Map p 68.*

JK Bakery BANFF DELI

Build your own sandwiches to take for a picnic at this busy little cafe beneath the local movie theater.

There are also well-priced daily lunch specials, such as lasagna and chili, and superb baked goods. *229 Bear St.* ☎ *403/760-0800. Lunch C$9–C$15. Mon–Sat 8:30am–5pm. Map p 68.*

Juniper Bistro BANFF CANA-

DIAN The main draw to this bistro just out of Banff is its sunny patio, one of the nicest in town. The menu has hearty pub food, such as dark-ale bison ribs and a fish hot-pot. *Bottom of Mt. Norquay Rd., in the Juniper Hotel. www.thejuniper. com.* ☎ *403/763-6205. Entrees C$28–C$34. Daily 7:30am–9:30pm. Map p 68.*

The Keg at Caribou Lodge

BANFF *STEAKHOUSE* It's got everything from filet mignon to rib steak, but the stars here are grilled sirloins and prime rib. Banff has two Keg locations (it's a chain across Canada), both along Banff Avenue. But the one inside the Caribou Lodge has a cozy, wood-framed atmosphere, great service, and consistently top-notch steaks. It's also open for breakfast. *521 Banff Ave. www.kegsteakhouse.com.* ☎ *403/762-4442. Entrees C$24–C$44. Daily 6:30am–midnight. Map p 68.*

Assorted fresh-baked cookies from JK Bakery.

The outdoor patio at Juniper Bistro.

★★ Maple Leaf Grill BANFF *CANADIAN* Canadian classics like rainbow trout and venison vie with Alberta bison and Atlantic salmon beneath a birchbark canoe in a room that feels more like a lodge. It's casual in atmosphere, but the food is decidedly upscale. The award-winning wine list features more than 100 Canadian labels. *137 Banff Ave. www.banffmapleleaf.com.* ☎ *403/760-7680. Entrees C$26–C$61. Daily 10am–2am. Map p 68.*

Miki Sushi BANFF *JAPANESE* Given the numbers of Japanese tourists and expats who flock here, it's no wonder that Banff has so many good sushi options. This tiny spot located at the very far end of town has the most authentic and expansive menu. A la carte sushi, noodles, and hot pots mean there's something for everyone. The food is fresh, and the service is friendly. Prices are good too! *The Inns of Banff, 600 Banff Ave.* ☎ *403/762-0600. Entrees C$15–C$33. Daily 5–10pm.*

Nourish BANFF *VEGETARIAN* If you're weary of steak and game meats, this friendly second-floor restaurant in the Sundance Mall has organic, vegan, wheat-free, and gluten-free choices. Even nonvegetarians will like the nacho platter or wild-mushroom ravioli with lavender sauce. The decor is funky and colorful. *215 Banff Ave. www.nourishbistro.com.* ☎ *403/760-3933. Entrees C$16–C$26. Daily 11:30am–10:30pm. Map p 68.*

kids Old Spaghetti Factory BANFF *ITALIAN* Expect no-frills Italian specialties, such as lasagna and pesto linguini. Entrees include soup or salad, garlic bread, and an ice cream dessert. There are always great specials and bargains here, especially for families. *Cascade Plaza, 317 Banff Ave., second floor. www.oldspaghettifactory.ca.* ☎ *403/760-2779. Entrees C$15–C$22. Daily 11:30am–10pm. Map p 68.*

★ The Outpost LAKE LOUISE *PUB* This English-style pub happens to be joined to one of Canada's finest dining establishments, the Post Hotel. So you can expect no-fuss (burgers, pizzas, quesadillas) with exquisite standards. I recommend the veal bratwurst with rosti potatoes and onion sauce. *200 Pipestone Rd., the Post Hotel. www.posthotel.com.* ☎ *403/522-3989. Entrees C$18–C$28. Mon–Fri 4:30pm–midnight; Sat–Sun noon–midnight. Map p 68.*

Miki Sushi at the Inns of Banff.

★ Park Distillery BANFF

REGIONAL Arguably the most fun eatery in town. Eat such family-style, campfire-inspired meals as barbecued ribs, pork 'n' beans, and coleslaw. And don't miss the cornbread with maple butter. You can also sample the in-house vodkas, ryes, and whiskeys. It also offers plenty of good options for vegans and kids. *219 Banff Ave. www.park distillery.com.* ☎ *403/762-5114. Entrees C$19–C$50. Daily 11am–midnight. Map p 68.*

★★★ Post Hotel LAKE LOUISE

REGIONAL Blending fine dining with a rustic elegance, the Post is helmed by Swiss chef Hans Sauter, who uses European techniques and regional ingredients—mainly such meats as veal tenderloin, caribou striploin, and rack of lamb. Service is first-class. The real star, though, is the massive wine cellar. *200 Pipestone Rd., the Post Hotel. www. posthotel.com.* ☎ *403/522-2167. Entrees C$52–C$89. Daily 11:30am–2pm & 5:30–10pm. Map p 68.*

★★ Sky Bistro BANFF

REGIONAL The view from this restaurant, perched atop the Banff Gondola at 7,510 ft., is unbeatable. The food, which is local, seasonal, and fresh, has a wow factor of its own. A meal here is an unforgettable experience. You must ride the Gondola up—look for packages that include admission. You can also catch a free shuttle from downtown Banff. *700 Tunnel Mountain Rd., at the Buffalo Mountain Lodge. www.banffjaspercollection.com.* ☎ *403/760-4484. Entrees C$28–C$43. Apr 17–May 16 daily 11am–8:30pm; May 17–June 27 & Sept 3–Oct 14 daily 11am–9:30pm; June 28–Sept 2 daily 11am–10:30pm. Map p 68.*

Dine with a view at Three Ravens Restaurant.

★ **Three Ravens Restaurant & Wine Bar** BANFF *REGIONAL* Up here at the top of the Sally Borden Building in the impressive Banff Centre is a thoughtful and lovely place for dinner. The intricate, high-end menu features quality ingredients from across western Canada. A slightly less expensive buffet-style option is right next door—or just come for a drink and tapas at the wine bar before taking in a show. *Top floor, Sally Borden Building, 107 Tunnel Mountain Dr. www.banff centre.ca/dining.* ☎ *403/762-6300. Entrees C$32–C$58. Daily 5–9pm; wine bar daily 4pm–midnight. Map p 68.*

★★ **Vermillion Room** BANFF *FRENCH* The newest renovation at the Fairmont Banff Springs has brought a bold and upscale brasserie-styled bistro to town. Think coq au vin, bison bourgignon, duck confit, and *moules* (mussels), Plus some amazing cocktails to go with it all! *In the Fairmont Banff Springs Hotel, 405 Spray Ave. www.fairmont. com/banffsprings.* ☎ *403/762-6860. Entrees C$28–C$66. Daily 7am–11am & 6–9pm; Sat brunch 11:30am–1:30pm; Sun brunch 11am–2pm. Map p 68.*

★★ **Whitebark Café** BANFF *CAFE* Finally, a first-rate espresso bar in Banff! This is the place to grab a latte, cappuccino, or macchiato; catch up on the local paper;

Try one of the excellent sandwiches at the Wild Flour Bakery.

and enjoy the sunny morning patio in summer. In classic espresso-bar style, it's a small spot, with only a stand-up bar inside. But the coffee is worth it. It also has a great, affordable light lunch special (usually a quiche or quinoa salad). *401 Banff Ave. www.whitebarkcafe.com.* ☎ *403/762-7298. Lunch C$7–C$12. Daily 6:30am–7pm. Map p 68.*

★ **Wild Flour Bakery and Café** BANFF *CAFE* Bustling from dawn to dusk, this is Banff's best bakery and a great spot for lunch. The sandwiches are excellent—try the pulled pork with apple barbecue sauce or the gourmet grilled cheese. There's always a soup and focaccia of the day. Grab a protein bar for an afternoon snack. *221 Bear St. www.wildflourbakery.ca.* ☎ *403/760-5074. Entrees C$9–C$15. Daily 7am–4pm. Map p 68.*

Lodging in Banff National Park

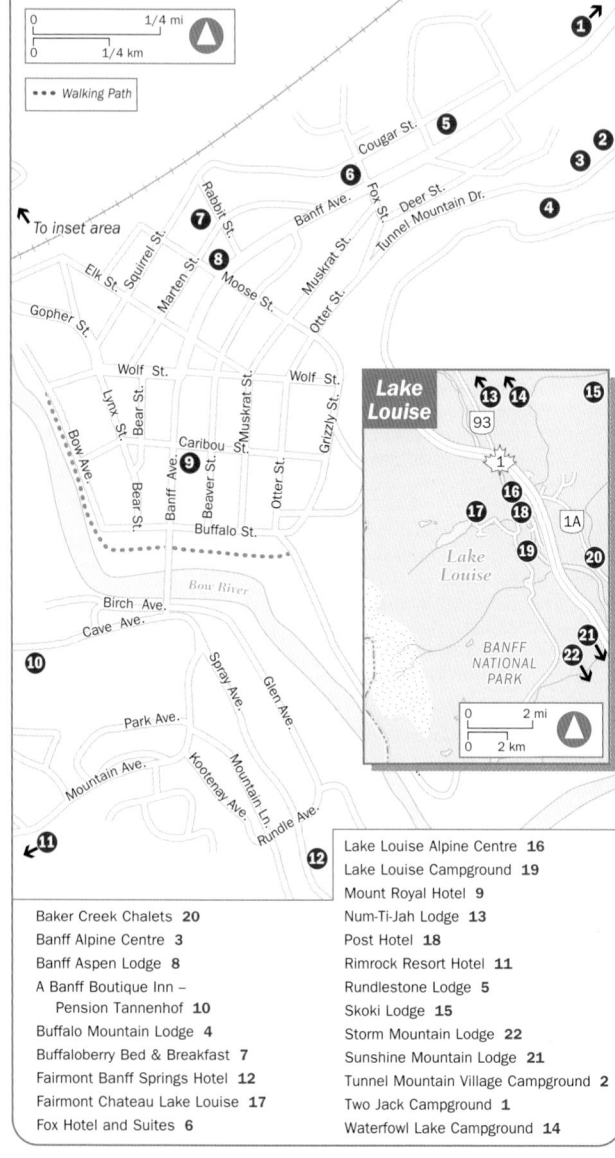

0	1/4 mi
0	1/4 km

••• Walking Path

To inset area

Lake Louise

Lake Louise

BANFF NATIONAL PARK

0	2 mi
0	2 km

Baker Creek Chalets **20**
Banff Alpine Centre **3**
Banff Aspen Lodge **8**
A Banff Boutique Inn –
   Pension Tannenhof **10**
Buffalo Mountain Lodge **4**
Buffaloberry Bed & Breakfast **7**
Fairmont Banff Springs Hotel **12**
Fairmont Chateau Lake Louise **17**
Fox Hotel and Suites **6**

Lake Louise Alpine Centre **16**
Lake Louise Campground **19**
Mount Royal Hotel **9**
Num-Ti-Jah Lodge **13**
Post Hotel **18**
Rimrock Resort Hotel **11**
Rundlestone Lodge **5**
Skoki Lodge **15**
Storm Mountain Lodge **22**
Sunshine Mountain Lodge **21**
Tunnel Mountain Village Campground **2**
Two Jack Campground **1**
Waterfowl Lake Campground **14**

Lodging Best Bets

One of the family-friendly guest rooms at Baker Creek Chalets.

Best **Backcountry**
★★ Skoki Lodge $$ *In Banff National Park; access from trail head at Temple Lodge next to Lake Louise Ski Resort (p 81)*

Best **Boutique Hotel**
★ A Banff Boutique Inn—Pension Tannenhof $$ *121 Cave Ave. (p 79)*

Best **on a Budget**
Banff Aspen Lodge $ *401 Banff Ave. (p 78)*

Best **for Business**
★ Rimrock Resort Hotel $$$ *300 Mountain Ave. (p 81)*

Best **Downtown Location**
★ Mount Royal Hotel $$ *138 Banff Ave. (p 80)*

Best **Historic Charm**
★★ Post Hotel $$$ *200 Pipestone Rd. (p 81)*

Best **for Families**
Fox Hotel and Suites $$ *46 Banff Ave. (p 80)*

Best **for Meeting Hiking Partners**
Banff Alpine Centre $ *801 Hidden Ridge Way (p 78)*

Best **for Skiers**
Sunshine Mountain Lodge $$ *At Sunshine Village Ski Resort (p 82)*

Best **Spa**
★★ Willow Stream at the Fairmont Banff Springs $$$ *405 Spray Ave. (p 79)*

Best **View**
★★ Fairmont Chateau Lake Louise $$$ *111 Lake Louise Dr. (p 79)*

Best **for Wildlife Watching**
★ Baker Creek Chalets $$ *11km (6¾ miles) southeast of Lake Louise & 14km (8¾ miles) north of Castle Junction on Bow Valley Pkwy., Hwy. 1A. (p 78)*

Lodging A to Z

Travel Tip

All prices given are for summer rates, which are in effect from about June 15 to September 15. If you travel outside this peak season—except for around the Christmas holidays—rates should be lower. Check the hotel's websites for packages and deals.

★ kids Baker Creek Chalets

LAKE LOUISE   In a semisecluded spot just south of Lake Louise, this collection of red-roofed cabins and lodges is really in the wild—bears, elk, and deer routinely stroll by. Cabins mainly sleep four to six and have kitchenettes. It's the kind of place you want to settle in and spend an entire week, well worth at least a night or two away from busy Banff. The train runs sporadically throughout the day and night next to the property; if you are a light sleeper, ask for the quietest cabins. *11km (6¾ miles) southeast of Lake Louise & 14km (8¾ miles) north of Castle Junction on Bow Valley Pkwy., Hwy. 1A. www.bakercreek.com.*

Banff Alpine Centre.

☎ *403/522-2270. 35 units. Doubles C$328–C$685. Map p 76.*

Banff Alpine Centre

BANFF   Fun and reasonably priced, this hostel is just outside the Banff townsite on Tunnel Mountain Road. Dorm rooms sleep four to six people, and the five double rooms with private bathrooms are a good bargain. The pub is always lively. *801 Hidden Ridge Way. www.hihostels.ca/alberta.* ☎ *403/762-4123. 52 units, which accommodate 2–6 people, or 216 beds. Beds from C$37; private doubles from C$215. Map p 76.*

Banff Aspen Lodge

BANFF   An inexpensive option in a good location, this Banff Avenue hotel has undergone a pretty chic and hip upgrade. Rooms are well-priced, all looking out onto an interior patio with hot tubs. Breakfast is included. Start your day in the lobby at the town's best espresso bar. *401 Banff Ave. www.banffaspenlodge.com.* ☎ *403/762-4401. 89 rooms. Doubles from C$169, breakfast included. Map p 76.*

Relaxing in the hot tub at the Banff Aspen.

★ A Banff Boutique Inn—Pension Tannenhof
BANFF A local couple with a passion for inn-keeping has turned an old-fashioned building into a lovely inn, with modern decor and mountain hospitality. It's a breath of fresh air in Banff. Rooms have strange layouts, some with very small bathrooms, but the vibe is relaxing and the breakfasts superb. *121 Cave Ave. www. banffboutiqueinn.com.* ☎ *403/762-4636. 10 units. Doubles C$189–C$419. Breakfast included. Map p 76.*

★★ Buffalo Mountain Lodge
BANFF With peeled log frames, feather duvets over flannel sheets, fieldstone fireplaces, and log furniture, this collection of buildings on Tunnel Mountain has a preppy cottage feel. It's casually elegant and has an outdoorsy vibe too. *700 Tunnel Mountain Rd. www.crmr.com.* ☎ *800/661-1367 or 403/762-2400. 108 units. Doubles C$381–C$449. Map p 76.*

★ Buffaloberry Bed & Breakfast
BANFF The unpretentious owners of this little inn love the outdoors, and their B&B, in a building nestled in one of downtown Banff's quieter areas, may be the best sleep in town, thanks to soundproof rooms, blackout curtains, solid-core doors, and luxurious natural linens. Bathrooms are spacious. *417 Marten St. www.buffalo berry.com.* ☎ *403/762-3750. 4 units. Doubles C$465. Breakfast included. Map p 76.*

★★ Fairmont Banff Springs Hotel
BANFF One of the most famous buildings in Canada, this spectacular hotel is a true experience. Rooms are notoriously small, so don't plan on spending much time indoors. The Gold Floor has by far the nicest rooms. The list of amenities, from the Willow Stream Spa to a bowling center, horse stables, and nine restaurants, overwhelms. This is an unforgettable place to spend a few nights, but it doesn't come cheap. Packages including breakfasts and online specials help take the sting out of the high price tag. *405 Spray Ave. www.fairmont.com/banffsprings.* ☎ *800/441-1414 or 403/762-2211. 768 units. Doubles C$829–C$929. Map p 76.*

★★ Fairmont Chateau Lake Louise
LAKE LOUISE This award-winning landmark hotel is elegant, with a Swiss alpine feel, and more

Enjoying cocktails at the Buffalo Mountain Lodge.

comfortable than the Banff Springs. Rooms with lake views cost much more than those on the other side of the hall (which still have nice mountain views). The Gold Floor offers superior service. All the rooms and public spaces have been recently updated. The pool is nothing special, but the hotel's rich heritage, coupled with access to amazing hiking and skiing, is unmatched on the planet. *111 Lake Louise Dr. www.fairmont.com/lake-louise.* ☎ *800/441-1414 or 403/522-3511. 554 units. Doubles C$841–C$989. Map p 76.*

kids Fox Hotel and Suites

BANFF   More contemporary than most of the hotels in town, rooms are mostly suites with kitchenettes and one or two bedrooms. Loft-style second-floor units have mountain views. The courtyard has a stunning hot pool themed after the historic Banff springs. *46 Banff Ave. www.foxhotelandsuites.* ☎ *800/661-8310 or 403/760-8500. 117 units. Doubles C$429–C$559. Map p 76.*

Lake Louise Alpine Centre

LAKE LOUISE   Don't let the fact that this is a hostel turn you off a great value. Rooms range from small dormitories and simple doubles to larger rooms that sleep up to six. Communal bathrooms and showers are down the hall. *203 Village Rd. www.hihostels.ca.* ☎ *403/522-2201. 45 units. Dorms from C$57; private rooms from C$172. Map p 76.*

Lake Louise Campground LAKE

LOUISE   This campground is downhill from the Fairmont Chateau Lake Louise, away from the lake. The tent area is in the trees near the river. The trailer area is more open and closer to the highway and railway line. It's a 10-minute walk to Lake Louise Village. *58km (36 miles) northwest of Banff townsite on Trans-Canada Hwy. 1. Exit at Lake Louise & turn left after passing under the railway bridge onto Fairview Rd. Reservations at www.pccamping.ca.* ☎ *877/737-3783. Lake Louise Tent: 206 sites. No RV hookups. C$28. Closed Sept 30–May 25. Lake Louise Trailer: 189 sites. Electrical hookups only. C$32. Open year-round. Map p 76.*

★ Mount Royal Hotel

BANFF   One of the original hotels in town underwent a stylish renovation in 2018. It's now loaded with upscale amenities—including rooftop hot tubs with major wow

The Fairmont Banff Springs Hotel is one of the most famous buildings in Canada.

Relaxing by the firepit at Lake Louise Alpine Centre.

factor—and a location right in the heart of all the action. *138 Banff Ave. www.banffjaspercollection.com.* ☎ *877/862-2623 or 403/762-6700. 130 units. Doubles from C$359. Map p 76.*

★ **Num-Ti-Jah Lodge** ICEFIELDS PARKWAY Banff's most scenic lodge is rustic, historic, and secluded. You'll pay for the location and the expensive dining room (the only option), not the amenities. The stairs creak as you climb them, and the walls are thin. Rooms are clean, although quite basic. Heaps of character and history manage to cover up the need for a major upgrade. *40km (25 miles) north of Lake Louise on Icefields Pkwy. www.num-ti-jah. com.* ☎ *403/522-2167. 25 units. Doubles C$450–C$510. Map p 76.*

★★ **Post Hotel** LAKE LOUISE A quintessential and exquisite mountain inn, the Post Hotel combines beautiful guest rooms and excellent service in a peaceful location. Guest rooms are simple but luxurious, with fireplaces, down quilts, and heated slate floors in the bathrooms. The Temple Mountain Spa is the best in Lake Louise. *200 Pipestone Rd. www. posthotel.com.* ☎ *800/661-1586 or 403/522-3989. 92 units. Doubles C$445–C$895. Map p 76.*

★ **Rimrock Resort Hotel** BANFF Modern and slick, the Rimrock has a great view and fine lodgings. The lobby is graced by a giant marble fireplace, cherry oak walls, leather chairs, and big windows offering views you can't get even in the penthouses of other local hotels. Peaceful and elegant, rooms are airy, luxurious, and large. Request one on the east face of the south wing for the choicest views. *300 Mountain Ave. www.rimrock resort.com.* ☎ *800/661-1587 or 403/762-3356. 346 units. Doubles C$478–C$543. Map p 76.*

Rundlestone Lodge BANFF There is a long line of midsize hotels and motels along Banff Avenue. This one stands out for its modern feel. The gym, pool, and spaciousness of standard rooms add value. Predictable but clean, with bonus points for the very friendly service. *537 Banff Ave. www.rundlestone.com.* ☎ *800/661-8630 or 403/762-2201. 96 rooms. Doubles from C$309. Map p 76.*

★★ **Skoki Lodge** BACKCOUNTRY This is a classic backcountry lodge built nearly a century ago, so you must ski or hike 11km (6.8 miles) to get here, arriving to a gorgeous valley behind the Lake

A peaceful sitting room at the Post Hotel.

Louise ski area. The lodge is rustic; there is no electricity or running water. There are, however, incredible trails at your doorstep and true Rocky Mountain seclusion. *Banff National Park. www.skokilodge.com.* ☎ *800/258-7669. Sleeps up to 22 guests. From C$240 per person, including meals. Map p 76.*

Storm Mountain Lodge BANFF OUTSKIRTS A collection of old-fashioned cabins halfway between Banff and Lake Louise has been nicely restored with large tubs, crackling fireplaces, and comfy beds. Unit nos. 9 and 10 are farthest from the sometimes-noisy Hwy. 93. Nos. 11 and 14 have great views of Castle Mountain. *On Hwy. 93 just west of Castle Junction. www. stormmountainlodge.com.* ☎ *403/762-4155. 14 units. Cabins C$369–C$395. Map p 76.*

Travel Tip

Remember that sites at Lake Louise (tent and trailer) and at all Tunnel Mountain campgrounds should be reserved at www.pccamping.ca. All other sites are on a first-come, first-served basis.

Sunshine Mountain Lodge SUNSHINE VILLAGE Banff's only ski-in/ski-out hotel is located at the top of the gondola at Sunshine Village ski resort. Rooms are luxurious, ranging from quite affordable little doubles to spacious two-story suites. The biggest bonus? You get fresh tracks each morning. Open winter only. There's a 3-night minimum during peak season. *1 Sunshine Rd. www.sunshinemountainlodge. com* ☎ *403/705-4000. 84 rooms. Ski-&-stay packages start at C$322 per person. Map p 76.*

Tunnel Mountain Village Campground BANFF You can walk to Banff Avenue in the park's biggest campground. It's divided into three sections: a mixed tent and RV camp 2.5km (1½ miles) east of town; an RV mecca 4km (2½ miles) east of town; and a trailer- and tenter-friendly section to the east of the RV area. *4km (2½ miles) east of Banff townsite on Tunnel Mountain Rd. Reservations at www.pccamping.ca.* ☎ *877/737-3783. Tunnel Mountain Village I: 618 sites. No RV hookups. C$27. Closed Oct. 2–May 7. Tunnel Mountain Village II: 188 sites. Electrical hookups only. C$32. Open year-round. Tunnel Mountain Trailer Court: 321 sites. Full hookups. C$38. Closed Oct 2–May 7. Map p 76.*

New Twist on Camping

New to camping but keen to give it a try? Banff's oTENTiks are part cabin and part tent and require no set-up. The setting, at Two Jack Lakeside, is also fabulous. There's lighting, electricity, indoor heat, and plenty of room for families up to six. Fun! The cost C$120 per night. Make reservations at www.reservation.pc.gc.ca.

Two Jack Campground MINNE-WANKA LOOP There are two areas here. The main area (which is larger and busier) is just off the road in a densely wooded forest 13km (8 miles) northeast of Banff townsite, on the Minnewanka Loop. It's quite private, although there are no great views. The second area is next to the lake and is very popular because it is the most scenic and peaceful campground near the Town of Banff. The lakeside campground also boasts 10 oTENTiks, a unique cross between a tent and an A-frame cabin, which will appeal to first-time campers and families. They're far from luxurious but are homey, comfortable, warm, dry, and low maintenance. *12km (7½ miles) from Banff townsite on Minnewanka Loop Rd. Reservations at www.pccamping.ca.* ☎ *877/737-3783. Two Jack Main: 380 sites. RV-friendly but no RV hookups. C$22. Closed Sept 9–May 4. Two Jack Lakeside: 74 sites. No RV hookups. C$27. Closed Sept 15–May 14. Map p 76.*

Waterfowl Lake Campground ICEFIELDS PARKWAY This is my favorite in the park because of the scenery and peacefulness. There is an open area on the lakeshore for relaxing or playing games, plus amazing views of the surrounding mountains and glaciers. *57km (35 miles) north of Lake Louise on Ice-fields Pkwy., Hwy. 93. www.pc.gc.ca/ en/pn-np/ab/banff/activ/camping/ waterfowl. No reservations. 116 sites. No RV hookups. C$22. Closed Sept 8–June 18. No credit cards. Map p 76.*

The oTENTiks at Two Jack Campground are a cross between a tent and an A-frame cabin.

Shopping, Arts & Nightlife

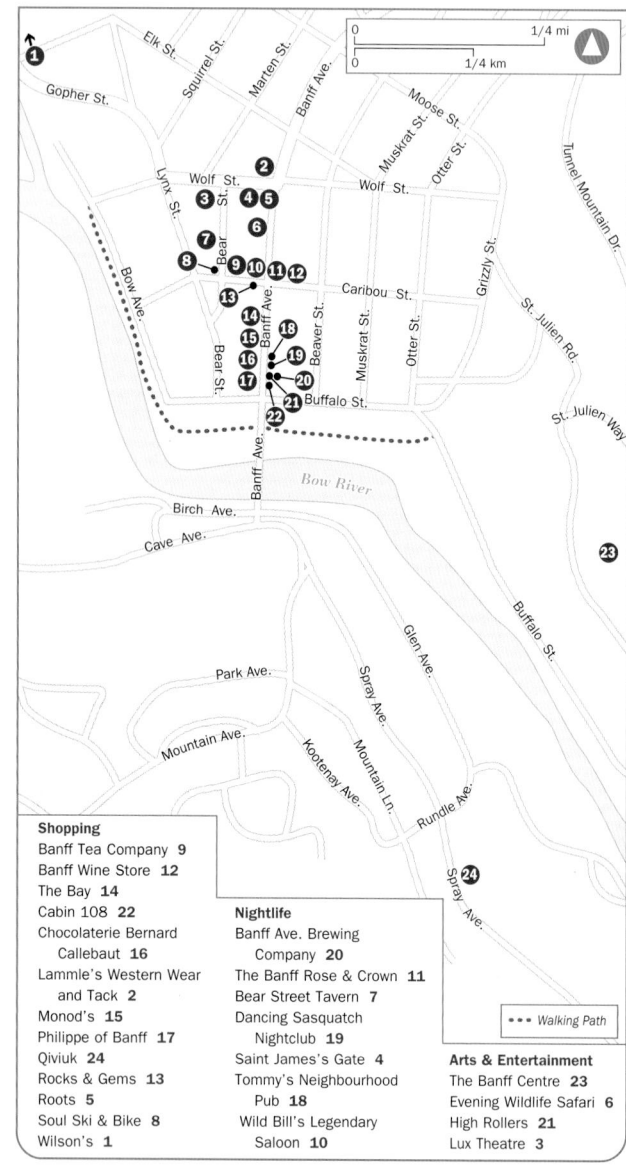

Shopping
Banff Tea Company **9**
Banff Wine Store **12**
The Bay **14**
Cabin 108 **22**
Chocolaterie Bernard
 Callebaut **16**
Lammle's Western Wear
 and Tack **2**
Monod's **15**
Philippe of Banff **17**
Qiviuk **24**
Rocks & Gems **13**
Roots **5**
Soul Ski & Bike **8**
Wilson's **1**

Nightlife
Banff Ave. Brewing
 Company **20**
The Banff Rose & Crown **11**
Bear Street Tavern **7**
Dancing Sasquatch
 Nightclub **19**
Saint James's Gate **4**
Tommy's Neighbourhood
 Pub **18**
Wild Bill's Legendary
 Saloon **10**

••• *Walking Path*

Arts & Entertainment
The Banff Centre **23**
Evening Wildlife Safari **6**
High Rollers **21**
Lux Theatre **3**

Shopping & Nightlife Best Bets

Banff Tea Co. offers a wide range of leaf teas.

Best **Cowboy Culture**
★ Wild Bill's, *201 Banff Ave. (p 90)*; and Lammle's Western Wear, *317 Banff Ave. (p 87)*

Best **Dance Floor**
Dancing Sasquatch, *120 Banff Ave. (p 89)*

Best **Outdoor Fashion**
Monod's, *129 Banff Ave. (p 87)*

Best **Ski Shop**
Soul Ski & Bike, *203A Bear St. (p 88)*

Best **Ladies' Fashion**
Cabin 108, *108 Banff Ave. (p 86)*

Best **Jazz**
★★ The Banff Centre, *107 Tunnel Mountain Rd. (p 88)*

Best **Low-Key Après Ski**
Tommy's Neighbourhood Pub, *120 Banff Ave. (p 90)*

Best **Local Microbrewery**
★ Banff Ave. Brewing Co, *205 Wolf St. (p 89)*

Best **Wine & Tapas**
Bear Street Tavern, *211 Bear St. (p 70)*

Shopping, Arts & Nightlife A to Z

Shopping

Banff Tea Company

BANFF   With more than 180 teas from around the world, from oolong to souchong, you're sure to find something to keep your thermos tasty while you're out exploring the Rockies. The Rocky Mountain Blend has two kinds of black teas and some Rooibos. It's brought to you by the same folks that run the **Plain of the Six Glaciers Teahouse** (p 146), and a portion of the proceeds is donated to local charities. *208 Caribou St. www.banffteaco.com.* ☎ *403/762-8322. Map p 84.*

Banff Wine Store

BANFF   The staff at this basement-level shop is incredibly knowledgeable and friendly. Ask for tips on a posthike pinot or an après-ski cabernet. There are wines from more than a dozen countries, including Canadian ice wine, and a wide price range. They also deliver to your hotel! *302 Caribou St.* ☎ *403/782-3465. Map p 84.*

A wide selection at Banff Wine Store.

The Bay

BANFF   The Hudson's Bay Company is a Canadian institution established in 1670. Today, the Bay sells everything from cosmetics to Cuisinarts in its three-level department store. Souvenirs here include maple candies, the famous Hudson's Bay blankets, and Olympic uniforms. *125 Banff Ave. www.hbc.com.* ☎ *403/762-5525. Map p 84.*

Cabin 108

BANFF   An independently owned fashion boutique that has plenty of finds at good prices. Come here to pick up a new outfit before hitting the clubs or wine bars later. *108 Banff Ave.* ☎ *403/762-2108. Map p 84.*

Chocolaterie Bernard Callebaut

BANFF   This Belgian-born Calgarian is a fifth-generation chocolate maker who says he eats at least six different chocolates each day. His Banff store, inside the Harmony Lane Mall, is practically an education in all things chocolate. Choose from 48 flavors, including dark chocolate–coated ginger,

Colorful towels, tote bags, and more on display at the Bay.

ganache cream, and truffles. *111 Banff Ave. www.bernardcallebaut. com.* ☎ *403/762-4106. Map p 84.*

Lammle's Western Wear and Tack BANFF   For true-blue cowboy gear, head upstairs in Cascade Plaza. Start with a Shady Brady cowboy hat and a pair of Wrangler jeans with a silver belt, and then wrap up the whole outfit up with a pair of Dan Post cowboy boots. It also has kidswear for junior saddle ropers. *Cascade Plaza, 317 Banff Ave. www.lammles.com.* ☎ *403/762-5460. Map p 84.*

Monod Sports BANFF   Banff's oldest outdoor clothing and equipment retailer is a busy, jam-packed shop staffed by keen outdoorsy types. Hiking boots are upstairs at the back, along with fly-fishing rods, while climbing harnesses and tents are downstairs, and cold-weather wear is right in the middle. Fleeces, puffy vests, or zip-off pants, anyone? *129 Banff Ave. www. monodsports.com.* ☎ *403/762-4571. Map p 84.*

Philippe of Banff BANFF   Because Banff is the jewel of the Rockies, it's only appropriate that you'll find diamonds at this fine jeweler's atelier. Banff goldsmith Philippe Plourde handcrafts stunning jewelry that honors tradition yet

embraces modern styles. *130 Banff Ave.* ☎ *403/760-8744. Map p 84.*

Qiviuk BANFF   Celebrities and fashion influencers have discovered that it's softer than cashmere, warmer than beaver or fox fur, and lighter than wool. The supple and plush pelt from the Canadian Arctic musk ox comes from the Far North, making qiviuk the world's rarest natural fiber. This store in the Banff Springs sells sweaters, coats, hats, shawls, and scarves. *Fairmont Banff Springs Hotel, 405 Spray Ave. www. qiviuk.com.* ☎ *403/762-4460. Map p 84.*

Fashion boutique Cabin 108 on Banff Avenue.

Rocks & Gems BANFF   Bring the kids to scour the big bin of tumbled stones and take home a small souvenir. There are two giant amethyst geodes on display. *137 Banff Ave. www.rocksandgemscanada. com.* ☎ *403/762-9330. Map p 84.*

Roots BANFF   Canada's iconic leather and casual clothing shop is a great place for a maple leaf–inspired souvenir, from hoodies to baby sleepers. It's lately started dabbling in yoga wear and linens but maintain its, um, roots with sweats. This is your chance to adapt to the Canadian lifestyle with genuine leather and always-stylish purses, jackets, and shoes. *277 Banff Ave. http://canada.roots.com.* ☎ *403/762-9434. Map p 84.*

Soul Ski & Bike BANFF   In a town packed with ski shops, this one stands out for its large selection of skis and snowboards in winter and bikes in summer. Plus, the service is friendly, and there's plenty of inspiration here to help get you outside and active. *203A Bear St. www.soulskiandbike.com.* ☎ *403/760-1650. Map p 84.*

Wilson Mountain Sports LAKE LOUISE   Carrying everything from tents and hiking poles to fleeces and snowshoes, this is a great one-stop shop in the village at Lake Louise for all your outdoor needs. Camping, hiking, skiing, climbing, biking—they have almost everything here. *Building A, Samson Mall, 201 Village Rd. www.wmsll.com.* ☎ *403/522-3636. Map p 84.*

Arts & Entertainment
★★★ The Banff Centre
BANFF   For inspiring concerts featuring world-class jazz, dance, pop, folk, and world music, keep an eye on the calendar; something wonderful is bound to be happening during your visit. *St. Julien Rd.* ☎ *403/762-6301. www.banffcentre. ca. Wed & Fri–Sun 9pm–2am. Admission varies. Map p 84.*

★ Evening Wildlife Safari
BANFF   Seasonal 2-hour van-based wildlife tours run by **Discover Banff Tours** depart Banff each evening, taking full advantage of what is perhaps the best time for wildlife sightings. The guides are very good, and binoculars are provided. *Discover Banff Tours' office is in Sundance Mall, 215 Banff Ave. www. banfftours.com.* ☎ *403/760-5007. Adults C$56, kids ages 5–12 C$32. Apr–Oct daily at 6:30pm. Map p 84.*

Van tour during an Evening Wildlife Safari with Discover Banff Tours.

Bowling at High Rollers.

★★ kids High Rollers BANFF

Looking for a fun evening activity?
Head straight to this bowling alley
with major vibes on Banff Avenue.
It's also got great pizza and beer.
*110 Banff Ave. www.highrollersbanff.
com.* ☎ *403/7622695. Mon–Thurs
4pm–2am; Fri–Sat noon–2am. Bowling lanes from C$49/hr. Map p 84.*

Lux Theatre BANFF   Banff's ven-
erable but aging cinema plays
mainly first-run Hollywood hits, and
there's always a family-friendly
blockbuster running. *229 Bear St.
www.luxbanff.com.* ☎ *403/762-
8595. Adults C$13, kids ages 11 &
under C$10. Map p 84.*

Nightlife
Banff Ave. Brewing Company

BANFF   It's "all about the beer" at
this second-story microbrewery,
particularly lively in the après-ski, or
après-work (yes, people in Banff do
work) hours. A sampler lets you try
its half-dozen specialties. The menu
is staple pub food—try the meatloaf or a huge serving of poutine.
*111 Banff Ave., 2nd floor. www.
banffavebrewingco.com.*
☎ *403/762-1003. Free admission.
Daily 11:30am–2am. Map p 84.*

The Banff Rose & Crown

BANFF   With a spacious rooftop
patio and a long list of beers on
tap, this is a laidback favorite with a
lowbrow style. There is often live
music, including Maritime Mondays
for fans of the East Coast. *202 Banff
Ave., upstairs. www.roseandcrown.ca.*
☎ *403/762-2121. Admission C$4–
C$12. Daily 11am–2am. Map p 84.*

Dancing Sasquatch BANFF   The
best spot for late-night dancing
and a funky techno atmosphere.
There's a cigar room, a martini bar,
and stag and stagette groups min-
gling with ski bums. *110 Banff Ave.,
downstairs. www.banffnightclubs.ca.*
☎ *403/760-5300. Admission C$6–
C$15. Map p 84.*

★ Saint James's Gate BANFF

This Irish pub was named for the
birthplace of Guinness, and much
of its interior woodwork was
imported from Dublin. Selecting a
draught here is just about the
toughest challenge in Banff—it has
33 beers on tap as well as 50 sin-
gle-malt scotches and 10 Irish whiskeys. Live music is usually Celtic
and always a blast. *205 Wolf St.
https://stjamesgatebanff.com.*
☎ *403/762-9355. Admission C$4–
C$14. Daily 11am–2am. Map p 84.*

Live music and dancing at Wild Bill's Legendary Saloon.

Tommy's Neighbourhood Pub

BANFF   Locals here are happy to share stories of what it's like to live in such a storied town. This is a friendly place where you can actually have a conversation without yelling. *120 Banff Ave. www.tommys neighbourhoodpub.com.* ☎ *403/762-8888. Free admission. Daily 11am–2am. Map p 84.*

★ Wild Bill's Legendary Saloon

BANFF   This local cowboy hangout is fun and not necessarily all about the yee-haw. What can I say? Head here if you want to drink beer and do some line dancing. Wednesday nights brings line-dance lessons. *201 Banff Ave., upstairs. www.wbsaloon.com.* ☎ *403/762-0333. Admission C$5–C$18. Daily 11am–2am. Map p 84.* ●

Kananaskis Country

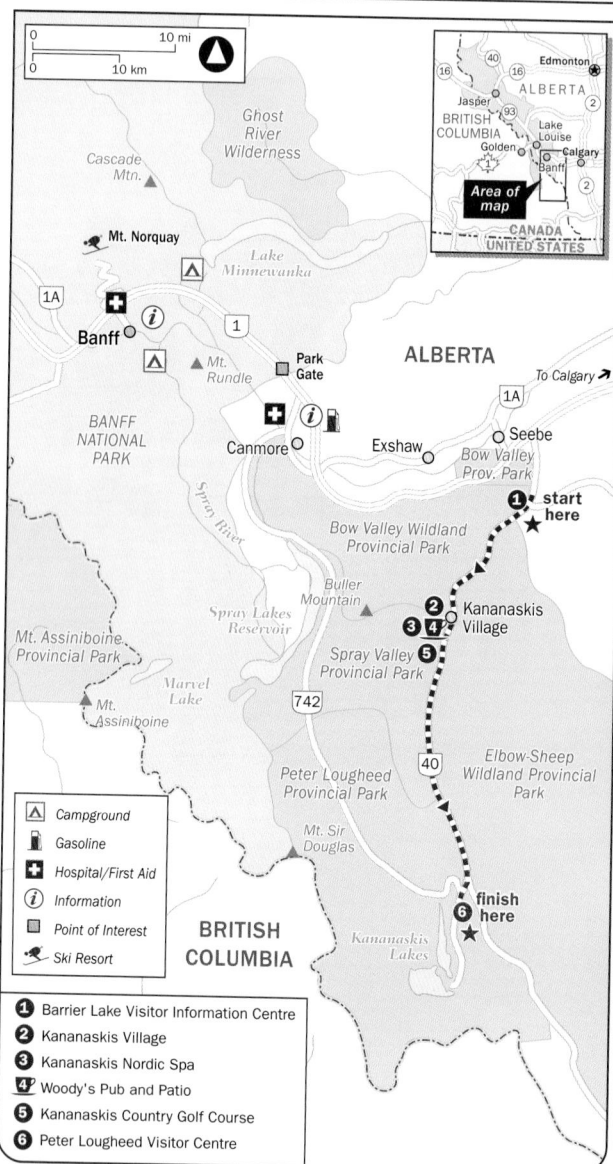

Legend:
- ⛺ Campground
- ⛽ Gasoline
- ✚ Hospital/First Aid
- ⓘ Information
- ▪ Point of Interest
- 🎿 Ski Resort

1. Barrier Lake Visitor Information Centre
2. Kananaskis Village
3. Kananaskis Nordic Spa
4. Woody's Pub and Patio
5. Kananaskis Country Golf Course
6. Peter Lougheed Visitor Centre

Previous page: Sunset on Moraine Lake in the Canadian Rockies.

Kananaskis Country is a vast area of rugged mountain wilderness that contains nine Alberta provincial parks and "multiple-use" land where forestry, cattle-grazing, and petroleum development are permitted. Roads and trails are quiet here compared to those at Banff, drawing mainly weekenders from Calgary. Kananaskis is named for a Cree native who was reportedly struck by an axe but survived, and it offers a good variety of outdoor activities, gorgeous scenery, and excellent infrastructure.

From Banff, take Trans-Canada Hwy. west 55km (34 miles). Turn south on Hwy. 40, the Kananaskis Trail.

❶ Barrier Lake Visitor Information Centre. This is a good first stop, at the entrance to Kananaskis Country on Hwy. 40. Pick up brochures and maps. ⏱ *15 min. Hwy. 40, 8km (5 miles) south of Trans-Canada Hwy. 1. www.alberta parks.ca.* ☎ *403/678-0760. Early Apr to late June Mon–Fri 9am–4pm, Sat–Sun 9am–5pm; late June to early Sept 9am–6pm; early Sept to early Apr Mon–Fri 9am–4pm, Sat–Sun 9am–5pm.*

Continue south on Hwy. 40 for 16km (10 miles). Turn right toward Kananaskis Village & left on Centennial Dr., following this for 2.5km (1½ miles).

❷ Kananaskis Village. The heart of "K-Country" is home to a golf course, tennis courts, tour and equipment rental outfitter, hotels, a

The Kananaskis Country Golf Course.

Helicopter ride above Kananaskis Country.

cafe, a hotel and conference center, a spa, and plenty of trails. It's a year-round resort hub that offers a pleasant stroll and a handful of shops. *26km (16 miles) south of Trans-Canada Hwy. 1 on Hwy. 40. Turn right on Mt. Allen Dr. & left on Centennial Dr. Follow directions to parking lot.*

❸ Kananaskis Nordic Spa. This is the Rockies take on a traditional Scandinavian spa, and it's a real

Chinook Country

Don't be surprised by quick and drastic rises in temperatures in wintertime here. When warm Pacific air comes funneling through to the foothills and slams into a cold high-pressure air mass, dry air is compressed and heated, dropping quickly and producing a phenomenon known as a "chinook." Local temperatures can go up as much as 40°C (72°F) in 20 minutes. Most winters bring 20 chinook days a year to the eastern edge of the Canadian Rockies near Kananaskis Country.

treat. Plan a few hours to make the most of this alpine oasis, with five outdoor pools plus saunas and steam cabins. Visit Monday through Thursday to avoid the weekend crowds. *1 Centennial Dr., Kananaskis Village.* ☎ *403/591-6800. www. knordicspa.com.*

4️⃣ **Woody's Pub & Patio.** Pop into the Pomeroy Kananaskis Mountain Lodge for lunch at Woody's Pub & Patio. The log cabin vibes are cozy, but the rooftop patio on a sunny day is even better. There's something for everyone, including plenty of locally sourced options, such as the Alberta beef brisket sandwich or quinoa and squash salad. *1 Centennial Dr., Kananaskis Village.* ☎ *403/591-6373. $$.*

Head north out of the Village & then turn left at the first stop sign.

5️⃣ **Kananaskis Country Golf Course.** Two 18-hole, par-72 courses make up one of the top-rated and most scenic golf resorts in Canada. Following serious flooding in 2013, the courses were lovingly restored and reopened in 2018. *Clubhouse is on Lorette Dr., south of Kananaskis Village. www. kananaskisgolf.com.* ☎ *877/591-2525 or 403/591-7070. Greens fees*

from C$118. Early May to mid-Oct 7am–10pm.

Continue south on Hwy. 40 for 30km (19 miles), turn west on Kananaskis Lakes Trail & travel 3.7km (2⅓ miles).

5️⃣ **Peter Lougheed Provincial Park/Visitor Centre.** Easy interpretive trails lead out from an excellent visitors center onto the shores of the lovely Upper and Lower Kananaskis Lakes. A more demanding hike goes up from the peninsula between the two lakes to alpine wildflowers and valley views at Three Isle Lakes (hiking boots are a must!). Mountain bikers come for the Pocaterra and High Rockies trails. ☎ *403/678-0760. July–Aug Mon–Thurs 9:30am–4:30pm, Fri–Sat 9:30am–5:30pm; Sept–June 9:30am–4:30pm.*

Mt. Kidd in Peter Lougheed Provincial Park.

Canmore

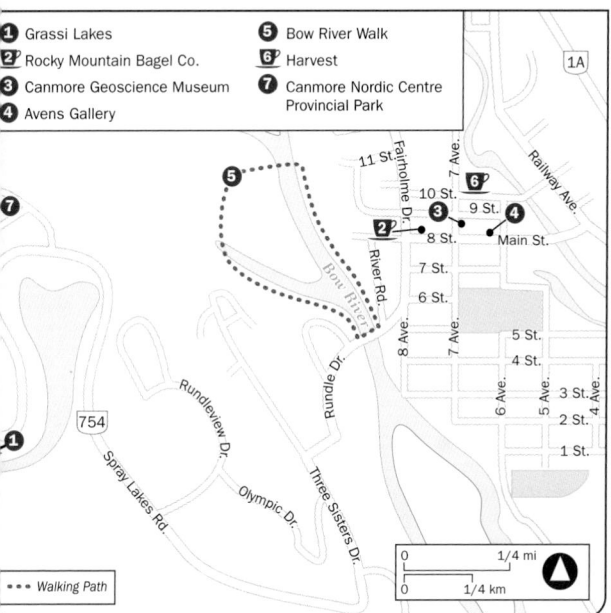

1. Grassi Lakes
2. Rocky Mountain Bagel Co.
3. Canmore Geoscience Museum
4. Avens Gallery
5. Bow River Walk
6. Harvest
7. Canmore Nordic Centre Provincial Park

••• Walking Path

It's hard to beat Canmore. The town of 13,000 boasts beautiful scenery, world-class trails, plus a relatively short commute to Banff or Calgary. Mountains rise high in all directions, and the turquoise Bow River flows through town. Locals take pride in healthy living, the great cafes and restaurants, and the keen arts scene that have earned Canmore the nickname "Alberta's Aspen." Many visitors stay here for hotel rates that are typically lower than in Banff, making it a good place to begin day trips into the park. The best way to explore Canmore is on foot.

At the west end of Main St., turn left & drive over the Bow River. Turn left again at Three Sisters Dr. & right onto Spray Lakes Rd. One kilometer (⅔ mile) past the Nordic Centre, turn left into a parking lot for the trail head.

1 ★★ Grassi Lakes. Start the day with a moderate, short, but stunning hike just above town. It's a 4km (2.5-mile) loop that takes you up historic steps, past a waterfall and on to two small, jewel-like lakes. *Just past Nordic Centre on Smith Dorrien–Spray Lakes Rd.*

Head back down the hill, around the shore of the reservoir & into town. Park in the lot behind 8th St. & between ArtsPlace & the Information Centre.

Downtown Canmore.

2 **Rocky Mountain Bagel Company.** Reward yourself with breakfast on Main Street. There are many places to choose from, but the artisan bagels and other homemade treats at this longtime local operation are worth checking out. Plus, it's on the sunny side of the street. *830 Main St.* ☎ *403/675-9978. Daily 6am–6pm. $.*

Around the corner to the right, staying on the same block & inside the Civic Centre is:

3 **Canmore Geoscience Museum.** From coal mining to Olympic fame, there's human as well as geological history to discover in this museum. It's housed in Canmore's **Civic Centre,** which has won awards for its eco-friendly design. *902b 7th Ave. www.cmags. org.* ☎ *403/678-2462. Admission C$7 adults, C$5 students & seniors. Early June to early Sept Mon–Fri noon–4:30pm, Sat–Sun 11am–4:30pm; early Sept to mid-Oct*

Mon–Thurs noon–4:30pm, Fri–Sun 10am–4:30pm; mid-Oct to early June Mon & Wed–Fri noon–4:30pm, Sat–Sun 11am–4:30pm, closed Tues.

Stroll back to the left along Main St. for window shopping. On the south side is the:

6 **Avens Gallery.** For 30 years, this has been the premier art gallery in Canmore. There's small art (jewelry, sculpture, blown glass), but more impressive are the large canvases representing the inspiring local scenery. Also check out **Hive Gallery** and **Carter-Ryan Gallery** a few doors up the road. *101–710 Main St.* ☎ *403/678-4471. Mon–Sat 9:30am–5:30pm; Sun 10am–5pm.*

Continue down Main St. & keep straight as Main St. becomes Riverview Place. At the far end of the cul-de-sac, a sign marks the beginning of a walking trail.

5 **Bow River Walk.** At the end of Main Street, follow footpath signs to the Bow River Walk, which traces

Walkers cross a bridge over the Bow River.

Extreme Golf in the Rockies

Canmore has three outstanding golf courses. The oldest course in town is the friendly 18-hole **Canmore Golf and Curling Club** (2000 8th Ave.; www.canmoregolf.net; ☎ 403/678-4785), close to downtown, along the Bow River. The clubhouse has one of the best patios in town. Greens fees are C$89 per person. On the north side of Canmore is **SilverTip Resort** (1000 SilverTip Trail; exit at the main Canmore exit and take the first left before the lights; www.silvertipresort.com; ☎ 877/877-5444 or 403/678-1600). Calling what it offers "extreme mountain golf," this Les Furber–designed 18-hole, par-72 course is one of a kind. Greens fees range from C$135 to C$175. **Stewart Creek Golf Course** (1 Stewart Creek Rd., via the Three Sisters Pkwy. exit just east of Canmore; www.stewartcreekgolf.com; ☎ 877/993-4653 or 403/609-6099) is another "high mountain" course that winds along the picturesque lower slopes of the Three Sisters Mountain on the south side of the Bow Valley. Greens fees range from C$135 to C$215.

both sides of this turquoise alpine river while taking in dazzling mountain scenery. A gentle 30-minute loop takes you over the old railway bridge, past the TransAlta Plant, and back to town over Bridge Road.

Return to Main St., turning left on 7th Ave. & right on 10th St.

6 ★ **Harvest.** This is where locals grab a healthy and hearty lunch. Most sandwiches are grilled, croque monsieur–style. On weekends, there are homemade cinnamon buns. It's just off Main Street. *718 10th St.* ☎ *403/678-3747. Daily 8am–3:30pm. $.*

Get back in the car & retrace your route up toward Grassi Lakes. Take a right at the large signs.

7 **Canmore Nordic Centre Provincial Park.** The park was the host of the Nordic skiing and biathlon events for the 1988 Calgary Winter Olympics and is the only

A skier at the Canmore Nordic Centre.

Canadian stop on the Nordic World Cup tour. It has more than 65km (40 miles) of ski trails in winter, 100km (62 miles) of mountain-bike trails in summer, and a Frisbee golf course. *1.8km (1 mile) south of Canmore, take Rundle Dr. across the Bow River Bridge, go left at Three Sisters Dr. & right at Spray Lakes Rd.; follow signs.* ☎ *403/678-2400.*

Icefields Parkway (Jasper)

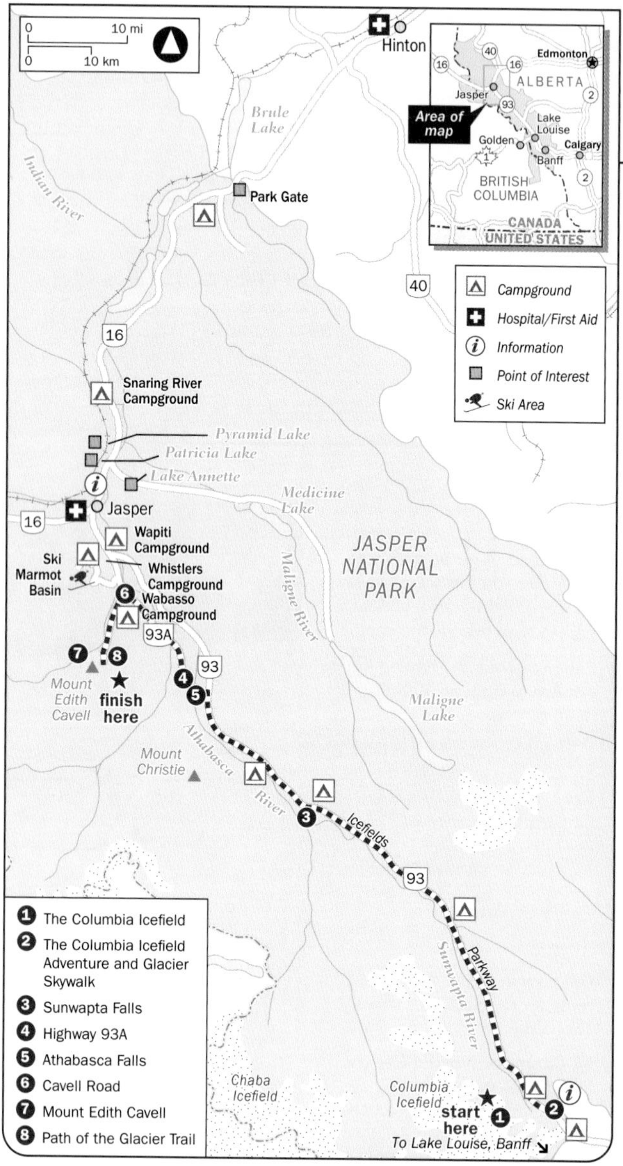

Scale: 10 mi / 10 km

Hinton

Brule Lake

Indian River

Park Gate

ALBERTA
Jasper, Edmonton
Lake Louise
Golden, Banff, Calgary
BRITISH COLUMBIA
CANADA
UNITED STATES

Area of map

40

◭	Campground
✚	Hospital/First Aid
(i)	Information
▣	Point of Interest
⛷	Ski Area

Snaring River Campground

Pyramid Lake
Patricia Lake
Lake Annette
Medicine Lake

Jasper

Ski Marmot Basin

Wapiti Campground
Whistlers Campground
Wabasso Campground

JASPER NATIONAL PARK

Maligne River

93A
93

Mount Edith Cavell
finish here

Mount Christie

Athabasca River

Maligne Lake

Icefields

93

Sunwapta River

Chaba Icefield

Columbia Icefield
start here

To Lake Louise, Banff

❶ The Columbia Icefield
❷ The Columbia Icefield Adventure and Glacier Skywalk
❸ Sunwapta Falls
❹ Highway 93A
❺ Athabasca Falls
❻ Cavell Road
❼ Mount Edith Cavell
❽ Path of the Glacier Trail

As you drive north on the Icefields Parkway, Hwy. 93, you enter Jasper National Park, the largest of the national parks in the Canadian Rockies at 10,878 sq. km (4,200 sq. miles). Large carnivores roam the wide valleys here, so drive slowly and keep an eye out for wildlife; the scenery sometimes more closely resembles the moon than the Rocky Mountains. This tour only covers the highway north of the Icefields Centre; for information on the southern half of the Parkway, see p 64.

❶ ★★★ The Columbia Icefield. The geographical heart of Icefields Parkway is a world-class natural wonder and living laboratory that examines glaciology and mountain geology. It's fantastically visitor-friendly and is located just north of the Banff National Park border, about a 90-minute drive south of the Town of Jasper. A **Parks Canada Visitor Information Centre** inside the Icefields Centre is open May through late September only, while the building itself is open early April through mid-October. *185km (115 miles) from Banff & 103km (64 miles) from Jasper.* ☎ *780/852-6288.*

❷ ★★ Columbia Icefield Glacier Adventure and Glacier Skywalk. These two complimentary attractions are intended to give the ultimate glacier experience. Giant "Ice Explorers" take you right on to the Athabasca Glacier, giving you a sense of the enormity of this icefield. You get about 15 minutes to walk on top of the 300m-thick

(984-ft.) sheets of ice. The Glacier Skywalk is a glass-floored walkway with a 918-foot drop offering spectacular views over an ancient glacier-carved valley and a chance to spot wildlife. There's plenty of interpretive information provided as well. Both tours start from the **Columbia Icefield Glacier Discovery Centre.** They include bus transfers; you can't drive yourself there. Choose from either the combo package or the Glacier Skywalk only—the Ice Explorer tour can't be done on its own.

Although tours depart every 10 to 15 minutes, the tours can be very busy, especially in summer, so reservations are highly recommended. *www.columbiaicefield.com.* ☎ *866/506-0515. Adults C\$114, kids ages 6–15 C\$57, free for kids ages 5 & under. Glacier Skywalk only: adults C\$37, kids ages 6–15 C\$19. Mid to late Apr 10am–4pm; early May to early June 10am–5pm; June–Aug 9am–6pm; early Sept to late Sept 10am–5pm; early Oct to late Oct 10am–4pm.*

Glacier Skywalk over the Columbia Icefield.

An aerial view of Sunwapta Falls.

Continue north on Icefields Pkwy. for 49km (30 miles).

❸ Sunwapta Falls. The Sunwapta River tumbles through a steep-walled limestone gorge, making a sharp turn from northwest to southwest. Follow a 2km (1.2-mile) trail along the north bank of the river for excellent views. *50km (31 miles) north of Icefields Centre & 55km (34 miles) south of Jasper townsite. Follow turnoff to parking lot.*

Continue north on Icefields Pkwy., turning northwest or left onto:

❹ Hwy. 93A. Icefields Parkway soon meets Hwy. 93A, a scenic road with less traffic that heads up toward Jasper. It's a good option if you have time. *30km (19 miles) from Jasper & 75km (47 miles) from Icefields Centre.*

Make a quick left into the parking lot at:

❺ ★ Athabasca Falls. The milky-blue Athabasca River pours through a narrow canyon cut out of quartzite rock. A nearby bridge offers phenomenal views of the thundering falls and Mt. Kerkeslin in the background. *Just past the 93A turnoff, on the south side of the road, 30km (19 miles) south of Jasper & 75km (47 miles) north of the Icefields Centre.*

Continue northwest on Hwy. 93A. After 8km (5 miles), turn left.

❻ ★ Cavell Road. Follow Hwy. 93A north along the west bank of the Athabasca River and over the Whirlpool River to Cavell Road. Turn left. Completed in 1924, this narrow, winding road is challenging to drive and is off-limits to most RVs and trailers (anything over 7m/23 ft.). It is also closed from October through June, depending on snow.

❼ Mt. Edith Cavell. At 3,363m (11,033 ft.), Mt. Edith Cavell, named after a World War I heroine, is the highest and arguably most scenic mountain in the vicinity of Jasper townsite. Angel Glacier saddles the northeastern slope and sends a tongue of ice off the cliffside. *28km (17 miles) from Hwy. 93A on Cavell Rd.*

❽ ★★ The Path of the Glacier Trail. From the parking lot at the base of Mt. Edith Cavell, this trail takes you over boulders, shrubbery, pebbles, and sand through a landscape that, less than a century ago, was covered by a glacier. New plants, trees, shrubs, and wildflowers have slowly returned to the area, known as a terminal moraine. *It's an easy 1.6km (1-mile) loop that will take 45 min.*

Drive back down Cavell Rd. & turn left on Hwy. 93A, which will take you back to Jasper.

Mt. Edith Cavell.

Maligne Valley Road

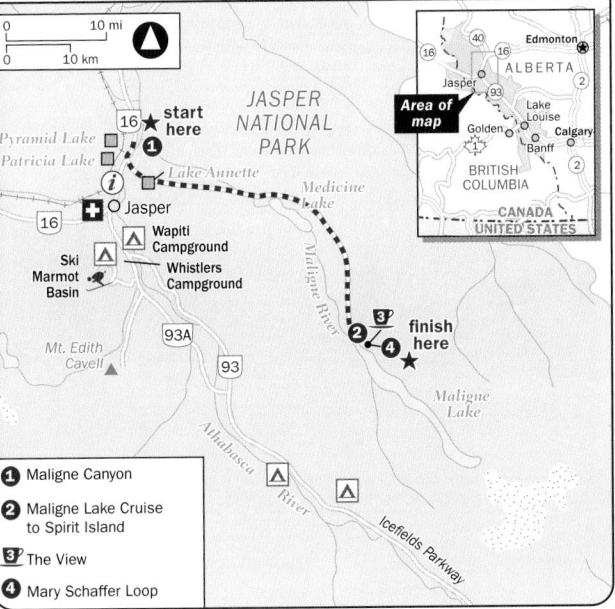

1 Maligne Canyon

2 Maligne Lake Cruise
to Spirit Island

3 The View

4 Mary Schaffer Loop

This road takes you through the **Maligne Valley** and ends at the picturesque Maligne Lake. Wildlife can often be spotted on this half-day outing, including bighorn sheep, deer, elk, moose, grizzly bear, and black bear. With a handful of stops, some short hikes, and a boat cruise, it will take you most of the day. START: **Town of Jasper.**

Drive east on Connaught St., turning left onto Hwy. 16. After 4km (2½ miles), turn south onto Maligne Lake Rd.

1 **Maligne Canyon.** A spectacular example of the cutting power of moving water, this is a very long, gradual waterfall through a deep limestone canyon. A series of bridges takes you back and forth down the canyon. *2.3km (1.4 miles) on Maligne Lake Rd. to the Sixth Bridge parking lot.*

Continue on Maligne Lake Rd. to its end.

2 ★★ kids **Maligne Lake Cruise to Spirit Island.** This is the best boat tour in the Canadian Rockies. From the deck of the glass-enclosed boats (which are heated on chilly days), watch for eagles, mountain goats, and even the odd avalanche. The cruise makes a stop halfway up the lake at the mysterious Spirit Island and then returns to the dock. You can

A Hot Springs Soak

Head out for one of Jasper's best hikes (the Sulphur Skyline) and then soak your tired bones in the hot mineral-rich pools of **Miette Hot Springs** ★ (www.hotsprings.ca/miette-hot-springs; ☎ 780/866-3939). From Jasper townsite, follow Yellowhead Hwy. 16, 42km (26 miles) east to Miette Road. Follow Miette Road 17km (11 miles) south to the end of the road. *Admission is adults C$7, children C$5, seniors C$6, family pass C$21. It's open May 1 to June 13 and Sept 3 to Oct 14 10:30am to 9pm; and June 14 to Sept 2 9am to 11pm; closed Oct 15 to April 30.*

Soaking in the mineral-rich Miette Hot Springs.

also rent canoes at the historic boathouse, built by legendary Jasper trapper and guide Curly Phillips. *At the end of Maligne Lake Rd.* www.malignelake.com. ☎ 888/900-6272. *Adults C$79, kids ages 6–15 C$40. Cruises depart frequently between 9:30am & 3pm from late May to late June & early Sept to early Oct, 9:30am–5:45pm in July & Aug.*

3 **The View.** Visit for lunch and take in the views of this stunning valley, which you'll hear called "Hall of the Gods," from the lakeside patio at the View. This is the most gourmet of the dining options at Maligne Lake. If you're tight on time, consider the Lake House Café instead. *Inside the day lodge at the end of Maligne Lake Rd.* ☎ 888/900-6272. $$$.

4 **Mary Schaffer Loop** (also known as Loop Trail). A pleasant hike around the north side of Maligne Lake, the largest lake in the Canadian Rockies, reaches a viewpoint with an interpretive display about explorer Mary Schaffer, the first woman of European descent to set eyes on the lake, in 1908, and the most prolific writer about the place. It's a 3.2km (2-mile) loop that will take you just over an hour.

Canadian Rockies goat.

Town of Jasper

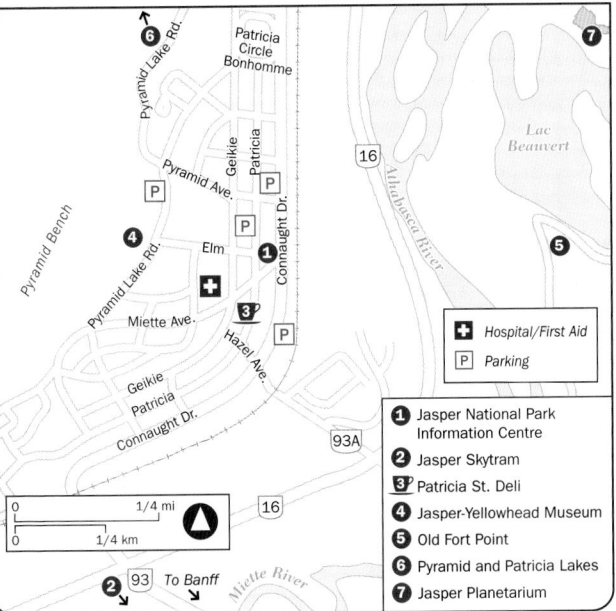

✚	Hospital/First Aid
P	Parking

1. Jasper National Park Information Centre
2. Jasper Skytram
3. Patricia St. Deli
4. Jasper-Yellowhead Museum
5. Old Fort Point
6. Pyramid and Patricia Lakes
7. Jasper Planetarium

Located in the heart of the park, the Town of Jasper came into being in anticipation of a transcontinental railway that now runs up the Athabasca Valley and over the Yellowhead Pass. The Canadian National Railway built a series of cabins on the shores of Lac Beauvert, which later became the Jasper Park Lodge. The town today feels very different from the Town of Banff—it's less crowded and more laidback and lacks the swanky shops and nightclubs of its southern counterpart.

❶ Jasper National Park Information Centre. In this cozy and central heritage building, get your bearings and get information from the Friends of Jasper, Parks Canada, and Tourism Jasper, all of which have booths at the information center. **Tourism Jasper** (☎ 780/852-6236) can inform you about hotel, restaurant, and outfitting options in the park.

500 Connaught Dr. www.pc.gc.ca/en/ pn-np/ab/jasper. ☎ *780/852-6176. Mid-May to mid-Oct daily 9am–7pm; mid-Oct to mid-May daily 9am–5pm.*

Drive south 4km (2½ miles) from the townsite, on Hwy. 93A; turn west at Whistlers Rd.; & continue for 2.5km (1½ miles) to the Tramway terminal, following clearly marked signs to:

The Jasper-Yellowhead Museum is a great escape on a rainy day.

❷ ★★ kids Jasper Skytram.

Your quickest and easiest way to the high alpine terrain, this 7-minute gondola ride takes you up 973m (3,192 ft.), just short of the summit of the Whistlers. From the top, the views of the Athabasca and Miette Valleys are stunning. There's a well-marked, although quite steep, 45-minute trail to the summit of the mountain, and the view is more outstanding with each step upward. Dress warmly and wear good walking shoes. At the summit, the panoramic view takes in six mountain ranges, including Mt. Robson, the highest point in the Canadian Rockies. Rides leave every 10 minutes or so. *www.jasper skytram.com.* ☎ *780/852-3093. Adults C$49, kids ages 6–15 C$26, free for kids 5 & under. Late Mar to mid-May 10am–5pm; mid-May to late June 9am–8pm; late June to early Sept 8am–9pm; early Sept to late Oct 10am–5pm. Closed late Oct to late Mar.*

Return to town by the same route. Park on Patricia St.

❸ Patricia St. Deli.

You'll find some of the best sandwiches—and some of the friendliest people—in Jasper at this deli right in the heart of town. "Two slices of bread with heaven in between," they say. A sandwich and a home-baked cookie make for a great picnic. *610 Patricia St.* ☎ *780/852-4814. $.*

Turn left on Pyramid Lake Rd. & left again on Bonhomme St.

❹ Jasper-Yellowhead Museum.

Good for a rainy day, this museum exhibits artifacts from the park's early days, including fur-trade and mountaineering

You can walk to the Whistlers summit from the Jasper Skytram.

The stairs up to Old Fort Point.

equipment. You'll find legendary guide Curly Phillips's hand-built cedar-strip canoe, Métis beaded deerskin jackets, and the gear used during the first ascent of Mt. Alberta in 1925. *400 Bonhomme St. www.jaspermuseum.org.* ☎ *780/852-3013. Adults C$7; seniors, students & kids ages 6–18 C$6, family pass C$15; free for kids ages 5 & under. Daily 10am–5pm in summer; closed Mon–Wed in winter.*

Drive 5 min. south of Jasper townsite via Hwy. 93A or Hazel Ave., crossing Hwy. 16. Turn east (left) on Old Fort Point Rd. & park in the first parking lot after the bridge.

⑤ ★★ Old Fort Point. The climb up the stairs at Old Fort Point is steep but worthwhile. Jutting out into the Athabasca River, the point offers great views that take in Jasper townsite, Lac Beauvert, and the Fairmont Jasper Park Lodge. From here, you can also catch sight of Mts. Kerkeslin and Hardisty to the southeast and the snowy triangle of Mt. Edith Cavell, shining above all others, to the south. The trail head is just across the river bridge on Old Fort Point Road.

Head back to town, east (right) on Connaught Dr. & north (left) on Pyramid Lake Rd.

⑥ Pyramid and Patricia Lakes. Head out in the early evening to spot wildlife on land (elk, deer, and moose) and in the water (beavers and ducks) just above town. Fishing is also a draw. Pyramid Island has a nice, short interpretive loop, great for watching the day come to an end. *From town, turn north (left) to follow Connaught Dr./Hwy. 16 out of town for 3.5km (2 miles). Turn right on Maligne Lake Rd. & right again on Old Lodge Rd. Drive to the end of the road & park at the Fairmont Jasper Park Lodge.*

⑦ Jasper Planetarium. Explore the night sky of this famed Dark Sky Preserve, beginning with the planetarium theater experience and ending with an outdoor telescope viewing. Don't miss the largest telescope in the Rockies. *www.jasperplanetarium.com.* ☎ *780/931-3275. Adults C$59, kids ages 4–17 C$25. May 1–June 14 9:45pm; June 15–Sept 16 3:30pm, 4:30pm & 10pm; Sept 17–Oct 27 & Dec 1–Apr 21 9pm.*

Yoho National Park

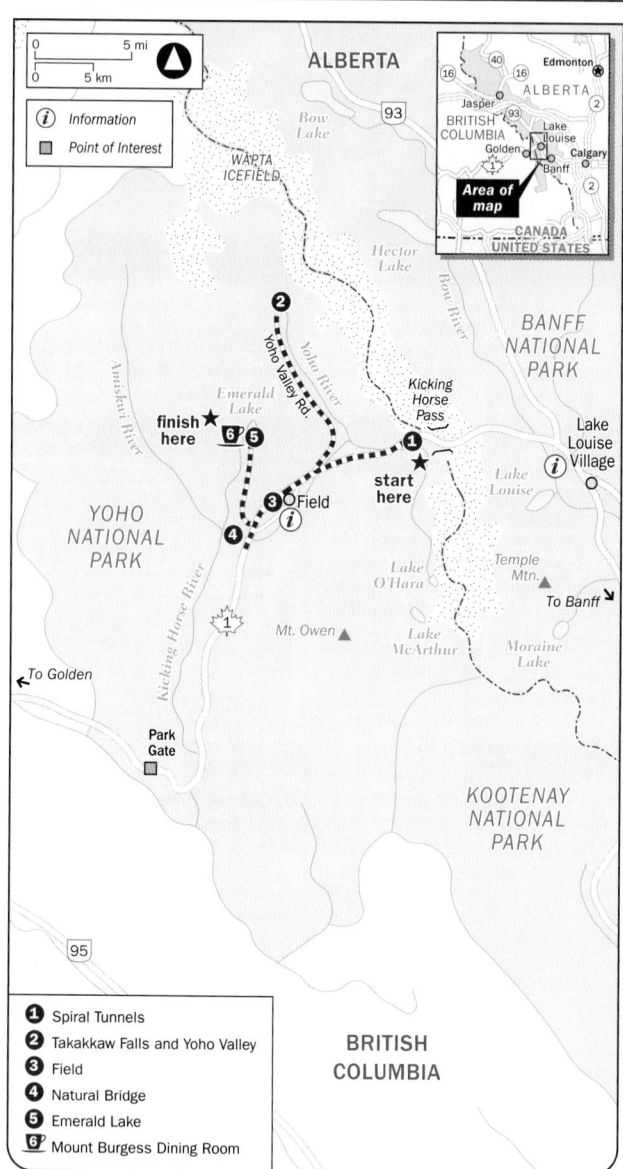

0 · 5 mi
0 · 5 km

ALBERTA

93

Bow Lake

WAPTA ICEFIELD

Hector Lake

Area of map

Edmonton
Jasper
ALBERTA
BRITISH COLUMBIA
Lake Louise
Golden
Calgary
Banff
CANADA
UNITED STATES

(i) Information
▪ Point of Interest

❷

Yoho Valley Rd.

Yoho River

Amiskwi River

Emerald Lake

finish here ★
❻ ❺

BANFF NATIONAL PARK

Kicking Horse Pass

❶
start here ★

Lake Louise
(i) Lake Louise Village

❸ ○ Field
(i)

❹

Kicking Horse River

①

Mt. Owen ▲

Lake O'Hara

Lake McArthur

Temple Mtn. ▲

To Banff ↘

Moraine Lake

YOHO NATIONAL PARK

← To Golden

Park Gate ▪

KOOTENAY NATIONAL PARK

95

❶ Spiral Tunnels
❷ Takakkaw Falls and Yoho Valley
❸ Field
❹ Natural Bridge
❺ Emerald Lake
❻ Mount Burgess Dining Room

BRITISH COLUMBIA

Yoho National Park makes a great base for exploring the Rockies. You're midway between the Columbia Icefield and the Town of Banff, next door to Lake Louise, and yet in a less traveled area. "Yoho" is an expression of awe and wonder in the Cree language, and that's just what you'll experience in the park. This drive takes you from Lake Louise southwest on Trans-Canada Hwy. 1 through the park toward Golden, British Columbia.

Take Trans-Canada Hwy. 1 west from Lake Louise 9.2km (5¾ miles) to the border between Alberta and British Columbia. Continue 8.7km (5½ miles) west of the border and turn off into the roadside interpretive display at the:

❶ ★ Spiral Tunnels. The first trains to make it over Kicking Horse Pass had really difficult ascents going toward Lake Louise or wild rides descending the steep west slope. Engineers developed a groundbreaking plan: The Spiral Tunnels take trains through two loops inside Cathedral Mountain, easing the steepness substantially. View the Spiral Tunnels from two lookouts: The first (and best) is on the side of Trans-Canada Hwy. 1 just up the hill from Field and has excellent interpretive signs; the second is on Yoho Valley Road just past the Cathedral Mountain Lodge.

Continue down the hill on Trans-Canada Hwy. another 3.7km (2⅓ miles), turning right at Yoho Valley Rd. Continue to the end.

❷ ★★ Takakkaw Falls & the Yoho Valley. If you love waterfalls, you've come to the right place: "Takakkaw" means magnificent in Cree. At 380m (1,247 ft.), this is the fourth-highest waterfall in Canada and originates at the Daly Glacier high above. There's a great picnic spot at the base. Looking to the north, you can often see the Yoho Glacier on a clear day. This is

Takakkaw Falls.

also the trail head for some superb hiking, ranging from an hour to Laughing Falls to 4 hours on the Iceline Trail.

Drive back out to Trans-Canada Hwy. 1, continuing 1.8km (1 mile) west to the turnoff for Field.

❸ ★ Field. This tiny town is the service center for Yoho National Park. It makes a good place to stop for lunch but isn't worth a visit in and of itself. Stop by the Yoho National Park Visitor Centre, grab a sandwich and a coffee, and maybe pop into the pottery shop and keep moving.

Turn left (west) on Trans-Canada Hwy. & continue 2km (1¼ miles) to the turnoff for Emerald Lake Rd.

Lake O'Hara: Getting to Paradise

In Yoho National Park, the best hiking trails are at magical Lake O'Hara, a region that makes locals misty-eyed just at its mention. There are some easy, shorter hikes around the lake itself, and a handful of excellent 3- to 6-hour trails that take you above Lake O'Hara to some of the equally spectacular surrounding lakes. The best bet is to connect all the short hikes into a challenging day hike known as the ★★★ **Lake O'Hara Alpine Circuit** (p 4).

Just on the other side of Lake Louise, O'Hara is accessed by a 11km (7-mile) road that can be hiked or cross-country-skied in the winter. But daily Parks Canada–run bus rides (mid-June to mid-Oct) will take you up to the warden station on the shores of Lake O'Hara in a painless 15 minutes. That'll give you the rest of the day for hiking. You must reserve a spot on the bus by going online at www.reservation.parkscanada.gc.ca or calling 📞 **877/737-3783.** Reservations open in mid-April and often fill up right away. There are no restrictions on the number of people hiking the somewhat-boring access road.

While you're on the line, you can also reserve a campsite at the **Lake O'Hara Campground** (bookable only by phone) to enjoy a calm and quiet night at the lake. It's good for families—it's in the backcountry but accessible by bus.

Bus tickets cost C$15 for adults and C$7 for children, round-trip. Buses leave the parking lot daily at 8:30 and 10:30am. The last bus out departs the campground at 6:30pm.

The parking lot is 1km (½ mile) west of the Alberta–British Columbia border, just off the south side of Trans-Canada Hwy. 1. Turn south at the sign to Lake O'Hara and west into the parking lot. Reserve campsites well in advance; the reservation line opens April 1 at 8am MDT. Visit www.pc.gc.ca/yoho. Lake O'Hara Lodge has its own private bus service (p 137).

The Burgess Shale

The Rockies' greatest contribution to archaeology is the 515-million-year-old Burgess Shale, a fossil bed discovered at the base of Mt. Stephen. This discovery transformed our understanding of the evolution of life on Earth and revealed the amazing biodiversity that existed before the mass extinction of species—half of the animal groups seen in the shale have disappeared from the planet. You can get here only on a full-day guided hike organized by Parks Canada or the Burgess Shale Geoscience Foundation. This is a must for archaeology buffs, but you cannot visit it on your own; you must hike in to either the Walcott Quarry or Mt. Stephen on an official tour with a registered guide, and you must be quite fit. Kids over 8 years old will enjoy the shorter hike to the Mt. Stephen Fossil Beds. Make reservations at www.pc.gc.ca/yoho or ☎ **877/737-3783.**

The Walcott Quarry hike costs C$55 to C$70 adults, C$28 to C$35 kids ages 8 to 16, C$46 to C$60 seniors. Hikes are available Friday through Monday early July to September 15, with additional daily hikes until August 31. The groups take only 12 fit hikers on one trip per day.

Canoeing on Emerald Lake.

4 Natural Bridge. Just south of Field is the Natural Bridge, where the Kicking Horse River meets with U-shaped sedimentary rock that has so far kept the river from breaking open a deep canyon. The river did manage to erode a small canyon of softer rock just upstream from the tougher section, creating a crooked bridge. Visit it soon—it may be gone in a matter of centuries!

Drive 7km (4⅓ miles) to reach:

5 ★★ Emerald Lake. Up the road from the Natural Bridge is the glacier-fed Emerald Lake, featuring hiking trails, canoe rentals, and the lovely Emerald Lake Lodge (see p 137). A visit to Emerald Lake could fill an album worth of photos.

6 ★ Mt. Burgess Dining Room. The seasonal fine dining inside this historic lodge is all about rustic Rocky Mountain cuisine with artistic flair. The menu focuses on local game, including elk, bison, and caribou, and the award-winning wine list has more than 400 labels. *Emerald Lake Lodge, Emerald Lake Rd., 8km (5 miles) off Trans-Canada Hwy. 1, at a turnoff 2km (1¼ miles) south of Field.* https://crmr.com/emerald. ☎ *800/663-6336. $$$.*

Golden, British Columbia

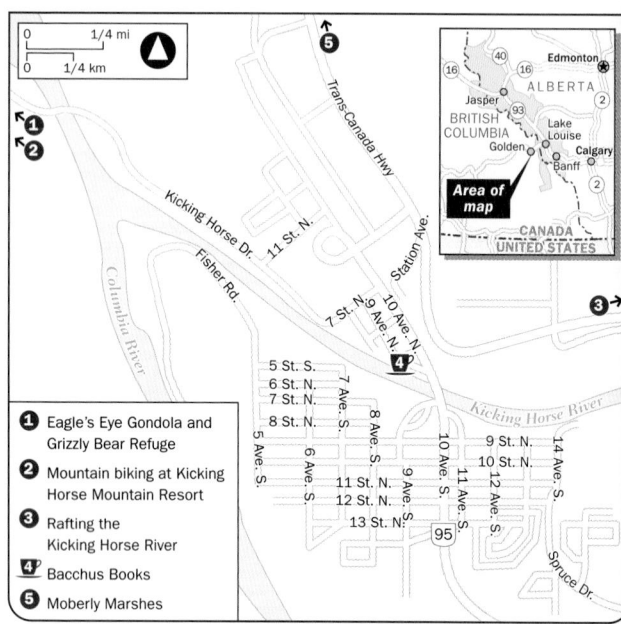

1 Eagle's Eye Gondola and Grizzly Bear Refuge

2 Mountain biking at Kicking Horse Mountain Resort

3 Rafting the Kicking Horse River

4 Bacchus Books

5 Moberly Marshes

Golden is just off Trans-Canada Highway (Hwy. 1) at the confluence of the Kicking Horse and Columbia rivers. The small town (pop. 4,200) is home to the Kicking Horse Mountain Resort, frequently ranked as one of the best ski resorts in North America. Golden is the gateway to Yoho National Park, 20km/12 miles east.

1 ★★ **Eagle's Eye Gondola & Grizzly Bear Refuge.** Soar up to 2,350m (7,700 ft.) for views of the Rocky and Purcell mountains. Hike the Terminator Ridge. The gorgeous restaurant opens for lunch in summer. Combine a gondola ride with a visit to the world's largest protected grizzly bear refuge near the gondola's base, home to Boo the grizzly. *From Hwy. 95, turn west at blue sign for Kicking Horse Mountain Resort in downtown Golden, 13km (8 miles) uphill. www.* kickinghorseresort.com. ☎ 866/754-5425 or 250/439-5425. *Gondola & Refuge package rate: C$48 adults, C$40 kids ages 13–17 & seniors, C$24 kids ages 6–12. Gondola only: C$43 adults, C$37 kids ages 13–17 & seniors, C$21 kids ages 6–12. Grizzly Bear Refuge only: C$31 adults, C$26 kids ages 13–17 & seniors, C$15 kids 12 & under. Late June to early Sept daily 9:30am–4:30pm.*

2 **Mountain Biking.** When the snow leaves Kicking Horse Mountain Resort, the trails are opened to

Boo, a beautiful rescued grizzly bear, in the Grizzly Bear Refuge.

❸ Whitewater Rafting. The Kicking Horse River rapids are some of the best in British Columbia. You'll see the valley from a totally different perspective. **Kootenay River Runners** runs a half-day trip. *1km (⅔ mile) west of the western gates of Kootenay National Park. www.kootenayriverrunners.com.* ☎ *800/599-4399 or 250/347-9210. Rates start at C$128. No children ages 11 & under.*

Back in Golden, turn right onto 6th Ave. & take a quick left onto 9th St.

world-class downhill biking. Stick your bike on the gondola and cruise down twisty single-track trails. *At the base of Kicking Horse Mountain Resort. www.kicking horseresort.com.* ☎ *866/754-5425 or 250/439-5424. Full-day bike ticket C$57 adults, C$43 kids & seniors, C$28 kids ages 7–12.*

From Kicking Horse Mountain Resort, head back into Golden. Drive through town and up the hill on Trans-Canada Hwy. 1. Twenty-five kilometers (16 miles) from Golden, turn right at the sign for Beaverfoot Lodge.

❹ Bacchus Books. Sure, the eclectic first floor is chock-a-block with unique books, but follow your nose upstairs to the cafe and you'll discover fresh baked treats, hearty homemade soups, and a tasty glory bowl. *409 9th Ave. N. www.bacchus books.ca.* ☎ *250/344-5600. $.*

❺ kids Moberly Marshes. The Gadsden Provincial Park houses the largest remaining wetlands area in North America and home to more than 260 resident and migratory bird species. Bring your binoculars. *10km (6.2 miles) north of Golden along Trans-Canada Hwy. 1.*

Whitewater rafting on the Kicking Horse River.

Kootenay National Park

Legend:

- ⬛ Campground
- 🛢 Gasoline
- ✚ Hospital/First Aid
- ⓘ Information
- ⬛ Point of Interest
- ⛷ Ski Area

1 Fireweed Trail
2 Stanley Glacier
3 Marble Canyon
4 The Paint Pots
5 Kootenay Park Lodge
6 Radium Springs Pools
7 Sinclair Canyon

0 — 5 mi
0 — 5 km

A **drive through Kootenay National Park makes a great day trip** from Banff National Park. Established in 1920, the park is quite long and narrow (94km/58 miles long; 8km/5 miles across) and has a remarkably diverse landscape. The main road through the park traverses the scars of the massive 2003 forest fire; two large lightning-caused fires eventually merged and burned 12.6% of the park. It's a quiet park, with some interesting stops along the Banff–Windermere Highway. It'll take you about 90 minutes to drive back from Radium Hot Springs directly to Banff, but this tour runs southwest, starting at the border of Banff National Park.

Take Hwy. 93 west toward British Columbia.

❶ kids **Fireweed Trail.** Just past the Continental Divide and over the Alberta–British Columbia border, make a stop at the Vermillion Pass to hike the longer of two Fireweed Trail loops, a short 30-minute loop with interpretive signs that explain why natural forest fires are healthy and good for the environment and are no longer suppressed by Parks Canada. *On the south side of Hwy. 93, at the provincial border.*

Continue west on Hwy. 93.

❷ ★★ **Stanley Glacier.** Taking you from fire to ice in only 8km (5 miles), this is a relatively short and only moderately steep half-day hike

Trees along the Fireweed Trail.

Water flowing through Marble Canyon.

on the crest of the Continental Divide. The family-friendly trail takes you up to a hanging valley with a giant glacier clinging to the limestone cliffs at the back. There are impressive views throughout the entire hike. Great in the morning, as the small parking lot fills up quickly. *On the south side of Hwy. 93, 3.2km (2 miles) past the provincial border.*

Continue west on Hwy. 93.

❸ ★★ **Marble Canyon.** If it's a hot day, you'll particularly enjoy a short hike on this narrow trail of

Radium

A small town (population 675) at the southern end of Kootenay National Park, Radium Hot Springs—often simply called Radium—is named for (you guessed it) its famous hot springs, which draw visitors to soak in the reputedly healing waters. The town is essentially a strip of motels and restaurants, but if you explore some of the back roads, you'll discover spectacular scenery and bump into more than a few Calgary residents who make this their second home. It's also a good area for golfing and hiking—the **Radium Golf Group** (www.radiumgolf.ca; ☎ **800/667-6444** or 250/347-6200; map p 134) has an 18-hole championship course located along the cliffs that border the Columbia River. You can also hike the **Juniper Trail** past Sinclair Canyon or the **Valley View Trail,** which starts at Redstreak Campground.

limestone carved by two retreated glaciers. The farther up the trail you walk, the more impressive the canyon. It's cool and shady here. And don't be fooled by the name: There is no marble, only white and gray dolomite rock. Kids will find the hike intriguing, but keep an eye on them because the trail can get very slippery. *On the north side of Hwy. 93, 7km (4⅓ miles) past the provincial border.*

Continue west on Hwy. 93.

❹ **The Paint Pots.** A brief and beautiful walk takes you to this fascinating area where First Nations people gathered ocher, an iron-based mineral that was baked, crushed, mixed with grease, and used as a paint for tepees, pictographs, and personal adornment. There is an excellent, wheelchair-friendly, 30-minute interpretive trail. *On the north side of Hwy. 93, 10km (6¼ miles) past the provincial border.*

Vintage cars parked outside the Kootenay Park Lodge.

The popular Radium Hot Springs Pools have been in business since 1914.

5 **Kootenay Park Lodge.** The only place to stop for a coffee inside Kootenay National Park is at this historic lodge. The restaurant is only open for dinner, but the General Store has fresh coffee and simple deli-style sandwiches to go. *Hwy. 93 at Vermillion Crossing, 42km (26 miles) west of Castle Junction, 61km (38 miles) east of Radium Hot Springs.* ☎ *250/434-9648. www. kootenayparklodge.com. $.*

Continue west on Hwy. 93.

6 ★ **Radium Hot Springs Pools.** These "sacred mountain waters" have been drawing visitors to the Columbia Valley since 1914. There is one hot pool (104°F/40°C); and a cooler swimming pool. The hot pool is settled in a canyon rich with oxide, giving the walls a permanent orange-sunset look. *3km (1¾ miles) northeast of the Town of Radium on Hwy. 93. www.hotsprings. ca.* ☎ *800/767/1611 or 250/347-9485. Adults C$7, kids ages 3–17 C$5, seniors C$6. Mid-May to mid-Oct daily 9am–11pm; mid-Oct to mid-May Mon–Fri 1–9pm, Sat–Sun 10am–9pm.*

Driving through the red cliffs of Sinclair Canyon.

Continue west on Hwy. 93.

7 **Sinclair Canyon.** Kootenay closes with a bang at the spectacular red cliffs of Sinclair Canyon, which welcome you to the Columbia Valley just after the Radium Hot Springs pools.

Calgary in One Day

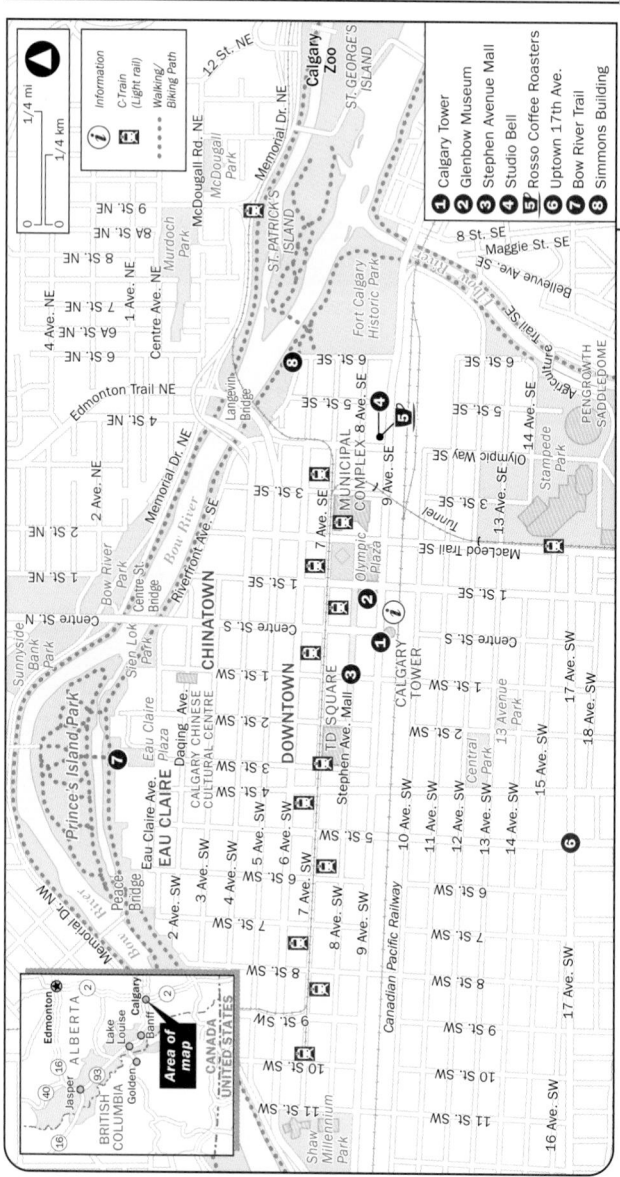

1. Calgary Tower
2. Glenbow Museum
3. Stephen Avenue Mall
4. Studio Bell
5. Rosso Coffee Roasters
6. Uptown 17th Ave.
7. Bow River Trail
8. Simmons Building

With more than a million people, a vibrant economy, and plenty of personality, the city of Calgary invites you to "be part of the energy." Safe, clean, and young, Calgary has an identity that goes beyond white cowboy hats and rodeos. And while hipsters may snicker at the cowboy schtick, it is really authentic here. Western hospitality is legendarily friendly, upbeat, and relaxed. It's a fun and exciting city that is quite simple to discover. With a day or two, you can take in the main sites and even have time to wander in one of the city's top neighborhoods—East Village and Inglewood stand out.

❶ ★★ Calgary Tower. Come here first to get your bearings 191m (627 ft.) in the sky. You can spot the Stampede Grounds and Scotiabank Saddledome (where the NHL's Calgary Flames play) to the southwest, the Bow River winding through town, and the snow-capped Rocky Mountains on the western horizon. *9th Ave. & Centre St. www.calgary tower.com.* ☎ *403/266-7171. Elevator ride C$18 adults, C$16 seniors, C$9 kids ages 4–12. June–Aug 9am–10pm; Sept–May 9am–9pm.*

Walk 1 block east on 9th Ave. SE, turning left on 1st St. SE.

❷ Glenbow Museum. The walls and halls of this storied museum downtown tell the story of the West, from the past to the present. Start in the Blackfoot Gallery to learn about indigenous cultures; then continue to the Mavericks Gallery, which represents what it

means to be Albertan today. *130 9th Ave. SE, at 1st St. www.glenbow. org.* ☎ *403/268-4101. C$18 adults, C$12 seniors & students, C$11 kids ages 7–17. Mon–Thurs & Sat 9am–5pm; Fri 9am–8pm; Sun noon–5pm.*

Turn left on 1st St. SE & left again at 8th Ave. SE, also known as Stephen Ave.

❸ Stephen Avenue Mall. A pedestrian avenue that is lined by banks, high-end shops like Holt Renfrew and Birks, lively eateries, and some interesting public art, this is a great spot for lunch. Try **Bank & Baron P.U.B.** (125 8th Ave. SW; ☎ 587/293-9688) for a modern twist on Alberta's historic roots; the **Guild** (200 8th Ave. SW, ☎ 403/770-2313) for wood-fired meats; or the chic **Blink** (111 8th Ave. SW; ☎ 403/263-5330).

From Stephen Ave., head 1 block south to 9th Ave. SW & then left along 9th Ave. to 4th St. SE.

Calgary city skyline at night.

Stephen Avenue Mall in downtown Calgary.

❹ Studio Bell National Music Centre.

The award-winning home of Canada's music culture is located in the former industrial area turned architectural playground known as the East Village. Discover the stories behind Canadian music culture in the four Halls of Fame and take in a musical demonstration. And don't leave without checking out the view from the fifth-floor East Village Skybridge. *850 4th St. SE. www.studiobell.ca.* ☎ *403/543-5115. C$18 adults, C$14 seniors & students, C$11 kids ages 3–12. Daily 10am–5pm.*

Bikers trail on Bow River.

Visit the National Music Centre's ❺ **Rosso Coffee Roasters** location for a taste of this Calgary coffee institution. *850 4th St. SE. www. rossocoffeeroasters.com.* ☎ *403/476-1667.*

From the museum, walk 2 blocks south to turn right on 12th Ave. SW. Walk 6 blocks west through Central Memorial Park & 2 blocks south.

❻ Uptown 17th Avenue.

Cross south and venture through a lively neighborhood towards the eclectic, trendy stretch of 17th Avenue. Fashion boutiques, vintage stores, clubs, coffee shops, and great bistros draw fashionistas, foodies, and those just looking for a nice stroll. *17th Ave. SW btw. 10th St. & 4th St. SW.*

Hop in a cab or turn left at 4th St. SW & go north 13 blocks, turning right on 2nd Ave. SW.

❼ Bow River Trail.

This wide, paved pathway is where Calgarians come to walk, run, bike, push strollers, inline skate, and get fresh air. Rent a bike at **Rapid Rent** (from C$10/hr., in the Eau Claire Market, Barclay Parade SW; www.rapidrent. ca; ☎ 403/444-5845), then ride or

The Calgary Stampede

If you're in Calgary during the first 2 weeks of July, well, yeehaw! The world-famous **Calgary Stampede,** calling itself the "Greatest Outdoor Show on Earth," takes over the city in a major way. It's the richest rodeo around, with C$2 million in prizes. From morning stampede breakfasts and parades to a roller-coaster midway and live concerts, there is a lot to soak in. Visit www.calgarystampede.com for more information on the event and how to get tickets.

The 10-day Calgary Stampede draws a million visitors annually.

walk from the 9th Street pedestrian bridge downriver as far as the George C. King Bridge near the zoo.

Stop in for a drink & food at:

8 Simmons Building. Inside a beautifully refurbished historic warehouse on the riverbank, you'll find some of Calgary's finest food. There's the outstanding **Sidewalk Citizen Bakery, Phil & Sebastian Coffee Roasters,** and the **Charbar** restaurant (p. 123). It's the heart of the dynamic East Village neighborhood development. *Confluence Way, near 2nd Ave. SW & 3rd St. SW.*

Then bike over the George C. King pedestrian bridge, back on the north side of the river, completing the loop by crossing the Peace Bridge.

The short ribs at Charbar.

Calgary in Two Days

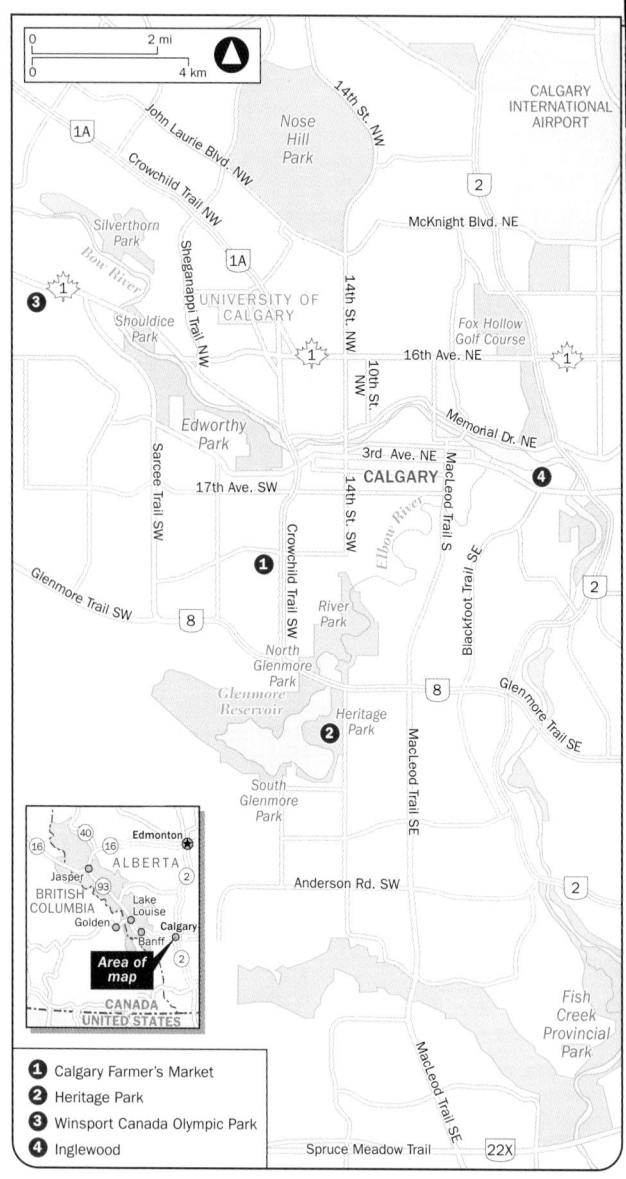

- ❶ Calgary Farmer's Market
- ❷ Heritage Park
- ❸ Winsport Canada Olympic Park
- ❹ Inglewood

You've seen all the main highlights of Calgary and its bustling downtown core. A second day will let you branch out to roam the wider regions of Calgary. But you'll need a vehicle for today's trip.

❶ Calgary Farmer's Market. A year-round indoor market has rows of seasonal produce, organic meat, and artworks from some 100 vendors. *510–77 Ave SE. www.calgary farmersmarket.ca.* ☎ *403/240-9113. Free admission. Thurs–Sun 9am–5pm.*

Continue south on Crowchild Trail, turning east on Glenmore Trail. Turn south on 14th St. SW into the Glenmore Park.

❷ Heritage Park. A re-created pioneer village covers the years from 1860 to 1940. Ride on a steam train or paddle-wheeler or take a ride on the antique midway. *1900 Heritage Dr. SW. www.heritagepark. ca.* ☎ *403/268-8500. Adults C$27, kids ages 7–15 C$19, kids ages 3–6 C$14. Daily 10am–5pm.*

Head north out of Glenmore Park onto 14th St. SW, turning west or left on Glenmore Trail. Follow until it meets up with Trans-Canada Hwy. 1. Go west to the next exit.

❸ Winsport Canada Olympic Park. The slopes that hosted the 1988 Olympics have a small ski hill open to all during the winter. In summer, it turns into a playground with mountain biking, ziplining, and great views from the top of the Ski Jump Tower. There's also Canada's Sports Hall of Fame. *88 Canada Olympic Rd. SW. www.winsport.ca.* ☎ *403/247-5452. Free admission; pay per activity. Hours vary.*

Take Trans-Canada Hwy. 1 east back toward the city. Turn east at Memorial Dr., following the Bow River all the way past the Calgary Zoo to turn south on Deerfoot Trail & east on 17th Ave. SE.

❹ Inglewood. Calgary's oldest neighborhood has stories to tell. Wander the original main street and the aptly named Music Mile to explore music venues, shops, and boutique eateries. Refuel with a wood-fired rotisserie meal at **The Nash,** 925 11th St. SE (www.the nashyyc.com; ☎ 403/984-3365). The historic hotel is an Inglewood landmark, brought back to life by a passionate culinary team.

Heritage Park is a living museum and re-created pioneer village.

Calgary **Dining & Lodging**

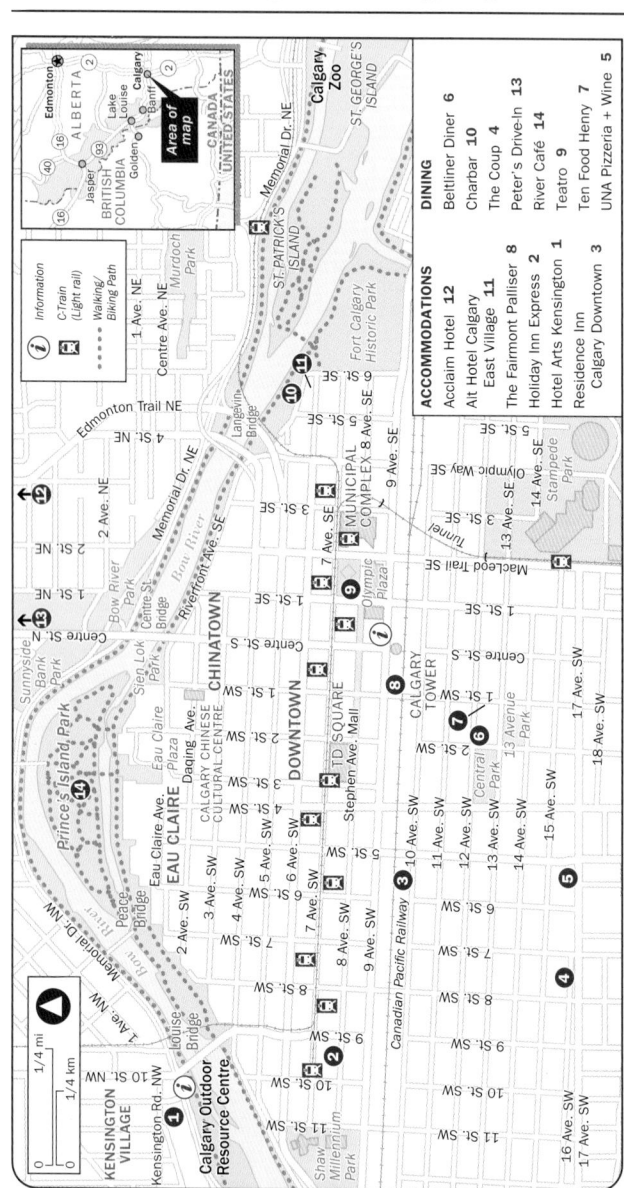

ACCOMMODATIONS

Acclaim Hotel **12**
Alt Hotel Calgary
East Village **11**
The Fairmont Palliser **8**
Holiday Inn Express **2**
Hotel Arts Kensington **1**
Residence Inn
Calgary Downtown **3**

DINING

Beltliner Diner **6**
Charbar **10**
The Coup **4**
Peter's Drive-In **13**
River Café **14**
Teatro **9**
Ten Food Henry **7**
UNA Pizzeria + Wine **5**

Dining & Lodging A to Z

Restaurants

★ Beltliner Diner NORTH OF 17TH AVENUE *DINER*   There are plenty of places for brunch in Calgary, but this is my current favorite. It's a stylish, modern version of a classic diner, with plenty of old-school entrees like Eggs Bennie and more current options like chicken and waffles and lamb merguez sausage and eggs. Come early to beat lineups. *242 12 Ave SW. www.thebeltliner.com.* ☎ *587/955-1555. Entrees C$14–C$20. Tues–Sat 7am–10pm; Sun–Mon 7am–3pm. Map p 122.*

★★ Charbar EAST VILLAGE *STEAKHOUSE*   A beautiful old warehouse has been transformed into a hip Argentine-style grill next to the Bow River. Slow-grilled meats are the stars here. Order a grass-fed Alberta butcher steak, with parilla-beef fat fries or fried Brussels sprouts on the side. There's also a large selection of ceviche, the other house specialty. Or just come for a drink and tapas and enjoy the rooftop patio on a summer evening. *618 Confluence Way SE. www.charbar.ca.* ☎ *403/452-3115. Entrees C$19–C$38. Mon–Thurs 11:30am–10pm; Fri 11:30am–midnight; Sat 10am–midnight; Sun 10am–10pm. Map p 122.*

★ The Coup 17TH AVENUE *VEGETARIAN*   Healthy, fresh, creative fusion food stars at this hip spot on 17th Avenue. Most ingredients are vegetarian, organic, and local. There are jam-packed salads, falafel quesadillas, and a noodle and veggie bowls aplenty. There's also a fun cocktail list. *924 17th Ave. SW. www.thecoup.ca.* ☎ *403/541-1041. Entrees C$17–C$23. Mon & Wed–Thurs 11am–3pm & 5–9pm; Fri 11am–3pm & 5–11pm; Sat 10am–3pm & 5–11pm; Sun 10am–3pm & 5–9pm. Map p 122.*

kids Peter's Drive-In NORTH OF DOWNTOWN *DINER*   If you're en route to Banff from the Calgary airport (or vice-versa), drop by this legendary and truly retro (it's been around since 1964) "drive-in" just off the Trans-Canada Highway for burgers, fries, onion rings, and a shake. You can be served in the car or go through the drive-through window. *219 16th Ave. NE. www.petersdrivein.com.* ☎ *403/277-2747. Entrees C$4–C$7. No credit cards. Daily 9am–midnight. Map p 122.*

★★ River Café PRINCE'S ISLAND PARK *REGIONAL*   From the picturesque setting in a wooden lodge on an island in the Bow River

Breakfast at the Beltliner Diner.

The bar at The Coup.

to a menu that exemplifies regional and seasonal Alberta cuisine, this is a rich experience. Start with the emblematic fish and game platter. Then opt for bison or beef. If you're only in town for 1 night and it's not storming out, then this should be your choice for dinner. *Prince's Island Park. www.river-cafe.com.* ☎ *403/261-7670. Entrees C$36–C$52. Mon–Fri 11am–11pm; Sat–Sun 10am–11pm. Map p 122.*

★★ **Teatro** DOWNTOWN *EUROPEAN* For a refined, romantic meal, come to this dazzling room inside the historic Dominion Bank building. It's mainly Italian food, since the owner is Italian, but there's a delicate high-end French influence. Pastas come with scallop béchamel or uni emulsion sauces, for example. Drop in for a martini or a glass of wine before going to a show, or later for a nightcap. *200 8th Ave. SE, Olympic Plaza. www.teatro.ca.* ☎ *403/290-1012. Entrees C$25–C$55. Mon–Fri 11:30am–10pm; Sat 5–11pm; Sun 5–10pm. Map p 122.*

★ **Ten Foot Henry** BELTLINE *REGIONAL* The casually earthy vibe at this eatery is brought to life not just by the soft lighting and hanging plants, but also by the incredibly friendly servers. They'll happily advise you in ordering a range of small plates from a menu that's primarily veggie-based, with creative pasta dishes and seafood options mixed in. It's a modern Western twist on tapas, and it's good. *1209 1st St. SW. www.tenfoothenry.com.* ☎ *403.475.5537. Entrees C$17–C$27. Daily 11am–11pm. Map p 122.*

★★ **UNA Pizza + Wine** 17TH AVENUE *PIZZA* Great service, fabulously simple Italian food, a casual and bustling atmosphere, NHL hockey players possibly sitting nearby, even a kids' menu—the only problem at UNA is that you can't make reservations. Come before 6pm or after 7:30pm or be prepared to stroll 17th Avenue while you wait. *618 17th Ave. SW. www.unapizzeria.com.* ☎ *403/453-1183. Entrees C$15–C$19. Daily 11:30am–1am. Map p 122.*

One of the creative pastas at Ten Foot Henry.

Accommodations

Acclaim Hotel AIRPORT   If all you need is a good bed before or after your flight, this stylish airport hotel is a great choice. Complimentary shuttle, big fluffy beds, a rooftop hot tub, and a fitness club will ease your travel-weary bones. It's way out of town, though. *123 Freeport Blvd. NE. www.acclaimhotel.ca.* ☎ *866/955-0008 or 403/291-8000. 123 units. Doubles C$130–C$260. Map p 122.*

Alt Hotel Calgary East Village

EAST VILLAGE   New to the East Village area, the Alt Hotel is exactly what you would expect in this buzzing cultural district. Aiming for "no frills chic," the hotel offers a new hipster take on boutique—and it works. The rooms are bright and comfortable, the well-equipped fitness room is open 24 hours, and the café (run by the local celebrity chefs at the Charbar group) is top-notch. *635 Confluence Way SE. www.althotels.com.* ☎ *833/258-6635. 143 rooms. Doubles C$189–C$249. Map p 122.*

★ The Fairmont Palliser

DOWNTOWN   Opened in 1914, this historic landmark has deep roots in the Calgary community. Rooms here are notoriously cramped, as in most urban hotels of this vintage, but are recently renovated and still retain an old-world elegance typical of Fairmont. The Fairmont Gold rooms have extra value with a private concierge, private check-in, and a separate dining area. *133 9th Ave. SW. www.fairmont.com.* ☎ *866/540-4477 or 403/262-1234. 407 units. Doubles C$309–C$559. Map p 122.*

kids Holiday Inn Express

DOWNTOWN   My choice for best mid-range hotel in town, this Holiday Inn includes the predictable high-rise hotel experience found in

Stately guest room at the Fairmont Palliser.

many hotels, plus free parking and breakfast. The rooms are average and the location good. There's a small fitness center. Kids eat free in the grill next door. *1020 8th Ave. www.hiexpress.com.* ☎ *877/660-8550 or 403/269-8262. 56 units. Doubles C$158–C$280. Map p 122.*

★★ Hotel Arts Kensington

KENSINGTON   This boutique inn—on the north side of the river a short walk from downtown—is private, expensive, design-forward, and chic. The rooms are large, the ambience is cool, and the restaurant is one of the best in town. *1126 Memorial Dr. NW. www.hotelarts kensington.com.* ☎ *877/313-3733 or 403/228-4442. 19 units. Doubles C$224–C$434. Map p 122.*

Residence Inn Calgary Downtown

DOWNTOWN   Built on the foundations of the historic Alberta Boot Company, these modern apartment-style studios and one-bedroom suites are perfect for a longer stay. The central location is convenient, and the included hot breakfast is a step above the usual. *610 10th Ave. SW. www.marriott.com.* ☎ *587/885-2288. Doubles C$189–C$239. Map p 122.*

Alberta Rockies **Dining & Lodging**

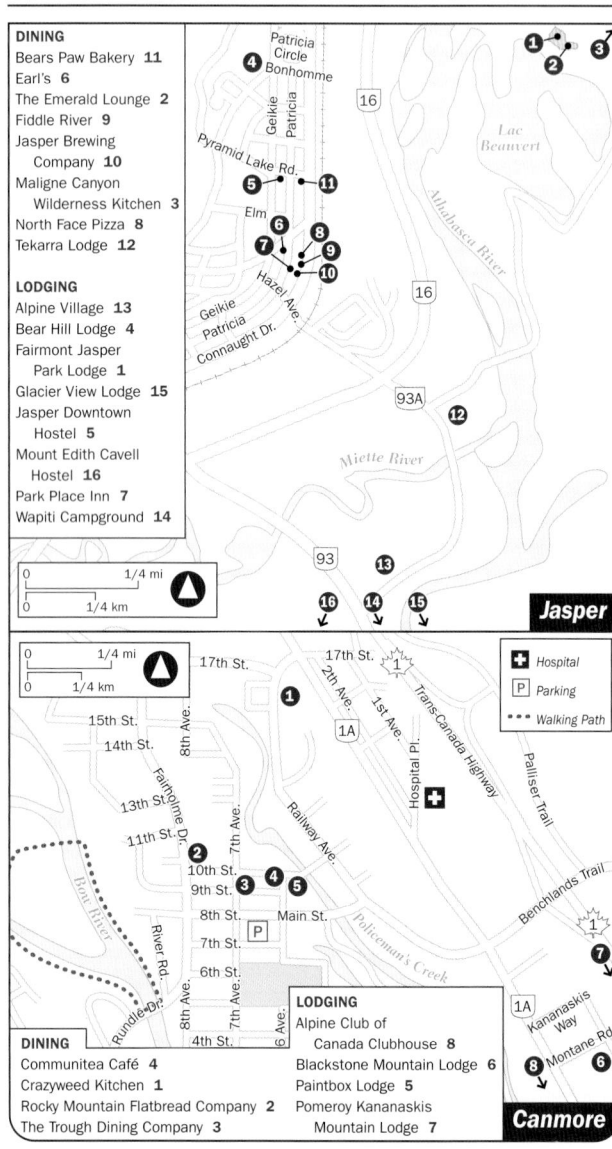

DINING

Bears Paw Bakery **11**
Earl's **6**
The Emerald Lounge **2**
Fiddle River **9**
Jasper Brewing
  Company **10**
Maligne Canyon
  Wilderness Kitchen **3**
North Face Pizza **8**
Tekarra Lodge **12**

LODGING

Alpine Village **13**
Bear Hill Lodge **4**
Fairmont Jasper
  Park Lodge **1**
Glacier View Lodge **15**
Jasper Downtown
  Hostel **5**
Mount Edith Cavell
  Hostel **16**
Park Place Inn **7**
Wapiti Campground **14**

Patricia Circle
Bonhomme
Geikie
Patricia
Pyramid Lake Rd.
Elm
Hazel Ave.
Geikie
Patricia
Connaught Dr.

16

Lac Beauvert
Athabasca River

16

93A

Miette River

93

Jasper

17th St.
17th St.
15th St.
14th St.
13th St.
11th St.
10th St.
9th St.
8th St.
7th St.
6th St.
4th St.
8th Ave.
7th Ave.
6 Ave.
Fairholme Dr.
8th Ave.
7th Ave.
2th Ave.
1st Ave.
Railway Ave.
Main St.
Hospital Pl.
Trans-Canada Highway
Palliser Trail
Benchlands Trail
Kananaskis Way
Montane Rd.
Policeman's Creek
Bow River
River Rd.
Rundle Dr.

1A

P

Hospital
P Parking
••• Walking Path

DINING

Communitea Café **4**
Crazyweed Kitchen **1**
Rocky Mountain Flatbread Company **2**
The Trough Dining Company **3**

LODGING

Alpine Club of
  Canada Clubhouse **8**
Blackstone Mountain Lodge **6**
Paintbox Lodge **5**
Pomeroy Kananaskis
  Mountain Lodge **7**

Canmore

Dining & Lodging A to Z

Restaurants

Bear's Paw Bakery JASPER
BAKERY/CAFE With two locations, this bakery is very popular. It has fresh sandwiches, granola to go, superb fruit tarts, and a huge variety of cookies, bars, and yummy delights—including dog treats. You'll find their freshly baked bread at countless restaurants around town. *610 Connaught Dr. & 4 Pyramid Rd. www.bearspawbakery.com.* ☎ *780/852-3233. Sandwiches C$7– C$12. Daily 7am–6pm. Map p 126.*

★★ Communitea Café
CANMORE *CAFE/VEGETARIAN* Choose from more than 80 blends of loose-leaf tea at this funky hangout. Breakfasts and lunches are healthy, affordable, and tasty. Build your own rice bowl with organic brown rice, steamed veggies, and flavorful Asian sauces. There are also great snacks like sushi, shrimp rolls, organic edamame—and quite possibly the best lattes in town, brewed in a one-of-a-kind espresso machine. This is a place with heart. *117–1001 6th Ave., corner of 10th St. www.thecommunitea.com.* ☎ *403/688-2233. Entrees C$8– C$15. Daily 8am–7pm. Map p 126.*

Bear's Paw Bakery.

★ Crazyweed Kitchen CAN-
MORE *GLOBAL/FUSION* Slightly unpredictable and always provocative, Crazyweed is both chaotic and creative. The food here could just be the most incredible of your life, particularly the ahi ceviche and the Thai grilled chicken. But service is erratic, either pompously absent or

"Classic Avocado Side Up" sandwich at the Communitea Café.

Outdoor dining on the deck of Maligne Canyon Wilderness Kitchen.

delightfully charming. *1600 Railway Ave. www.crazyweed.ca.* ☎ *403/609-2530. Entrees C$19–C$46. Tues–Sun 11:30am–10pm. Map p 126.*

Earl's JASPER *CANADIAN* A real crowd-pleaser, Earl's is a good choice for just about anybody—families, couples, or friends. Part of a popular Western Canada chain, there's a bit of Mexican, Asian, and European served here, from burgers to Thai curries to brick-oven pizzas. It also has the nicest outdoor patio in town, warmed by heaters on chilly evenings. *600 Patricia St., upstairs. www.earls.ca.* ☎ *780/852-2393. Reservations recommended in summer. Entrees C$13–C$53. Daily 11am–1am. Map p 126.*

★★ The Emerald Lounge JASPER *CANADIAN* Spacious seating areas dotted around a river-rock fireplace and the mountain-chic decor inspire a delightful sense of old-world nostalgia. On sunny days, sit on the patio to look out over Lac Beauvert. The cocktails here are the best, and there's a good range of salads, sandwiches and entrees (and to-die-for desserts). If you love it here as much as I do, treat yourself at other Jasper Park Lodge dining outlets like ORSO Trattoria and the Moose's Nook Chophouse. *In the Fairmont Jasper Park Lodge, Old Lodge Rd. www.fairmont.com/jasper.* ☎ *780/852-3301. Entrees C$22–C$49. Sun–Thurs 11:30am–midnight; Fri–Sat 11:30am–1am. Map p 126.*

Fiddle River JASPER *CANADIAN* Upstairs, above Connaught Street, is an ever-changing menu that's founded in seasonal produce and almost always showcases Canadiana favorites like Alberta-raised beef and wild game meatloaf, as well as pumpkin-seed halibut and a seafood kettle. The service is casual and friendly, and the views are divine. *620 Connaught Dr., upstairs. www. fiddleriverrestaurant.com.* ☎ *780/852-3032. Entrees C$25–C$44. Daily 5pm–midnight. Map p 126.*

Jasper Brewing Company JASPER *BREWPUB* A warm and cozy place for a pint and a burger, this brewpub has big-screen TVs and a blazing fireplace. The bartender will suggest the fish and chips or sirloin steak burger. Highly regarded ales, pilsners, and stouts are brewed in the back; a sample of six costs C$16. *624 Connaught Dr. www. jasperbrewingco.ca.* ☎ *780/852-4111. Entrees C$13–C$32. Daily 11am–2am. Map p 126.*

Maligne Canyon Wilderness Kitchen JASPER *REGIONAL* Located at the trail head to the

Maligne Canyon interpretive trail, this is a good option for a riverside patio lunch or an evening away from the (relatively speaking) busy Jasper downtown streets. The menu features locally sourced staples like venison sausage, Alberta beef brisket, and rainbow trout. There's a free shuttle from town. *Maligne Lake Road, 10km (6 miles) from downtown. www.maligne canyon.com.* ☎ *888/773-8888. Entrees C$20–C$28. May–Sept 8am–10pm; Oct–Apr Sun–Fri 9am–4pm, Sat 9am–10pm. Map p 126.*

North Face Pizza JASPER *PIZZA* If you want to order in, do so from Jasper's best pizza joint. It offers free delivery anywhere in town. There are also burgers, salads, pastas, sandwiches, and wings on offer, plus locally brewed beer from Big Rock Brewery on tap. Eat in (order at the counter) if you want to mingle with the local under-30 crowd. *618 Connaught Dr. www.northfacepizza. com.* ☎ *780/852-5830. Pizzas C$12–C$22. Daily 11am–2am. Map p 126.*

kids Rocky Mountain Flat-bread Company CANMORE *MEDITERRANEAN* The wood-fired clay oven here is reportedly the largest in Canada. Handcrafted flatbread pizzas are made with organic flour, regional cheeses, and fresh, creative toppings. Try the Pesto Shrimp or Apple Chicken or build your own creation. Salads are big and creative. Pint-sized portions for kids and a kid-friendly play area, where they can bake their own pretend pizzas, are available. *838 10th St. www.rockymountainflatbread.ca.* ☎ *403/609-5508. Entrees C$14–C$28. Sun–Thurs 11:30am–9pm; Fri–Sat 11:30am–10pm. Map p 126.*

★★ Tekarra JASPER *INTERNATIONAL* This little cabin inside the sprawling lodge of the same name draws Jasper's keenest foodies.

The menu spans from locally sourced ingredients like bison and Alberta beef to lamb and rainbow trout, always with a creative flair that's both rustic and refined. All the smoking, curing, and baking is done in-house. *In Tekarra Lodge, Hwy. 93A, 1km (½ mile) south of Jasper townsite. www.tekarrarestaurant. com.* ☎ *780/852-4624. Reservations recommended. Entrees C$19–C$45. Daily 5:30–9:30pm. Open late May to early Oct. Map p. 126.*

★★ The Trough Dining Co. CANMORE *BISTRO* With a relaxed and intimate vibe, this is Canmore's top restaurant. Flavors are powerful and intense in every dish. Labor-intensive entrees include jerk-spiced Alberta baby-back ribs and pan-roasted chicken with herb gnocchi, both chock-full of fresh ingredients and surprising tastes. Staff is highly professional, and the wine list is extensive. If you're on a budget, come in for a glass of wine and dessert. *725 9th St., behind Main St. btw. 6th & 7th aves. www.thetrough.ca.* ☎ *403/678-2820. Reservations highly recommended. Entrees C$24–C$46. Tues–Sun 5:30–9pm. Map p 126.*

Charcuterie plate at Tekarra.

Alpine Club of Canada Clubhouse.

Accommodations
Alpine Club of Canada Clubhouse
CANMORE   The national headquarters for Canada's Alpine Club is just outside Canmore and houses a sweet hostel-style inn. It's a budget-friendly choice and a hub for meeting fellow hikers, skiers, and adventurers. It offers a kitchen, barbecue grills, a laundry, and a great view. *201 Indian Flats Rd. www.alpineclubofcanada.ca. ☎ 403/678-3200. 12 units. C$30–C$35 for club members, C$40 for nonmembers. Map p 126.*

★★ **Alpine Village** JASPER   On the banks of the rushing Athabasca River, these rustic yet stylish log cottages make a cozy, romantic base, good for simply enjoying the natural beauty of the park. They range from brand-new deluxe bedroom suites to quaint cabins dating back to 1941. Most have some form of a kitchenette. Cabins farthest from the road are quieter, but those along the river (next to the road) have the best views. *2.5km (1½ miles) south of Jasper townsite on Icefields Pkwy., Hwy. 93, at the junction with Hwy. 93A. ☎ 780/852-3285. www.alpinevillagejasper.com. 41 units, 28 with kitchenettes. Cabins C$190–C$510. Closed mid-Oct to Apr. Map p 126.*

Bear Hill Lodge JASPER   What appears at first to be a hodgepodge of different cabins is actually a well-laid-out village just outside the downtown area. There are options for just about every traveler and budget, from affordable lodge rooms to cozy small cabins to the luxurious white-pine log cabins known as the "homesteads." Many units have kitchens, and those that don't include a continental breakfast during summer months. *100 Bonhomme St. www.bearhilllodge. com. ☎ 780/852-3209. 27 units. Cabins from C$249. Map p 126.*

Blackstone Mountain Lodge
CANMORE   Settle into your own condo at this vacation rental property. The decor is urban chic, but the views are definitely all natural. Fully equipped units have one, two, or three bedrooms, private balconies, granite countertops, stainless steel appliances, and even a wine cabinet. A good base if you're coming for a week or more. *170 Kananaskis Way. www.blackstone lodge.ca. ☎ 888/830-8883 or 403/609-8098. 123 units. Doubles from C$280, 2-bedroom suites from C$489. Map p 126.*

★★★ **Fairmont Jasper Park Lodge** JASPER Built in 1923, this historic lodge epitomizes the pampered wilderness experience. It's like an upscale summer camp for adults spread over the largest commercial property in the Canadian Rockies (with a revered golf course, gorgeous lake, stables, and outdoor pool). The guest rooms are mostly in single-story cabins and cottages spread throughout the property. The luxurious spa is well worth a visit if you're looking to treat yourself. Ask about packages and promotions. *4km (2½ miles) east of Jasper on Hwy. 16, 3.2km (2 miles) southeast off Maligne Lake Rd. www. fairmont.com/jasper.* ☎ *800/441-1414 or 780/852-3301. 446 units. Doubles C$509–C$820. Map p 126.*

★ **Glacier View Lodge** ICE-FIELDS PARKWAY The closest thing to backcountry luxury that's accessible by car. Staying here is the best way to experience the Columbia Icefield—without the daytime crowds. Fully renovated in 2019, the rooms and spectacular lounge invite all to linger. All-inclusive packages with meals and private tours on the Athabasca Glacier and Glacier Skywalk are costly, but worth it. *Columbia Icefield, Hwy. 93, 185km (115 miles) from Banff &*

103km (64 miles) from Jasper. www. banffjaspercollection.com/hotels/ glacier-view-lodge.* ☎ *888/770-6914. 30 units. Doubles from C$489. Map p 126.*

Jasper Downtown Hostel

JASPER This is the best choice for budget travelers still looking to stay central in Jasper. Not to be confused with the new HI Jasper Hostel, this home-style hostel has fewer new amenities but also doesn't feel as sterile. Dorms rooms range from four- to eight-bed with either shared or en-suite bathrooms, and private rooms are available. The sizeable kitchen is bright and well-stocked. *400 Patricia St. www.jasper downtownhostel.ca.* ☎ *780/852-2000. 15 dorms or private rooms. Dorms from C$45, private rooms from C$150. Map p 126.*

Mt. Edith Cavell Hostel JASPER

This simple and remote shelter is a good base for backpackers and hikers. It sleeps 32 people in two cabins. It also has no electricity or flush toilets, but there's a self-catering kitchen and awe-inspiring scenery all around. Private doubles are available. Members of Hostelling International receive a discount. Open mid-June to mid-September

The urban decor at Blackstone Mountain Lodge.

The cozy Artist Loft at Paintbox Lodge.

only. *On Cavell Rd.; take Hwy. 93A south from the townsite to Cavell Rd., turn west & continue for 13km (8 miles) to the hostel, on the east side of the road. www.hihostels.ca.* ☎ *866/762-4122 or 403/670-7580. 32 beds. Shared dorm C$34. Map p 126.*

★★ **Paintbox Lodge** CANMORE   A winner for its cozy vibe, friendly service, and location (just steps from Main St.), this is Canmore's best boutique-style inn. The eight guest rooms are all different and all comfortable; upstairs ones have high ceilings with a cozy sitting area. The two-bedroom suite is good for families. *629 10th St. www. paintboxlodge.com.* ☎ *888/678-6100 or 403/609-0482. 5 units. Doubles C$199–C$399. Map p 126.*

★ **Park Place Inn** JASPER   This is the only place in town one could call a boutique inn, with reasonable rates to boot. The 14 spacious rooms have a Western heritage theme, with comfortable beds, hardwood floors, huge tubs (many are claw-foot style), and plenty of space. Located upstairs on bustling Patricia Street, it has a downtown feel (if that's possible in Jasper). *623 Patricia St. www.parkplaceinn. com.* ☎ *866/852-9770 or 780/852-9770. 14 units. Doubles C$140–C$289. Map p 126.*

★ kids **Pomeroy Kananaskis Mountain Lodge** KANANASKIS   Recently reopened under new management after a massive renovation, this resort-style lodge is an unexpected delight in Kananaskis. The rooms aren't the high point here, but the hotel excels at providing kid-friendly amenities (dining, indoor waterpark, and more) without compromising the adult experience. Families will love the

Spa treatment at the Fairmont Jasper Park Lodge.

Jasper Downtown Hostel.

Children's Creative Centre, where kids can play while their parents visit the Kananaskis Nordic Spa next door. *1 Centennial Dr. www. lodgeatkananaskis.com.* ☎ *403/591-7711. 247 rooms. Doubles from C$269. Map p 126.*

Wapiti Campground JASPER
This is the only campground in the park that's open year-round. Of the 362 sites, 322 are for tents only. Seventy-five of the sites remain accessible in winter. There are often elk roaming about here—remember to keep your distance. A full reconstruction of the larger Whistlers Campground is underway and it's expected to reopen in 2021. *4km (2½ miles) south of Jasper townsite on Icefields Pkwy., Hwy. 93, on the east side. Summer: 362 sites, 40 with electrical hookup. C$28 tents; C$32 RVs. Open Victoria Day long weekend (late May) and mid-June to early Sept. Winter: 93 sites, 40 with electrical hookup. C$18 tents; C$22 RVs. Early Oct to early May. Map p 126.*

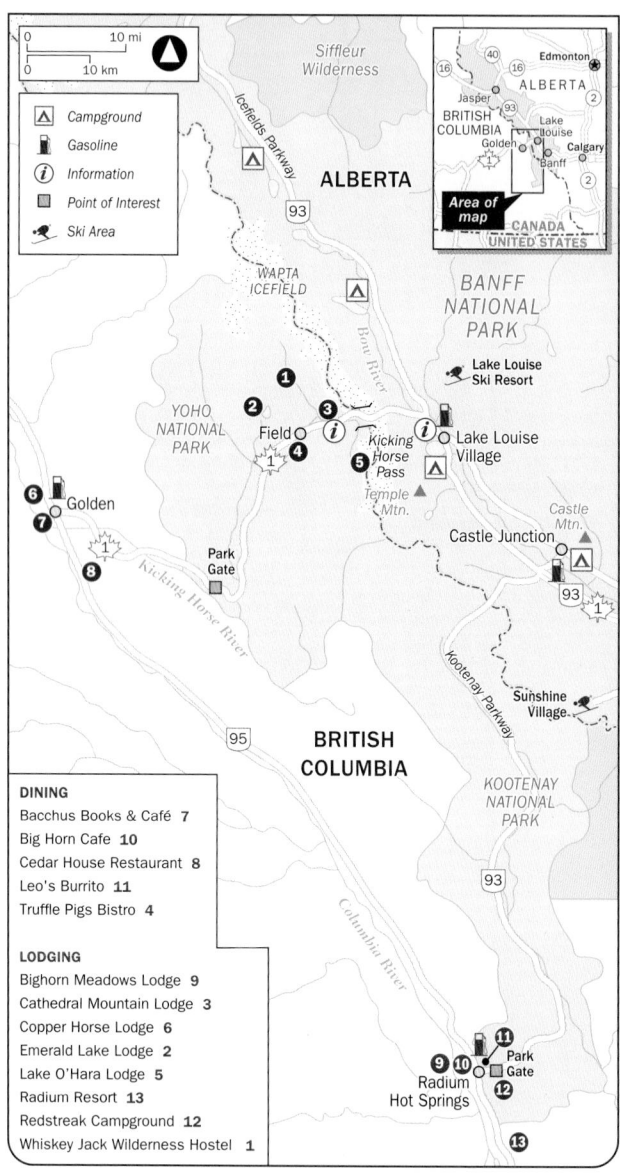

BC Rockies **Dining & Lodging**

DINING

Bacchus Books & Café **7**
Big Horn Cafe **10**
Cedar House Restaurant **8**
Leo's Burrito **11**
Truffle Pigs Bistro **4**

LODGING

Bighorn Meadows Lodge **9**
Cathedral Mountain Lodge **3**
Copper Horse Lodge **6**
Emerald Lake Lodge **2**
Lake O'Hara Lodge **5**
Radium Resort **13**
Redstreak Campground **12**
Whiskey Jack Wilderness Hostel **1**

Dining & Lodging A to Z

Restaurants
Bacchus Books & Café
GOLDEN *CAFE* A range of sandwiches (from seafood club to roasted veggie panini), daily homemade soups and specials, and loads of baked goods make this a cozy, friendly spot in the heart of Golden. *409 9th Ave N. www.bacchusbooks.ca.* ☎ *250/344-5600. Lunch C$7–C$12. Mon–Sat 9am–5:30pm; Sun 10am–4pm. Map p 134.*

Big Horn Cafe RADIUM *CAFE*
The options in Radium aren't great, but this cozy cafe has by far the best coffee and baked goods in the village. The quiche selection is excellent, and the sausage rolls make for good picnics. *7527 Main St., Ste. 6. www.bighorncafe.net.* ☎ *778/527-5005. Baked goods, breakfasts & sandwiches C$4–C$11. Daily 6am–4:30pm. Map p 134.*

★★ Cedar House Restaurant
GOLDEN *CANADIAN* Creating fresh and inspired food in a rural setting, the passionate chefs here work with local ingredients to prepare entrees like tamarind free-range chicken breast, slow-braised lamb shank, and a spectacular espresso and maple-syrup buffalo steak. Meats are all natural, and the fish is wild. The artfully crafted desserts taste as good as they look. *735 Hefti Rd. www.cedarhousechalets.com.* ☎ *250/344-4679. Entrees C$29–C$39. Reservations required. Wed–Sun 5–9pm. Map p 134.*

Leo Burrito RADIUM *MEXICAN*
Not much to look at from the outside, this little gem offers some of the best "fast" food in Radium. There are authentic burrito and taco options, and a few with a twist like the marinated tofu "Conrad Kain" burrito. *4951 Hwy 93. www.leoburrito.com.* ☎ *778/527-4999. Entrees C$10–C$16. Daily 11:30am–8pm. Map p 134.*

★★ Truffle Pigs Bistro FIELD
CAFE Field took center stage for foodies when this cafe became a bistro and moved across the street. The chef offers options like duck confit flatbread and a black-truffle pork loin. Handmade desserts and a good wine list make it the best dining stop between Lake Louise and Golden. *100 Centre St. www.*

The chefs at Truffle Pigs Bistro.

trufflepigs.com. ☎ 250/343-6303. Lunch C$9–C$26; dinner entrees C$18–C$40. Coffee & baked goods from 8am; lunch 11:30am–3:30pm; dinner 5–9pm; Map p 134.

Accommodations

Bighorn Meadows Resort

RADIUM   At last something besides a motel in Radium. These are vacation rentals at a condo development on the west side of town. They're modern, clean, and have great views. Units have private balconies with barbecues overlooking the golf course. Guest rooms are a bargain but don't have kitchens. *10 Bighorn Blvd., Radium Hot Springs, BC. www.bighornmeadows. com.* ☎ *877/344-2323 or 250/347-2323. 96 units. Apartments C$127–C$447. Map p 134.*

★★ Cathedral Mountain Lodge FIELD

If it's a cozy log cabin in a peaceful and powerful setting you're after, this is an excellent choice. The Cathedral Mountain lodge offers a beautiful blend of privacy and luxury tucked beneath its namesake mountain along the banks of the glacier-fed Kicking Horse River. Quintessential cabins are functional and cute (if somewhat close together), with fireplaces, modern bathtubs, and fluffy duvets. Afternoon tea and breakfast are included, and other perks include free canoe rentals at the sister property Moraine Lake Lodge. *Take Trans-Canada Hwy. 5km (3 miles) west from the Alberta–British Columbia border or 2km (1¼ miles) east of Field, BC, & turn northwest on Yoho Valley Rd.; continue 4km (2½ miles) to lodge. www.cathedralmountainlodge.com.* ☎ *866/619-6442 or 250/343-6442. 31 units. Cabins C$498–C$940. Map p 134.*

★ Copper Horse Lodge

GOLDEN   At the base of Kicking Horse Mountain Resort, this boutique-size inn has a stylish mountain vibe, lovely service, and a supremely relaxing feel. Built only a few years ago, it's a good choice if your aim is to rip it up on skis or mountain bikes at the resort or find some quiet romance. Otherwise, it's out of the way. *At end of Kicking Horse Mountain Rd.; turn right after the gondola. www.copperhorse lodge.com.* ☎ *877/544-7644 or 250/344-7272. 10 units. Doubles C$155–C$300. Map p 134.*

Bighorn Meadows Resort is located on the ninth fairway of the Springs Golf Course.

Guest cabin at Cathedral Mountain Lodge.

A room inside the Copper Horse Lodge.

★★ Emerald Lake Lodge

FIELD This luxurious but cozy lodge, made up of 24 buildings on a 5-hectare (12-acre) peninsula in the heart of Yoho National Park, is splendid. Each guest room has a fieldstone fireplace and warm, rustic decor, including dark green marble vanities in many bathrooms (although others remain in need of a facelift). Most rooms have a balcony. The real star, however, is Emerald Lake itself, a glow of turquoise that never escapes the corner of your eye. *1 Emerald Lake Rd., Field, BC. Take Trans-Canada Hwy. 2km (1¼ miles) south of Field to Emerald Lake Rd. turnoff; continue 8km (5 miles). www.crmr.com.* ☎ *800/663-6336 or 250/343-6321. 85 units. Doubles C$439–C$529. Map p 134.*

★★★ Lake O'Hara Lodge

YOHO NATIONAL PARK In a secluded alpine valley, where there are no phones, no television, no roads, and no cars (see the box "Lake O'Hara: Getting to Paradise," p 108), this is a paradise that is one of a kind. Cabins have comfortable beds and modern bathrooms; meals are included. It's a wonderful getaway for city slickers and a true mecca for mountain lovers of all ages. Reserve well in advance. *Access via the Parks Canada bus that leaves the Lake O'Hara parking lot. www.lakeohara.com. June–Sept:* ☎ *250/343-6418. Oct–May:* ☎ *403/678-4110. 16 units (8 lodge rooms, 8 cabins). Doubles C$730–C$1,035. Rates include all meals, tips, taxes & bus transportation. Credit cards accepted for reservation deposits only. Map p 134.*

Redstreak Campground

RADIUM HOT SPRINGS There's lots to do at Parks Canada's largest campground in Kootenay National Park, including nightly entertainment in the summer and a network

The Canadian Rockies

A room inside the Emerald Lake Lodge.

of trails heading into the park. It's located behind the Visitor Centre. *2.5km (1½ miles) southwest of Radium Hot Springs, turn east off Hwy. 93 at the sign. Reserve camp-site online at www.pccamping.ca or call ☎ 877/737-3783. ☎ 250/347-9505. 242 sites, 38 with electrical hookup only, 50 with full hookup.*

Guest room at the Truffle Pigs Lodge.

C$27–C$38. *Early May to mid-Oct. Map p 134.*

★ Truffle Pigs Lodge FIELD

This cozy and simple lodge located in the heart of the sweet little vil-lage of Field is a good choice. Rooms are quite basic, but the friendly vibes, great views, and good restaurant more than make up for that. There's a family suite for up to six. *100 Centre St., Field. www.trufflepigs.com. ☎ 250/343-6303. 13 units. C$212–C$300. Map p 134.*

Whiskey Jack Wilderness Hostel YOHO NATIONAL PARK

Hikers and adventurous sightseers will enjoy this rustic hostel way up the Yoho Valley Road. You'll share a 9-bed dorm room with others, but the hostel has indoor toilets and showers, kitchen facilities, and a great patio space. Walls are thin, though you're unlikely to mind as the main sound comes from the thundering Takakkaw Falls. *At the end of the Yoho Valley Rd. www. hihostels.ca. ☎ 866/762-4122 or 778/328-2220. 27 beds. Shared dorm C$33. Map p 134.* ●

The Best Hiking in Banff

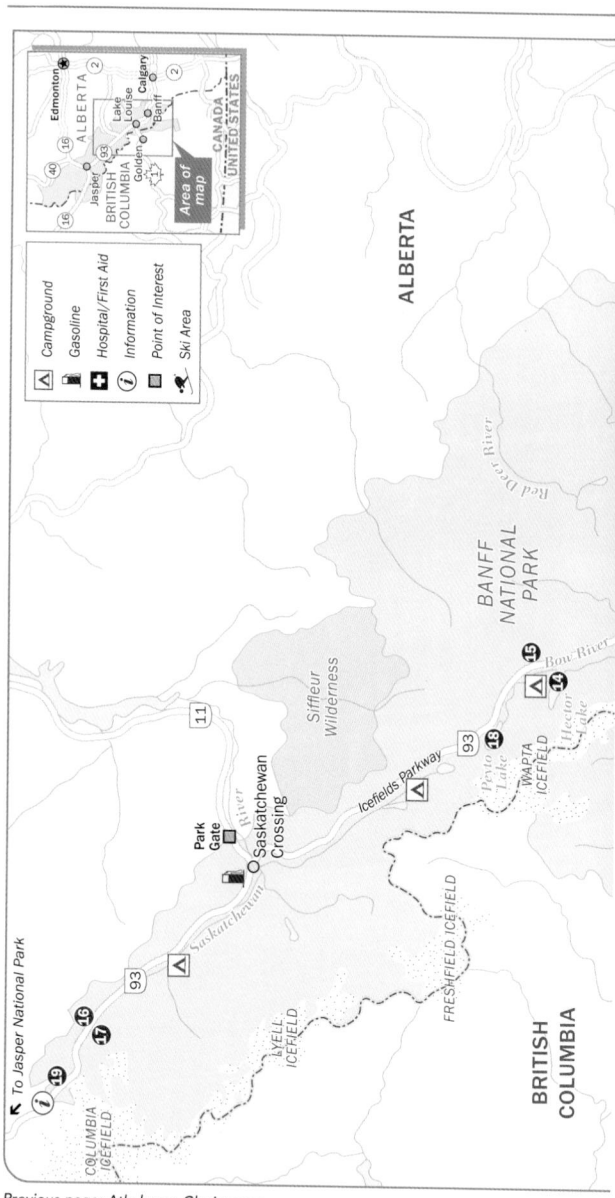

Previous page: Athabasca Glacier cave.

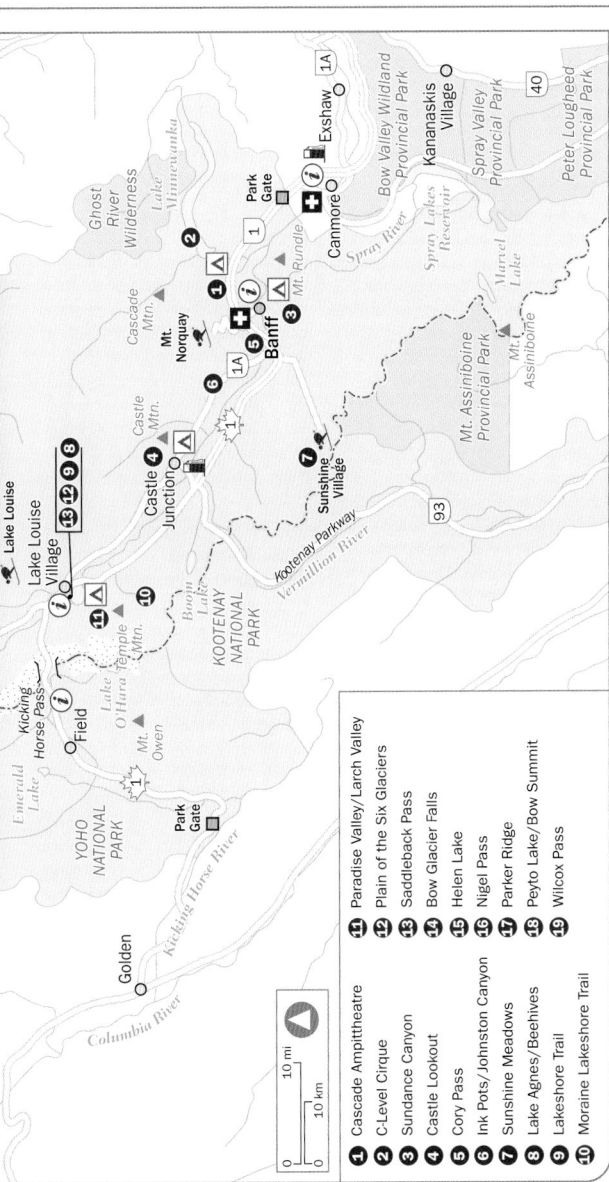

1. Cascade Ampitheatre
2. C-Level Cirque
3. Sundance Canyon
4. Castle Lookout
5. Cory Pass
6. Ink Pots/Johnston Canyon
7. Sunshine Meadows
8. Lake Agnes/Beehives
9. Lakeshore Trail
10. Moraine Lakeshore Trail
11. Paradise Valley/Larch Valley
12. Plain of the Six Glaciers
13. Saddleback Pass
14. Bow Glacier Falls
15. Helen Lake
16. Nigel Pass
17. Parker Ridge
18. Peyto Lake/Bow Summit
19. Wilcox Pass

The hiking season in Banff usually gets started in mid-June and winds down in October. Trails on the southern slopes and at lower elevations are free of snow earlier in the season and open earlier. In spring, trails are often extremely wet and muddy. In autumn, many days are sunny and warm, but the variability of the weather poses a new challenge, since snow may begin to accumulate over high passes.

Town of Banff Hikes

❶ ★ Cascade Amphitheater.

You can't miss Cascade Mountain, the beautiful pyramid-shaped peak at the northeastern end of Banff Avenue. One of the most rewarding day hikes in the townsite area, this is a demanding outing that starts (and later finishes) at the Mt. Norquay day lodge and takes you into a high alpine cirque in a hanging valley with a lush carpet of subalpine wildflowers. The trail crests at a dramatic point on the south edge of the meadows, on a small knoll of rockslide debris. *7.7km (4.8 miles) each way. Strenuous. Elevation gain is 640m (2,100 ft.). 6 hr. round-trip. Trail head is Mt. Norquay ski area. Map p 140.*

❷ ★ C-Level Cirque. This trail

has wonderful panoramic views and is a great afternoon getaway from busy Banff Avenue. After alighting on a stunning view of Lake Minnewanka, the trail heads back into the now-subalpine forest before ending in a small cirque (like a bowl with a circular ridge surrounding it) at the highest part of the valley. Look for calypso orchids, marmots, and pika as you climb to the treeless alpine zone. *3.9km (2.4 miles) each way. Moderate. Elevation gain 455m (1,493 ft.). 3 hr. round-trip. Trail head is Upper Bankhead picnic area parking lot, 3.5km (2.3 miles) on Minnewanka Rd. from the Minnewanka interchange on Trans-Canada Hwy. Map p 140.*

❸ kids Sundance Canyon. A

gentle hike that leaves from the Cave and Basin Historic Site is good in spring and fall. There are nice views of the Sawback Range and the pinnacle of Mt. Edith. The hike goes up a paved trail, turning at Sundance Creek and continuing to an extraordinary canyon with giant boulders. Head over the bridge and up the stairs for the best views. *4.3km (2.7 miles) each way. Easy. Elevation gain 143m (469 ft.). 3 hr. round-trip. Trail head at Cave & Basin Historic Site. Map p 140.*

Bow Valley Parkway & Sunshine Meadows

❹ Castle Lookout. This hike

gets you close to a former fire lookout on this scenic mountain. Short but steep, the trail offers an amazing panorama of the glacier-chiseled Bow Valley and Storm Mountain, which is often surrounded by its own gnarly weather system. This trail can be very warm on a sunny day and is a great shoulder-season choice. *3.7km (2.3 miles) each way. Strenuous. Elevation gain 520m (1,706 ft.). 3–4 hr. round-trip. Trail head is parking lot on the north side of the Bow Valley Pkwy. 1A, 5km (3 miles) west of Castle Junction. Map p 140.*

❺ ★ Cory Pass. This is one of

the most challenging hikes in Banff, but it's also by far the most spectacular one near the Town of Banff. The highlight is the 2,300m (7,546-ft.) monolithic limestone cliffs of the Sawback Range. The trail starts in a high, subalpine valley bottom and

Easy to Hard: Difficulty Ratings

Hiking times depend on a hiker's experience and fitness as well as the weather conditions. Hikers of an average fitness level can usually hike 2.5 to 3.5km (1.6–2.2 miles) in an hour. Steeper trails take longer, and you'll want to add in time for snack and rest breaks.

Easy: Hikes that are generally smooth and gentle, usually less than 6km (3.7 miles) long with an elevation gain of no more than 300m (984 ft.).

Moderate: Hikes up to 13km (8 miles) long on well-established trails with some exposure. Elevation gain can be up to 600m (1,969 ft.).

Difficult: Hikes longer than 13km (8 miles), with an elevation gain of more than 600m (1,969 ft.). Often on poorly defined trails, with obstacles and exposed terrain.

Lengths listed here are total distance from the start to the finish of the hikes. Elevation gain is the total ascent from the lowest point on the trail to the highest point.

ends in a high alpine zone well above the tree line—tremendous ecological diversity. Take a good map with you (see sidebar on p 144). *5.8km (3.6 miles) each way. Very strenuous. Elevation gain is 915m (3,002 ft.). 6–7 hr. round-trip. Trail head is Fireside Picnic Area at the eastern end of Bow Valley Pkwy. 1A. Map p 140.*

A hiker at Cory Pass.

6 Ink Pots/Johnston Canyon. Continue past the crowds at Johnston Canyon past the Upper Falls, twice the size of the lower ones. The trail opens into a lovely, wide valley and takes you to jade-colored natural springs. It's a magical place and very quiet after the rush of the canyon. *5.5km (3.4 miles) each way. Moderate. Elevation gain 243m (797 ft.). 4–5 hr. round-trip. Trail head is Johnston Canyon parking lot, 18km (11 miles) west of Banff on Bow Valley Pkwy. 1A. Map p 140.*

7 ★★ kids Sunshine Meadows. Located high in an alpine bowl that is also the site of the Sunshine Village ski resort, this alpine meadow is famous for its annual display of beautiful wildflowers, and is incredibly easy to get to—just take a shuttle to the Sunshine Village day lodge, where all trail heads are located. **Sunshine Village** (www.skibanff.com; ☎ 403/705-4000) runs a shuttle to the area.

Hiking To-Do List

1. **Select a trail.** Read through the hikes listed here, pick up a map and other hiking guides, and chat with the staff at the **Banff Visitor Centre** (224 Banff Ave.; www.pc.gc.ca/banff; ☎ **403/763-1550**) or the **Lake Louise Visitor Centre** (Samson Mall, 101 Lake Louise Dr.; ☎ **403/522-3833**) to find the right trail for you.

2. **Get a map.** The best are topographic maps, with a scale of 1:50,000. The Canadian government produces maps with lots of detail, but they are short on hiking trails. GemTrek Maps (www.gemtrek.com) produces the best hiking maps in the Canadian Rockies. Pick one up in Banff or order online. They're waterproof, tear-resistant, and have topographic contours, key for measuring elevation changes.

3. **Check the weather.** Get the up-to-date forecast by calling **Banff National Park** (☎ **403/762-1550**) or **Environment Canada** in Banff at ☎ **403/762-2088.**

4. **Check trail conditions.** Call or check online for the latest trail reports from the Park (www.pc.gc.ca/banff; ☎ **403/762-1550**), also posted around town. And be sure to find out about any bear warnings and area closures due to bear activity.

5. **Consider parking.** If you're heading to a popular spot like Lake Louise or Moraine Lake, consider taking the shuttle from the Town of Banff. You'll avoid headaches and wasted time. Visit the Banff Visitor Centre for more info or go to **www.roamtransit.ca**.

6. **Bring plenty of water.** Take at least 1 liter (2 pints) of water per person, more if you're going on a strenuous full-day hike.

7. **Go in a group.** Some areas of Banff are under bear warnings, and hikers must stay in groups of four or six at a time. It's safer, and often more fun!

8. **Tell someone about it.** Let someone know where you're going and when you'll be back.

The Rock Isle Lake trail leads you to the other side of the Continental Divide, into British Columbia's Mt. Assiniboine Provincial Park. Rock Lake is particularly lovely in the calm early morning, when it mirrors the surrounding scenery. It's a favorite of artists and photographers.

The Simpson Pass/Healy Meadows trail is worth an afternoon outing for views of Wawa Ridge, Mt. Assiniboine, and the Monarch, a pyramid-shaped peak. It's a wildflower lover's dream, and a favorite of old outfitters and pioneers, including Jim Brewster and "Wild Bill" Peyto, two of Banff's original mountain guides. *Rock Isle Lake Trail: 2.5km (1.6 miles) each way. Easy. Elevation gain is 105m (344 ft.). 2 hr. round-trip. Simpson Pass/Healy Meadows: 7.6km (4.7 miles) each way. Moderate. Elevation gain is 160m (525 ft.). 5 hr. round-trip. Map p 140.*

The Lake Agnes Teahouse.

Lake Louise Hikes

⑧ ★★ Lake Agnes/Beehives.

In a picturesque hanging valley above Lake Louise, Lake Agnes has been a favorite for more than a century. There are great views of the Bow Valley. The Lake Agnes Teahouse, on the shore of the lake, which serves freshly baked scones and tea in summer. From the teahouse, take the trail to the north shore of the lake to connect with the Big Beehive. *5.1km (3.2 miles) each way. Moderate. Elevation gain is 400m (1,312 ft.). 4 hr. round-trip. Trail head is Lake Louise shoreline trail, in front of Fairmont Chateau Lake Louise. Map p 140.*

⑨ kids Lakeshore Trail.

This broad, flat trail may be among the most well-trodden paths in Banff National Park. It leads you around the north shore of the lake to the base of Mt. Victoria and the shimmering Victoria Glacier. Benches along the trail let you sit and marvel at Lake Louise's color and beauty. Come early to beat the crowds. *1.9km (1.2 miles) each way. Easy. No elevation gain. 1 hr. round-trip. Trail head is in front of Fairmont Chateau Lake Louise. Map p 140.*

⑩ Moraine Lakeshore Trail.

Moraine Lake is a popular destination! This trail, along the western shore of the lake, is a pleasant way to enjoy the imposing Valley of the Ten Peaks and stretch your legs. The best views are at the start of the trail, but for a spectacular view of Moraine Lake at the end of the hike, head 5 minutes up to the Moraine Lake Viewpoint, at the south end of the parking lot, following the sign to Consolation Lakes. *1.2km (0.7 mile) each way. Easy. No elevation gain. 1 hr. round-trip. Trail head is Moraine Lake parking lot. Map p 140.*

⑪ ★★★ Paradise Valley/ Larch Valley.

A rewarding and challenging full-day hike. You'll hike past Lake Annette, Horseshoe Meadows, and the "Giant's Staircase" waterfall, then over Sentinel Pass and down through Larch Valley to Moraine Lake—all superb highlights. The trail ends at a different parking lot from where it begins, so you'll need to organize a shuttle. Parks Canada often requires hikers to stay in groups of six or more due to bear activity in the area. *17km (11 miles) each way. Strenuous. Elevation gain is 880m (2,887 ft.). 6–7 hr. Trail head is 2.5km (1.5 miles) south on Moraine Lake Rd. from Lake Louise Rd., in the Paradise Valley lot, on the right side of the road. Map p 140.*

Hiking Moraine Lake.

⓬ ★★★ Plain of the Six Glaciers. If you have time for only one half-day hike in Lake Louise, take this route through postcard-worthy scenery as it makes its way around Lake Louise and below mounts Victoria and Lefroy. It empties into a harsh glacier- and avalanche-scoured terrain before climbing into a lush meadow, where you can stop at the historic Plain of the Six Glaciers Teahouse for a warm drink and snack. *5.3km (3.3 miles) each way. Moderate. Elevation gain 365m (1,198 ft.). 4–5 hr. round-trip. Trail head is Lake Louise Shoreline trail in front of Fairmont Chateau Lake Louise hotel. Map p 140.*

⓭ Saddleback Pass. The trail takes you to a stupendous view of the colossal Mt. Temple from a pass between Saddle and Fairview mountains and switchbacks up to a flower-filled meadow. It's steep, so bring poles to ease the trip down. Continue a bit farther to Fairview's summit for a mile-high view of Lake Louise. *3.7km (2.3 miles) one-way to pass. Moderate to strenuous. Elevation gain is 595m (1,952 ft.). 4 hr. round-trip. Trail head is on the south shore of Lake Louise to the right of the old guide's cabin. Map p 140.*

Icefields Parkway Hikes

⓮ kids Bow Glacier Falls. When the Bow Glacier retreated, it left behind a majestic 120m (394-ft.) waterfall that simply hints at the massive icefield above it. The trail is broad and scenic alongside the flats skirting Bow Lake, a Rocky

The rushing Paradise Creek in Paradise Valley.

Traveling Safely in Bear Country

Banff National Park is home to both black and grizzly bears. You could see a bear from your car, from your hotel, or even while out exploring the mountains on foot. Be prepared! Avoid having an encounter with a bear while hiking by making your presence well known so as not to surprise the bear—sing, talk, clap your hands, call "Hey Bear!" every few minutes while you hike, especially in densely forested areas or when crossing avalanche paths. Carry bear spray and know how to use it. And keep your eyes and ears open at all times.

If you see a bear, try not to panic. Speak loudly and firmly to the bear and try to appear large by waving your arms. Back away slowly: Do not run! For more information, visit **www.pc.gc.ca/banff-bears**.

Wild Eastern Slopes grizzly bear taking a rest in Banff.

Mountain gem. At the western shore of the lake, there are views of the stunning Crowfoot and Bow glaciers. *4.7km (2.9 miles) each way. Easy. Elevation gain 95m (312 ft.). 3 hr. round-trip. Trail head is beside Num-Ti-Jah Lodge 36km (22 miles) north of the Lake Louise junction on Icefields Pkwy. 93. Map p 140.*

⓯ ★ **Helen Lake.** With tall peaks, alpine meadows, lakes, and wide views, this trail is diverse enough to draw you enthusiastically around every corner. This is a relatively quick and pain-free way to access the high alpine environment. The lakeside meadows draw friendly hoary marmots. *6km (3.7 miles) each way. Moderate. Elevation gain 455m (1,493 ft.). 4 hr. round-trip. Trail head is across the highway from the Crowfoot Glacier Viewpoint,*

Saddleback Pass in Lake Louise.

Backpacking Banff

It's a challenging undertaking—most people just starting to backpack will find the routes in Banff National Park demanding, thanks to the mountainous terrain. And you must be well-organized with what you bring on the trip. But a night under the stars in the Banff backcountry promises the ultimate Rocky Mountain high. The peak hiking season is from early July to mid-September; be sure to reserve your campsites in advance. Of the dozens of possible trips, the three listed here under "Backpacking Hikes" are my favorites.

33km (21 miles) north of the Lake Louise junction on Icefields Pkwy. 93. Map p 140.

⑯ ★ **Nigel Pass.** This hike tops out on a rocky 2,195m (7,201-ft.) ridge marking the boundary between Banff and Jasper national parks, rewarding you with great views of the Columbia Icefield. East of the pass, you can scramble over rocks to catch sight of the waterfall along the rocky north wall of Nigel Pass. *7.2km (4.5 miles) each way. Moderate. Elevation gain 365m (1,198 ft.). 5 hr. round-trip. Trail head is 2.5km (1.5 miles) north of the "Big Bend" switchback (114km/71 miles north of the Lake Louise junction) or 8.5km (5¼ miles) south of the Banff–Jasper boundary on Icefields Pkwy.*

Parker Ridge is a direct route to stunning views.

Admiring the scenery at Peyto Lake.

93. Parking lot is on northeast side of the highway. Map p 140.

⑰ ★★★ **Parker Ridge.** The best short day hike in the Icefields Parkway area, this open trail takes you high up and straight into the heart of the unforgiving alpine zone. In summer—which can last only a few weeks up here—the meadows turn a brilliant red with heather. Once you reach the summit, enjoy views of the Saskatchewan Glacier below you. *2.7km (1.7 miles) each way. Moderate. Elevation gain 250m (820 ft.). 3 hr. round-trip. Trail head is in the parking lot on the west side of Icefields Pkwy. 93, 4km (2.5 miles) south of the Banff–Jasper park boundary. Map p 140.*

⓲ Peyto Lake/Bow Summit.
This is the most popular short hike along the Icefields Parkway. Escape the crowds by continuing to the Bow Summit lookout; then hike down to the lake for an almost bird's-eye view of the Bow River's source. This trail takes you through the transition zone; what begins as a thick forest soon becomes a stunted one, getting sparser and sparser until you come to an area where there isn't a single tree growing. *Easy. Elevation gain 230m (755 ft.). 2 hr. round-trip. Trail head is the Bow Summit parking lot 41km (25 miles) north of the Lake Louise junction on Icefields Pkwy. 93. Map p 140.*

⓳ ★★★ Wilcox Pass. Starting just across the border in Jasper National Park, this trail gives you an almost bird's-eye view of the Columbia Icefield from the edge of a gorgeous alpine valley. It's an incredibly rewarding—albeit popular—trail since it's mostly above the tree line, offering nearly nonstop views and wildflowers in August. *12km (7.4 miles) return. Moderate. Elevation gain 335m (1,099 ft.). 5 hr. round-trip. Trail head is 2.5km (1.6 miles) south of the Icefields Centre on Icefields Pkwy. 93 at the Wilcox Pass campground. Map p 140.*

Backpacking Hikes
★★ Egypt Lake/Shadow Lake.
This is the most popular

backpacking area in Banff National Park, a multi-day exploration of Banff's highest-elevation hiking routes. With a series of passes along the Continental Divide encompassing cliffs, meadows, and lake-dotted alpine cirques, this trail takes you through some quintessential Canadian Rockies landscape. *40km (25 miles) return. Moderate. Elevation gain 790m (2,592 ft.). 2–3 days. Trail head is the Sunshine Village ski area.*

kids Glacier Lake. This overnight trip isn't too strenuous and gets you into the Icefields Parkway backcountry. It's a nice outing for families, since the hike is quite flat, and the elevation is relatively low. *8.9km (5.5 miles) each way. Easy. Elevation gain 210m (689 ft.). 2 days. Trail head is on the west side of Icefields Pkwy. 93, 1.2km (.8 mile) north of the junction with Hwy. 11, near Saskatchewan Crossing.*

★★★ Sunshine Meadows/Mt. Assiniboine. Showcasing the spectacularly colorful Sunshine Meadows and Mt. Assiniboine region, this route covers high alpine terrain, crosses dramatic passes, and runs alongside picturesque lakes. Head over Citadel Pass to admire Mt. Assiniboine (the highest mountain in Banff National Park. *62km (39 miles) return. Moderate to strenuous. Elevation gain 655m (2,149 ft.). 3–6 days. Trail head is the Sunshine Village ski area. Map p 140.*

A hiker pauses at Wilcox Pass, looking at the Columbia Icefield.

The Great Outdoors

Summer Sports

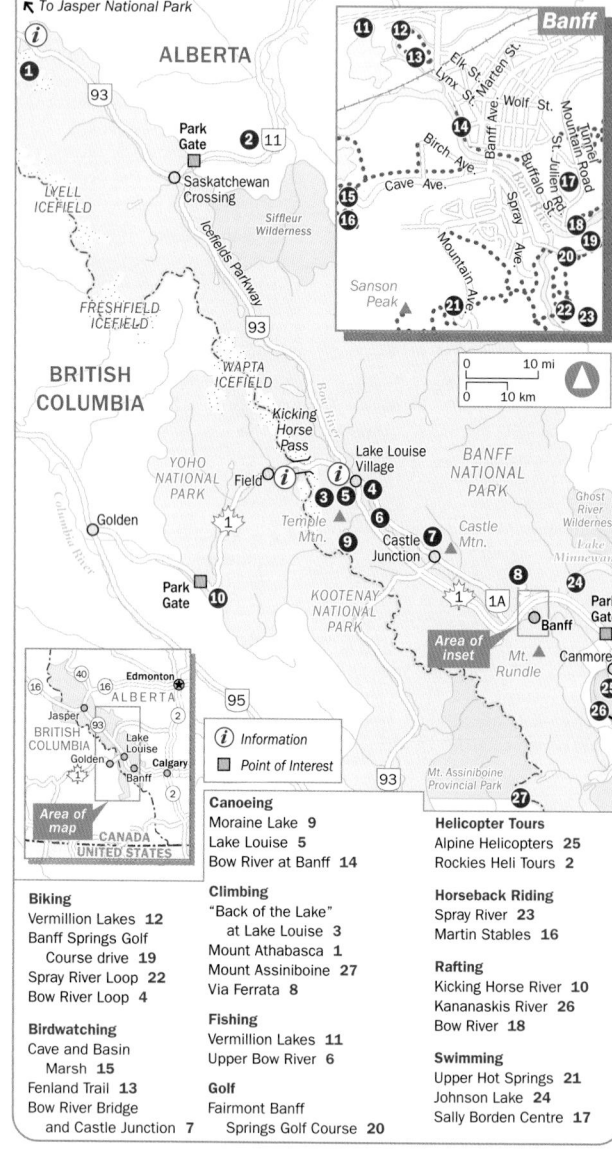

↖ To Jasper National Park

Banff

ALBERTA

Park Gate

Saskatchewan Crossing

LYELL ICEFIELD

Siffleur Wilderness

FRESHFIELD ICEFIELD

BRITISH COLUMBIA

WAPTA ICEFIELD

Kicking Horse Pass

YOHO NATIONAL PARK

Field

Lake Louise Village

BANFF NATIONAL PARK

Ghost River Wilderness

Golden

Temple Mtn.

Castle Junction

Castle Mtn.

Lake Minnewanka

Park Gate

KOOTENAY NATIONAL PARK

Banff

Area of inset

Mt. Rundle

Canmore

Park Gate

Elk St., Martin St., Lynx St., Wolf St., Banff Ave., Birch Ave., Cave Ave., Mountain Ave., Buffalo St., Spray Ave., St. Julien Rd., Tunnel Mountain Road, Sanson Peak

0 — 10 mi
0 — 10 km

Area of map

Edmonton, ALBERTA, Jasper, BRITISH COLUMBIA, Lake Louise, Golden, Banff, Calgary, CANADA, UNITED STATES

Mt. Assiniboine Provincial Park

(i) Information
◻ Point of Interest

Biking
Vermillion Lakes **12**
Banff Springs Golf Course drive **19**
Spray River Loop **22**
Bow River Loop **4**

Birdwatching
Cave and Basin Marsh **15**
Fenland Trail **13**
Bow River Bridge and Castle Junction **7**

Canoeing
Moraine Lake **9**
Lake Louise **5**
Bow River at Banff **14**

Climbing
"Back of the Lake" at Lake Louise **3**
Mount Athabasca **1**
Mount Assiniboine **27**
Via Ferrata **8**

Fishing
Vermillion Lakes **11**
Upper Bow River **6**

Golf
Fairmont Banff Springs Golf Course **20**

Helicopter Tours
Alpine Helicopters **25**
Rockies Heli Tours **2**

Horseback Riding
Spray River **23**
Martin Stables **16**

Rafting
Kicking Horse River **10**
Kananaskis River **26**
Bow River **18**

Swimming
Upper Hot Springs **21**
Johnson Lake **24**
Sally Borden Centre **17**

Banff offers a wide range of summertime activities, from hiking to biking to getting out on the sparkling lakes. This isn't a place for loungers. Give yourself a chance to sample a few of the adventures listed below. Get out and try something new!

Biking

With more than 190km (118 miles) of mountain-bike trails and numerous options for road biking, Banff is a friendly place for two wheels. Bike season runs from May to October. Note that not all hiking trails are open to bikers.

You can rent both road and mountain bikes in Banff National Park at **Soul Ski and Bike** (203 Bear St.; ☎ **403/760-1650**) and **Banff Adventures** (211 Bear St.; ☎ **403/762-4554**), which also has kids' bikes, trailers, and strollers. In Lake Louise, rent bikes at **Wilson Mountain Sports** (p 88).

Good routes around the Banff townsite area include the Banff Springs Golf Course drive and the Vermillion Lakes via the paved Fenland Trail. When you head out from the townsite, take the Bow Valley Parkway (Hwy. 93A). There's much less traffic than on the Trans-Canada Highway (Hwy. 1). If you're up at Lake Louise, try the old Great Divide Road, which leads into Yoho National Park—a quiet ride through mountain scenery.

Mountain biking is permitted on only a select number of the trails in Banff National Park. In fact, you are subject to fines if you are caught biking on hiking-only trails. In the Banff townsite area, the best ride for beginners and families is the 13km (7.8-mile) Spray River Loop. Near Lake Louise, families with kids will enjoy the relatively flat but very scenic 7.1km (4.4-mile) Bow River Loop, which leaves from the Lake Louise Campground. There are interpretive signs along the trail.

More advanced bikers will find thrills on the steep and narrow Stoney Squaw Loop or along the winding Toe Trail, near the Hoodoos.

Bird-Watching

Birding is a great activity for visitors of all ages. More than 260 species pass through the Canadian Rockies annually. Pick up a brochure from the **Banff Visitor Centre** in Banff townsite (224 Banff Ave.; ☎ **403/762-1550**). Great spots close to the Town of Banff include Cave and Basin March and Fenland Trail. Look for an osprey nest on

A mountain biker rides along the Spray River Loop.

The Great Outdoors

the Bow River Bridge and Castle Junction.

Canoeing

To canoe is to be Canadian, it's said. There are boathouses where you can rent canoes at both Moraine Lake and Lake Louise. The boathouse at the **Moraine Lake Lodge** (14km/8¾ miles south of Lake Louise on Moraine Lake Rd.; ☎ **403/522-3733**) rents canoes for C$120 per hour. The **Fairmont Chateau Lake Louise** (111 Lake Louise Dr.; ☎ **403/522-3511**) rents canoes for C$125 per hour. In the Town of Banff, rent a canoe at the **Banff Canoe Club** (end of Wolf St.; www.banffcanoeclub.com; ☎ **403/762-5005**) for C$45 per hour, where you can paddle straight into the placid Vermillion Lakes.

Be prepared if you're planning on canoeing the Bow River; experience is recommended, particularly in the section between Castle Junction and Banff, where there's a Class III rapid. The paddle from Banff to Canmore is intermediate-level and requires route-finding skills.

Climbing & Mountaineering

Visitors to Banff who've taken the time and energy to learn the ropes

Climbers take on the "Back of the Lake" route at Lake Louise.

Two hikers snowshoeing to a helicopter in the Canadian Rockies.

enjoy this highly technical sport. There are no specific regulations governing climbing or mountaineering in Banff National Park; however, Parks Canada does suggest you contact the **Banff Warden's office** (in Banff ☎ **403/762-1470**; in Lake Louise ☎ **403/522-1220**) for more information before you head out.

Banff has a number of excellent rock-climbing locations, including the "Back of the Lake," at Lake Louise. Classic mountain climbs include mounts Athabasca and Assiniboine—both are for experienced climbers only.

For advice on planning a climbing trip, contact the **Alpine Club of Canada** (www.alpineclubofcanada. ca; ☎ **403/678-3200**) or the **Association of Canadian Mountain Guides** (www.acmg.ca; ☎ **403/678-2885**). For private lessons and guiding, contact Canada's premier mountaineering school, **Yamnuska Inc.** (www.yamnuska. com; ☎ **403/678-4164**).

Via Ferrata

High on the ridges above Mt. Norquay is a unique opportunity to scale big mountains and get up really high. Via Ferrata is a series of ladders, cables, and a suspension

Share the Trail

Bike trails in Banff National Park are also hiking and horseback-riding trails. Expect to encounter people using the trail in other ways. Ride in control and always be prepared to stop. Slow down when you come upon a hiker. A friendly greeting will make them aware of your presence. Bikes can spook horses: When passing a horse, let the rider know you are coming. If a horse approaches you, move to the side of the trail, stop your bike, and let the horse pass. If you have a chance to stop and chat a little, ask the rider about the trail conditions ahead.

bridge that takes you (along with a certified guide) up to the beautiful Cliffhouse Bistro. The climb isn't as hard as it sounds, and it's great fun. No experience needed. *At Mt. Norquay, 2 Mt. Norquay Rd., Banff. www.banffnorquay.com.* ☎ *844/667-7829. From C$169/person. Departures throughout the day from 9am–3pm.*

Fishing
You need a permit to fish in Banff National Park. Pick one up at the **Banff Visitor Centre** in Banff town-site (224 Banff Ave.; ☎ **403/762-1550**). National Park fishing permits cost C$10 daily. An annual permit costs C$34. While the area has lots of lakes, few have any fish left in them. But the Bow River is one of the world's finest fly-fishing rivers

and the only area in Banff National Park open year-round.

Banff Fishing Unlimited (www.banff-fishing.com; ☎ **403/762-4936**) specializes in year-round fly-fishing, spin casting, and trophy lake-trout fishing. Their guides know all the secrets. **Alpine Anglers** (www.alpineanglers.com; ☎ 403/762-8223) offers top-notch instruction in the mild sensibilities of fly-fishing on the pristine, turquoise waters of the Bow River.

Golfing
The Fairmont Banff Springs hotel's 27-hole **Stanley Thompson Course** is world-famous (405 Spray Ave.; ☎ **403/762-6801**). The course has three tee-offs and an amazingly scenic location along the Spray and

The Fairmont Banff Springs Golf Course.

Saddle Up & Head High

If you're not sure about long days of hiking and carrying your own packs but you still want to explore the backcountry of Banff, consider an overnight horseback trip. From early May to late October, trail rides range from 1 night to 1 week. Some outfitters combine guided trail rides with stays at rustic but comfortable backcountry lodges, while others include overnights in wilderness tents situated in truly spectacular settings. This is one of the best ways to see the back corners of Banff—with considerably less effort than backpacking. For 2- to 5-day trips, ranging from C$679 to C$2,100, try **Banff Trail Riders** (132 Banff Ave.; www.horseback. com; ☎ **403/762-4551** or 800/661-8352). Starting at the Lake Louise Corral, **Timberline Tours** (www.timberlinetours.ca; ☎ **403/522-3743**) has overnight trips starting at C$650 per person.

Riding horses near Banff.

Bow rivers, beneath Mt. Rundle. It's expensive but legendary, and open to the public (meaning you don't have to be a guest at the hotel to play a round). Course fees range from C$199 in May and October to C$249 June through September, including cart. There's also a 9-hole course that lets you sample the experience with less commitment, starting at C$84. Watch for geese and elk!

Helicopter Tours

To get the ultimate bird's-eye view of the jaw-droppingly beautiful Rockies, you have to step just outside the boundary of Banff National Park. Near the Icefields Centre, **Rockies Heli Tours** (www.rockies heli.com; ☎ **888/844-3514** or 403/721-2100) has flights starting at C$278 per person. **Alpine Helicopters** (www.alpinehelicopters.com; ☎ **403/678-4802**) takes off just east of Banff in Canmore and flies to Mt. Assiniboine and back in 30 unforgettable minutes (C$330 per person). They also offer heli-hiking day tours starting at C$575.

Horseback Riding

Riding a horse in the Canadian Rockies is as logical as riding a camel in the Sahara Desert. Saddling up not only lets you explore the cowboy heritage of the Rockies but also takes you into parts of the Banff backcountry you may not otherwise have seen. Having said this, only a select few trails in Banff National Park are able to accommodate horses, so I recommend taking a trip organized by a local outfitter. They'll show you a good ol' time, while keeping you on course.

Timberline Tours (www.timberlinetours.ca; ☎ 403/522-3743) leads scenic trips at Lake Louise. A half-day outing is between C$159 and C$239, while overnight trips start at C$650. **Banff Trail Riders** (132 Banff Ave.; www.horseback.com; ☎ 800/661-8352 or 403/762-4551) has a corral at the Fairmont Banff Springs Hotel, where it runs 1-hour tours along the Spray River (C$64). It has another corral at Martin Stables (located on the banks of the Bow River across from Banff townsite), where 2-hour

Rafting down the Bow River.

trips head into the Sundance Range (C$119). It also organizes wonderfully fun wilderness cookouts, which include a Cowboy Cookout Lunch (C$152). All prices are per person.

Rafting

The gnarliest rapids in the Canadian Rockies are west of Banff on the Kicking Horse River (p 111, ❸) and east of Banff on the Kananaskis River. From the Town of Banff, you can hop on a gentle float trip down the Bow River. It's great for families. **Rocky Mountain Raft Tours** (www.banffrafttours.com; ☎ 403/762-3632) departs from just below Bow Falls and drops you at Canmore for C$60 for adults, C$20 for youth 15 and under.

Swimming

The spring-fed outdoor pools at the historic **Banff Upper Hot Springs** (p 14, ❼) make for a memorable dip any time of year. On a hot summer day, join the locals for an afternoon swim at **Johnson Lake** on the Minnewanka Loop. Throughout the year, the nicest indoor pool in Banff is at the sunny Banff Centre's **Sally Borden Centre** (St. Julien Rd.; ☎ 403/762-6450).

Going for a swim at Johnson Lake.

Winter Sports

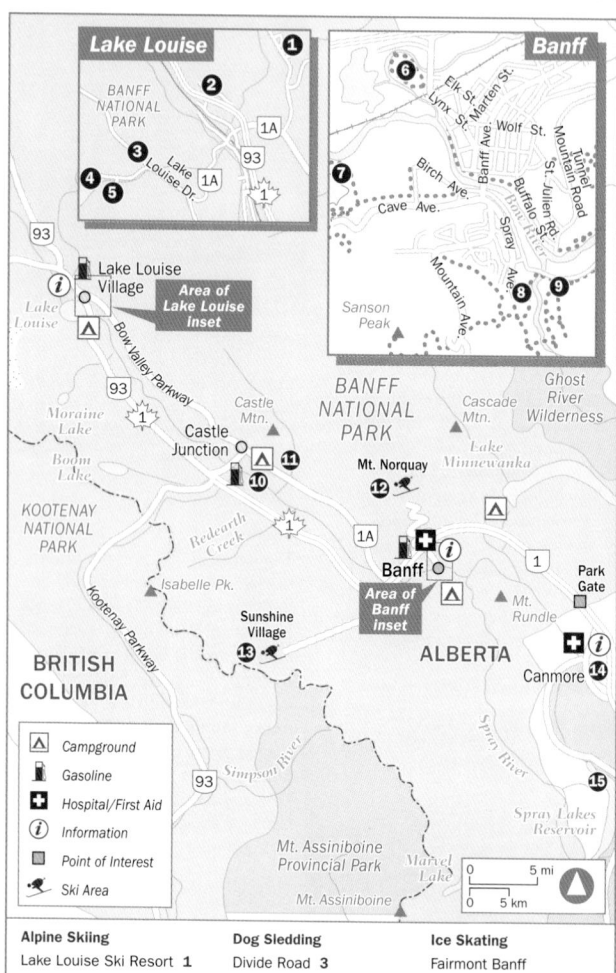

Alpine Skiing
Lake Louise Ski Resort **1**
Mt. Norquay **12**
Sunshine Village **13**

Cross-Country Skiing
Golf Course Trail/
Spray River Loop **9**
Pipestone **2**

Dog Sledding
Divide Road **3**
Spray Lakes **15**

Ice Climbing
Yamnuska Inc. **14**

Ice Walks
Johnston Canyon **11**

Ice Skating
Fairmont Banff
Springs Hotel **8**
Lake Louise **4**
Vermillion Lakes **7**

Snowshoeing
Fairview Lookout **5**
Fenland Trail **6**
Moose Meadows **10**

Winter is breathtaking in the Canadian Rockies, in both beauty and temperature. Days can drop to –15 °C (5°F) or lower, but you'll be too busy sampling the many adventures available—some you may have never experienced before—to care. Dress warmly, keep a pair of gloves and hat nearby, and make the most of the legendarily clear and sunny days and starry nights.

Alpine Skiing

Lake Louise Ski Resort. The views here will have you picking your jaw up off the glistening powder snow. Easy to access and full of varied terrain, Louise keeps folks loyal. Beginners will find a friendly ski and snowboard school, as well as some lovely green runs to get started. Head straight to the top of the Grizzly Express Gondola for more advanced blue runs. Larch is a great place for intermediates. Expert skiers should take to the Top of the World "Six-Pack" Chair and then the Summit Platter and enjoy powder bowls like West Bowl and Boomerang. There is a terrain park with jumps, obstacles, and railings. Cozy and rustic Temple Lodge, tucked in behind the resort below Whitehorn Mountain, is a good lunch restaurant while Whitehorn Lodge has amazing views. *Follow Whitehorn Rd. off Trans-Canada Hwy. 1 at the Lake Louise exit. www.skilouise.com.* ☎ *800/258-7669 or 403/522-3555.*

Downhill skiing at Lake Louise Ski Resort.

Mt. Norquay. At Banff's doorstep, this small resort has produced many world-class ski racers. It's got plenty of steep runs, and it's intimate and convenient, particularly their economical ski-by-the-hour deals (starting with 2 hr.), meaning you don't have to spend the entire day here to feel like you've gotten your money's worth. This is particularly appealing for beginners and families. On a powder day, head straight to the Memorial Bowl. It's open for night skiing on Fridays 5pm to 10pm. *At the end of Mt. Norquay Dr. www.banffnorquay.com.* ☎ *403/762-4421.*

Sunshine Village. Tucked high in the alpine zone in a series of scenic bowls centered around a "village" with a hotel, day lodge, ski school, and gondola station, Sunshine gets fabulous snow and has an abundance of space. It stays open weeks later than the other resorts in Banff, usually until the third week of May. Strawberry and Standish chairs are

Ski the Big Three

Ski packages that allow you to spend a day at each of Banff's three resorts are offered by the Ski Banff/Lake Louise partnership (P.O. Box 1085, Banff, AB T1L 1H9; www.skibig3.com; ☎ **877/754-7080** or 403/762-4561). Packages include lodging and lift tickets at each of the three resorts. The lift-ticket prices for adults range from C$329 for 3 out of 4 days to C$658 for 6 out of 8 days. It's a great deal and an excellent way to sample Banff's outstanding skiing. You can also book a guide or instructor to accompany you each day.

Rent downhill skis and equipment, as well as snowboarding equipment, in Banff at the **Ski Stop** (203A Bear St.; ☎ **403/762-1650**) or at the Fairmont Banff Springs Hotel (405 Spray Ave.; ☎ **403/762-5333**). In Lake Louise, rent skis, snowshoes, and snowboards at **Wilson Mountain Sports** (p 88). For a ski or snowboard tune-up, try **Ultimate Ski and Ride** (206 Banff Ave.; ☎ **403/762-0547**) or **Monod Sports** (p 87).

great for beginners. The Continental Divide has amazing views for intermediate skiers. Goat's Eye Mountain is great for advanced skiers. And only experts need attempt the aptly named Delirium Dive. Advanced snowboarders will find a lot of flat terrain at Sunshine, but the terrain park has grown steadily over the years and is a fun spot for catching some air. *8km (5 miles)*

Dog sledding across a frozen lake in Banff National Park.

west of Banff townsite at the end of Sunshine Rd. www.skibanff.com. ☎ 800/661-1676 or 403/762-6500.

Cross-Country (Nordic) Skiing

A wonderful way to explore the park in winter, cross-country skiing promises great exercise, views, and solitude, if you're seeking it. **Banff National Park** has more than 80km (50 miles) of managed trails, many of them within a half-hour drive of Banff townsite. The cross-country ski season runs from December to March.

Parks Canada regularly updates trail reports online at www.pc.gc.ca/banff and ☎ **403/762-1550** for Banff townsite area or ☎ **403/522-3833** for Lake Louise.

Rent cross-country ski equipment at the **Ski Stop** (see above). In Lake Louise; rent skis and snowshoes at **Wilson Mountain Sports** (p 88).

The **Golf Course Trail** has ungroomed trails that are wide open and easy for beginners. There are no defined trails and little elevation gain here, but it's a good place to

Banff offers some of the finest ice climbing in the Rockies.

Loops are a wide range of trails across the highway from the Lake Louise village, from 1.9 to 12km (1.2–7.8 miles). All are trackset. Check at the Lake Louise Visitor Centre for updates on trail conditions.

Dog Sledding
Just over the border from Banff National Park, another classic winter tradition matches tourists up with friendly huskies for a mush across a frozen lake. It's exhilarating. Try **Snowy Owl Sled Dog Tours** (104–602 Bow Valley Pkwy., Canmore; www.snowyowltours.com; ☎ 403/678-4369). For mushing tours near Lake Louise, contact **Kingmik Dog Sled Tours** (www.kingmikdogsledtours.com; ☎ 403/763-8887).

Ice Climbing
The frozen waterfalls of Banff National Park offer some of the finest ice climbing in the world. It's an extreme sport that requires proper preparation, but it's also

get a feel for the sport. At **Moraine Lake Road,** there are 8km (5 miles) of double trackset trails, ideal for a good workout. Flat and wide, trails branch off to the west on the slopes of Mt. Fairview.

The **Spray River Loop** is a 12km (7.8 mile) trail leading behind the Fairmont Banff Springs Hotel with a 200m (656-ft.) elevation gain. Tracks are set for both skate-skiing and classic skiing. It's a good place if you want to go fast. The **Pipestone**

Steep & Deep Runs Near Banff

Two other amazing ski resorts within a few hours of the Town of Banff are worth a visit, both in the Columbia Valley in British Columbia next door. **Panorama Mountain Resort** (from Hwy. 95, turn west at the Town of Invermere and right onto Panorama Dr., 18km/11 miles to uphill; www.panoramaresort.com; ☎ **800/663-2929** or 250/342-6941) has a whopping 1,220 vertical meters (4,000 vertical ft.) and some deliciously long cruiser runs, great for high-level intermediates. There's a cozy village of condos and hotels at the base. At **Kicking Horse Mountain Resort** (from Hwy. 95, turn west at blue sign in downtown Golden, 13km/8 miles uphill; www.kickinghorseresort.com; ☎ **866/754-5425** or 250/439-5400), the snow is so famously light it's called "champagne powder." The resort will appeal mainly to advanced skiers who aren't intimidated by steep terrain and deep snow. Most of the development here has happened since 2002, and the vibe is diehard and earthy.

an exhilarating experience—technical, exciting, and beautiful. Learn to climb with the guides at **Yamnuska** (www.yamnuska.com; ☎ **403/678-4164**).

Ice Skating

There are a number of places where you can skate outdoors under the winter sky. It's an exhilarating activity that's popular with families. Try the Vermillion Lakes in the early winter before the snow starts to pile up. There's also a public outdoor rink behind the Fairmont Banff Springs Hotel and one right in town at the Banff Community High School. At the Fairmont Chateau Lake Louise, an outdoor rink on the lake has a spectacular ice castle built right on top. It's a very scenic and romantic place to skate.

Ice Walks

The frozen walls at Johnston Canyon become a winter wonderland, thanks to ice cleats and the guides from **Banff Adventures** (211 Bear St.; www.banffadventures.com; ☎ **403/762-4554**), who take visitors out for a 4-hour intimate discovery of ice.

Snowshoeing

Strapping on a pair of snowshoes opens miles and miles of possibilities

Ice walking in Johnston Canyon.

in Banff, from short strolls near town to big backcountry bowls. Most snowshoe trails follow summer hiking trails—be sure to avoid cross-country trails (groomed or not groomed), as it interferes with the skiing, and be avalanche-aware. Near the townsite, try the flat Fenland Trail. Two other great spots are Moose Meadows on the Bow Valley Parkway and Fairview Lookout above Lake Louise. Well-priced guided snowshoeing trips are also organized by the **Lake Louise Ski Resort** (www.skilouise.com; ☎ **877/956-8473** or 403/522-3555). ●

Ice skating outside the Fairmont Chateau Lake Louise.

The **Savvy Traveler**

Before You Go

Tourist Office

The **Canadian Tourism Commission** (www.canada.travel; ☎ 604/638-8300) and **Travel Alberta,** 999 8th St., Calgary (www.travelalberta.com; ☎ **800/252-3782** or 780/427-4321) are useful sources of information. The Travel Alberta site is inspiring and helps you understand the breadth of attractions in this province. You can also check out the website for the **Banff Lake Louise Tourism Bureau,** Ste. 375, Cascade Plaza, Banff Ave. (www.banfflakelouise.com; ☎ **403/762-8421**).

The Best Time to Go

Unless you are a skier, summer is the most enjoyable time of the year to be in the Canadian Rockies. However, it's also the most crowded and expensive time. Most hotels double their prices during the high season, which stretches from June through September. So consider the "shoulder seasons." In **June,** the days are luxuriously long and you can catch the early wildflowers in bloom and perhaps even some migrating caribou. In **September,** aspen and larch trees turn golden, but the midday temperature stays gloriously warm.

The Canadian Rockies are also a great destination in winter, by turns cozy, romantic, and peaceful, but also brimming with fun outdoor activities. Banff's star ski resorts—**Sunshine Village, Mount Norquay,** and **Lake Louise**—are among the best in North America. Everything in the Town of Banff stays open year-round, with many hotels dropping their prices substantially

Previous page: Northern Lights, Cascade Banff.

during the winter season, which runs from **December to late March.** Road closures throughout the Canadian Rockies are often an issue due to winter snowfall, especially in the high mountain passes.

Festivals & Special Events

JANUARY. Ice Magic Festival (www.banfflakelouise.com; ☎ **403/762-8421**) is a stellar ice-carving competition held on the frozen shores of Lake Louise.

MARCH. Lake Louise Loppet (www.calgaryskiclub.org; ☎ **403/289-0386**) is a family-friendly annual cross-country ski race that also attracts Olympians and National Ski Team members.

APRIL. The longest-running ski race in the Canadian Rockies happens each year at Mount Norquay: the **Bruno Engler Memorial Race.** It brings out old-timers and young hot shots, and lots of locals dressed in retro ski costumes. (www.banffnorquay.com; ☎ **403/762-7703**).

MAY. Say farewell to winter with a splash at Sunshine Village's **Slush Cup Beach Party Weekend** (www.skibanff.com), the last weekend of the ski season. Outdoor concerts, a beer garden, and wild folks ski-jumping across puddles are highlights.

MAY–SEPTEMBER. Every Wednesday during the summer, rain or shine, come to the **Banff Mountain Market** (www.facebook.com/banff-mountainmarket; ☎ **403/762-1200**) in Central Park for food vendors, jewelry, artisans, vegetable and fruit sellers, and general fun vibes. There's often live music as well.

JULY. Held on July 1, **Canada Day** is the anniversary of the signing of the "British North America Act" with the United Kingdom, which created the united country of Canada. Following a free pancake breakfast in Banff's Central Park, pick a good spot on Banff Avenue to take in the late afternoon parade, with cowboys and marching bands. In the evening, listen to live music in the park as fireworks light up the sky.

AUGUST. During the first weekend in August, the peaks form an amazing backdrop for 3 days of music at the annual **Canmore Folk Music Festival** (www.canmorefolkfestival. com; ☎ 403/678-2524), Alberta's longest-running folk music festival.

Since 1926, Jasper has hosted the **Jasper Heritage Pro Rodeo** (www.jasperheritagerodeo.com; ☎ 780/852-4622), featuring bareback, saddle bronc, steer wrestling, and barrel racing. A Western dance, a barbecue, and a kid's rodeo are part of the festivities.

Banff's many heritage buildings welcome visitors during **Doors Open Banff** (www.doorsopen alberta.ca; ☎ 403/762-8421) for self-guided heritage tours.

SEPTEMBER. A Banff tradition that draws runners from across Western Canada, **Melissa's Road Race** (www.banffroadrace.ca) has a 10K (6.2-mile) and 22K (13.7-mile) road route, with proceeds going to the Banff community. It sells out months ahead of time, but spectators can catch the action at the finish line at the Banff Recreational Grounds.

OCTOBER–NOVEMBER. Each year, the Banff Centre hosts the **Banff Centre Mountain Film and Book Festival** (www.banffcentre.ca; ☎ 403/762-6301), celebrating the spirit of those who live in the mountains. If you're a keen armchair adventurer, it's best to buy a weekend pass, which gets you into

plenty of screenings and lectures and gives you a chance to rub shoulders with some of the finest adventurers from around the world.

NOVEMBER–DECEMBER. From a World Cup Alpine ski race to a Santa Claus Parade, a series of events ring in the winter—arguably the season locals love best (www. banfflakelouise.com; ☎ 403/762-8421).

The Weather
Despite the Canadian Rockies' northerly latitude, the climate actually resembles that of the Rocky Mountains south of the United States border because the altitude isn't as high as it is in the U.S. Rockies. Snow at lower elevations usually disappears by May but sometimes hangs around the higher elevations well into the summer. Although it often rains for at least a week in June, and you can expect a cold rain or wet snowfall in July, the summer climate is generally very pleasant, with warm days and low humidity. Evenings almost always require a sweater. Rain clouds often gather along the Continental Divide, so don't be disappointed to come all the way here and not be able to see the high peaks right away. July temperatures typically hit 68° to 77°F (20°–25°C). Spring and fall days are usually fine and bright, though evenings can be cool.

In January, though the lows can drop way down to –22°F (–30°C), the winter sunshine and blue skies are the stuff of legend.

Useful Websites
In addition to the websites at the opening of this chapter, check out:

• **www.parkscanada.gc.ca:** Incredibly useful information on all the area's national parks.

AVERAGE MONTHLY TEMPERATURES & RAINFALL

	JAN	FEB	MAR	APR	MAY	JUNE
High °F/°C	23/-5	32/0	40/4	49/9	57/14	72/20
Low °F/°C	5/-15	13/-11	18/-8	27/-3	31/2	41/5
Days of Precip.	12	10	11	11	16	18

	JULY	AUG	SEPT	OCT	NOV	DEC
High °F/°C	82/25	88/24	66/17	50/10	32/1	23/-5
Low °F/°C)	45/7	44/7	38/3	32/-1	18/-8	7/-14
Days of Precip.	19	14	11	11	13	12

- **www.banfflakelouise.com:** Comprehensive events and tips from the local tourism bureau.

- **www.crowfootmedia.com:** A site with inspiring stories and profiles of local characters that delves into what it means to live in this majestic place.

- **www.banff.ca:** The site for the Town of Banff has useful details for visitors, including information on the public-transit system.

Cellphones

The cellular phone coverage in the Canadian Rockies has improved dramatically. In the Town of Banff, as in other towns like Canmore, Lake Louise, and Jasper, coverage is good. In between these spots, though, coverage is not consistent, and service often drops. For example, your coverage will likely cut out as you drive from Banff to Lake Louise. Phones using CDMA network technology—currently the most common type in use in both Canada and the U.S.—will work in Canada in places with reception. GSM/GPRS phones—the dominant standard pretty much everywhere else—also work here, thanks to roaming agreements. Before leaving home, be sure to update your phone's roaming software to assure good connectivity. And check with your provider to see what kind of international usage fees may apply. For information on landlines and international calls, see "Telephones" in the "Fast Facts" section below.

Car Rentals

Most visitors to Banff and Jasper national parks will fly to either Calgary or Edmonton and rent a car to get to the parks. Though frequent and good shuttle service is available from the Calgary International Airport to several locations around Banff (see "By Plane" below), it's a good idea to rent a car to get around for the duration of your trip.

Getting There

By Plane

Both the **Calgary International Airport (YYC;** www.yyc.com; ☎ 877/254-7427 or 403/735-1200) and the **Edmonton International** Airport (**EIA;** https://flyeia.com; ☎ 800/268-7134) service the Canadian Rockies. If you are heading to Banff National Park, fly to Calgary and from there take the

Banff Airporter (https://banffair porter.com; ☎ 888/449-2901 or 403/762-3330; C$68 one-way or C$138 round-trip). Banff is 129km (80 miles) west of Calgary. It's about 90 minutes by car from the airport.

If you want to visit Jasper National Park first, fly to Edmonton (363km/225 miles east of Jasper; a 4-hr. trip by car). Many people visiting Jasper go first to Banff via Calgary and then drive north. Others do the trip in reverse.

By Car

If you're driving into Banff National Park from the east, take the **Trans-Canada Highway (Hwy. 1)** west from Calgary. The park's eastern gate is 129km (80 miles) west of the **Calgary International Airport,** just west of the Town of Canmore. If you are coming to Banff from the west, you have two options. From central British Columbia, you can take the Trans-Canada Highway east via the Town of **Golden, BC,** and Yoho National Park, and enter Banff just west of the village of Lake Louise.

The other option, from southeastern British Columbia, is to take Hwy. 93 north into Banff via the Town of **Radium Hot Springs, BC,** and Kootenay National Park. See chapter 5 for more information on planning a side trip to Golden, BC, or Radium Hot Springs, BC.

If you're approaching the parks from the city of Edmonton, which is to the north, you'll get to Jasper National Park first. Take **Hwy. 16** (the Yellowhead Hwy.) west to Jasper National Park's eastern gate (363km/225 miles west of Edmonton International Airport). From north-central British Columbia, you can take Hwy. 16 east to Jasper National Park via **Prince George, BC,** and Mount Robson Provincial Park.

Vancouver is 858km (532 miles) west of Banff and 863km (535 miles) west of Jasper.

By Train

VIA Rail Canada (www.viarail.ca; ☎ 888/842-7245) services Jasper National Park on its Edmonton–Vancouver run, which takes about 16 hours direct. Most trains from major Canadian and U.S. centers connect to this route. Check with VIA Rail Canada or with **Amtrak** (www.amtrak.com; ☎ 800/872-7245).

There is no VIA Rail Canada service to Banff or Calgary; however, **Rocky Mountaineer Railtours** (www.rockymountaineer.com; ☎ 877/460-3200) has a stunning overnight trip that departs from Vancouver and stops in either Banff or Jasper. (You select your destination at the changeover in Kamloops, British Columbia.)

By Bus

Onlt Regional Transit (www.onit regionaltransit.ca; ☎ 587/888-5275) connects Banff with Calgary and its bedroom communities like Okotoks and Cochrane. Operating during summers only.

Getting **Around**

By Bus

Banff's **ROAM** public bus system (www.roamtransit.com; ☎ 403/762-0606) is very good and runs regularly throughout the day and will take you to the Sulphur

5

Mountain gondola, the hot springs, the Fairmont Banff Springs Hotel, and up Tunnel Mountain Road. There is also an hourly public bus to the nearby Town of Canmore and to Lake Louise and Johnston Canyon. It's the best way to avoid parking hassles. Many Banff hotels offer free bus passes to their guests to help fight congested roads in peak season. One-way fares start at C$2.

By Shuttle

In an effort to reduce congestion, Parks Canada encourages visitors to ride shuttles to popular places like Lake Louise and Johnston Canyon. Visit **www.explorethepark.ca** for updated fares and schedules.

By Car

If you are staying in the Town of Banff and not really planning on trips outside of it, you can take a shuttle from the Calgary airport and then walk, ride the local ROAM public bus system, or take a short cab ride to most attractions in town. If you plan to visit Lake Louise and Moraine Lake, you'll either take the shuttles listed above straight from Banff or drive a car, park at designated areas, and then ride a parking shuttle to the main lakes and trail heads. And if Jasper's on your itinerary, a car will be essential.

Taxi services here are very expensive. The roads are in good condition most of the year (you don't really need to rent an expensive four-wheel-drive sport-utility vehicle except during major snowstorms), and driving here is a relaxing way to soak up the gorgeous scenery.

The one downside of renting a car is that parking can be a problem in the Town of Banff and at Lake Louise. Stick to the big parking lots (in Banff there is a covered multi-story parkade on Bear St. btw. Caribou and Buffalo sts.; in Lake Louise at the Samson Mall; and in Jasper beside the Heritage Railway Station). For more information, see chapter 4.

By RV

It's not for everyone, but most people who try it discover what a joy it is to travel by recreational vehicle. An RV affords a level of independence and comfort that car travel can't. And finding a quiet campground by a river is as close to the camping experience as you can get without giving up your pillow and mattress.

More than half of the campgrounds in Banff and Jasper national parks accommodate RVs, trailers, and camper vans, and you must stay in these designated areas. In addition to navigating around campgrounds, RVs (and their drivers) need to know how to get around town, too. In the Town of Banff, there is a trailer drop-off site in the industrial area at the northeast end of Banff Avenue. You can leave your trailer here and take the car or RV itself through the streets of town. A number of larger parking lots accommodate RVs, including one near the Mineral Springs Hospital on Gopher Street and another one across from the post office on Buffalo Street, along the Bow River.

Many people come to the Rockies in an RV they've rented at the airport in Edmonton or Calgary.

For RV rentals, contact **Cana Dream** (2510 27th St. NE, Calgary, AB T1Y 7G1; www.canadream.com; ☎ **800/461-7368** or 403/291-1000).

Fast **Facts**

ATMS Banff does have its share of Automated Teller Machines (ATMs), which operate on the worldwide **Cirrus** (www.mastercard.com; ☎ 800/424-7787), **PLUS** (www.visa.com; ☎ 800/843-7587), and **Interac** (www.interac.ca; ☎ 416/362-8550) networks. Know your personal identification number (PIN) before you leave home and be sure your daily withdrawal limit will cover the amount of cash you'll need. Note that ATM fees can be higher for international transactions than for domestic. **Alberta Treasury**'s branch is at 317 Banff Ave. (☎ 403/762-8505). In Lake Louise there is an ATM in Samson Mall (☎ 403/522-3678). The **Bank of Montreal** is at 107 Banff Ave. (☎ 403/762-2275), and the **Canadian Imperial Bank of Canada (CIBC)** is at 98 Banff Ave. (☎ 403/762-3317).

BANKING HOURS Banks are generally open Monday through Friday 9:30am to 4:30pm, though some branches have hours on weekends as well.

BIKE RENTALS Bike shops will likely try to rent you their most expensive bikes. If you're a beginner mountain biker, however, and will only be heading out on a few trails around town, you do not need a full-suspension bike. If you want to just cruise the main, paved trails of the townsite, go for an inexpensive bike.

You can rent both road and mountain bikes in Banff National Park at **Soul Ski & Bike** (203 Bear St.; www.soulskiandbike.com; ☎ 403/760-1650). In addition to renting regular-size bikes for adult riders, **Banff Adventures** (211 Bear St.; www.banffadventures.com; ☎ 403/762-4554) rents kids'

bikes, trailers, and strollers, too. In Lake Louise, rent bikes at **Wilson Mountain Sports** (Samson Mall; ☎ 403/522-3636). In Jasper, the folks at **Vicious Cycle** (630 Connaught Dr.; www.viciouscanada.com; ☎ 780/852-1111) are the local experts on two-wheeling. They rent front-suspension mountain bikes that can also be used on roads. You can rent both road and mountain bikes from **Jasper Source for Sports** (406 Patricia St.; ☎ 780/852-3654).

BUSINESS HOURS Hours vary by shop, but as a general rule most open daily around 10am and stay open until at least 6pm. Shops in the Town of Banff usually stay open later. Most are open daily, though some close on Sunday.

CONSULATES & EMBASSIES The **U.S. Consulate** is at Ste. 1000, 615 Macleod Trail SW, Calgary (☎ 403/266-8962). The **British Consulate** is at Ste. 3000, 150 6th Ave. SW, Calgary (☎ 403/705-1755). The **Irish Consulate** is at 3803 8th A St. SW, Calgary (☎ 403/243-2970). The nearest **Australian Consulate** is at 2050 1075 W. Georgia St., Vancouver (☎ 604/694-6160). The consulate of **New Zealand** is at 1050 W. Pender St., Vancouver (☎ 604/684-7388).

CURRENCY EXCHANGE Currency exchange counters can be found at the airport, but you'll get a better rate just using ATMs or at the **Custom House Global Foreign Exchange**, at 211 Banff Ave. (☎ 403/760-6630).

In Jasper, there is a currency exchange house in **Whistlers Inn** (105 Miette Ave.; ☎ 780/852-3361). Be sure to check current exchange rates before your trip via www.xe.com or any of the other major currency trackers.

CUSTOMS Non-Canadian residents will pass through **Canada Border Services** (www.cbsa-asfc.gc.ca; ☎ **800/461-9999** or 204/983-3500) upon arriving in the country. If you're concerned about items you intend to bring into the country, check the website's "Information for Visitors" section. U.S. citizens will pass through **U.S. Customs** (www.cbp.gov; ☎ **877/CBP-5511 [227-5511])** on departure from Canada. The standard personal duty-free allowance for U.S. citizens returning from Canada is US$800. There are also limits on the amount of alcoholic beverages (usually 1L), cigarettes (1 carton), cigars (100 total, and no Cubans), and other tobacco products you may include in your personal duty-free exemption. **Joint Customs declarations** are possible for family members traveling together. For instance, for a husband and wife with two children, the total duty-free exemption would be US$3,200. Note that most meat or meat products, fruits, plants, vegetables, or plant-derived products will be seized by U.S. Customs agents unless they're accompanied by an import license from a U.S. government agency.

For more specifics, visit the **U.S. Customs Service** website (www.cbp.gov). U.K. citizens should visit the **U.K. Customs and Excise** site (www.hmce.gov.uk), Australians should go to the **Australia Customs Service** (www.customs.gov.au), Kiwis should check the **New Zealand Customs Service** (www.customs.govt.nz), and citizens of Ireland should check the **Irish Revenue** site (www.revenue.ie).

DENTISTS Most major hotels have a dentist on call. **Banff Dental Care** is at 220 Bear St. (☎ **403/762-3979**). Call first for an appointment.

The clinic is open Monday and Wednesday 8am to 5pm, Tuesday and Thursday 9am to 6pm, and Friday 8am to 1pm.

DINING Eating out will be one of your highlights in Banff. For the most popular spots, reservations are recommended, and are essential on Saturday evenings or long weekends.

DOCTORS Hotels usually have a doctor on call. **Alpine Medical Clinic,** 201A-211 Bear St. (☎ **403/762-3155**), is a drop-in clinic open Monday through Thursday 8:30am to 7pm, Friday 8am to 5pm, and weekends 9am to 5pm.

ELECTRICITY Outlets and voltage (110 volts AC) are the same in Canada as in the United States, so laptops, chargers, hair dryers, and other small appliances from the U.S. will work just fine. Appliances from some other countries that work on a different voltage will require an adapter and/or converter.

EMBASSIES See "Consulates & Embassies" above.

EMERGENCIES For emergencies in Canada dial ☎ **911.**

EVENT LISTINGS Event listings are posted online by the **Banff–Lake Louise Tourism Bureau** at www.banfflakelouise.com. The free local weekly newspaper **Rocky Mountain Outlook** (www.rmoutlook.com) also is a great source for updated arts, sports, and community events. It's published on Thursdays and available throughout Banff.

FAMILY TRAVEL Banff and the Canadian Rockies are fantastically kid-friendly. Family travel websites include **Family Travel Forum** (www.familytravelforum.com), a comprehensive site that offers customized trip planning; **Family Travel Network** (www.familytravelnetwork.com), an online magazine providing travel tips; and **TravelWithYour Kids.com** (www.travelwithyourkids. com), a comprehensive site written by parents for parents offering sound advice for long-distance and international travel with children.

GAY & LESBIAN TRAVELERS **Banff Pride** (☎ **800/958-9621**) is a social networking group (www. facebook.com/BanffPRIDE) for Banff residents and visitors. **Banff Gay Weddings** (www.banffgay weddings.com; ☎ **403/609-3896**) organizes same-sex ceremonies and events. Banff and its neighboring towns are gay-friendly.

HOLIDAYS Alberta has 12 public holidays throughout the year, when banks, government offices, schools, and some shops are closed: New Year's Day (Jan 1), Family Day (third Mon in Feb), Good Friday (the Fri before Easter), Easter Monday (the day after), Victoria Day (the Mon before May 25), Canada Day (July 1), Heritage Day (first Mon in Aug), Labour Day (first Mon in Sept), Thanksgiving (second Mon in Oct), Remembrance Day (Nov 11), Christmas (Dec 25), and Boxing Day (Dec 26).

INSURANCE The cost of travel insurance varies widely, depending on the destination, the cost and length of your trip, your age and health, and the type of trip you're taking. You can get estimates from various providers through **Insure MyTrip.com** (www.insuremytrip. com). Enter your trip cost and dates, your age, and other information, for prices from more than a dozen companies.

Medical Insurance: Most U.S. health plans do not provide coverage outside of the U.S., and the ones that do often require you to pay for services upfront and reimburse you only after you return home. As a safety net, you may want to buy travel medical

insurance from providers like **MEDEX Assistance** (www.medex assist.com; ☎ **410/453-6300**) or **Travel Assistance International** (www.travelassistance.com; ☎ **800/821-2828**).

Trip-Cancellation Insurance: Trip-cancellation insurance typically covers you if you have to back out of a trip (due to illness, and so on), if your travel supplier goes bankrupt, if there's a natural disaster, or if your government advises against travel to your destination. Some plans cover cancellations for any reason. **TravelSafe** (☎ **888/885-7233;** www.travelsafe.com) offers both types of coverage. **Expedia** (www.expedia.com) also offers any-reason cancellation coverage for its air-hotel packages. Other recommended insurers include: **Access America** (www.accessamerica.com; ☎ **866/807-3982**); **Travel Guard International** (www.travelguard. com; ☎ **800/826-4919**); **Travel Insured International** (www.travel insured.com; ☎ **800/243-3174**); and **Travelex Insurance Services** (www.travelex-insurance.com; ☎ **888/457-4602**).

Lost-Luggage Insurance: If your luggage is lost, immediately file a lost-luggage claim at the airport, detailing the luggage contents. Most airlines require that you report delayed, damaged, or lost baggage within 4 hours of arrival. On international flights, baggage coverage is limited to approximately US$9.07 per pound, up to approximately US$635 per checked bag. If you plan to check items more valuable than what's covered by the standard liability, see if your homeowner's policy covers your valuables, or get baggage insurance as part of your comprehensive travel-insurance package.

INTERNET ACCESS Almost all hotels, cafes, and restaurants in the

Canadian Rockies now provide free Wi-Fi. There's even free Wi-Fi in some Parks Canada campgrounds.

LIQUOR LAWS The legal drinking age in Alberta is 18. In British Columbia it is 19. Bars, lounges, and restaurants that serve alcohol all close between midnight and 2am, depending on when they got their liquor license. Hard liquor, beer, and wine are available at privately owned liquor stores in Alberta. Specialty wine stores (p 86 lists some of the best) mostly stick to the grape, but usually also carry a small selection of beer and spirits.

LOST PROPERTY Lost items are often turned in to the **Town of Banff,** where they are kept for 30 days. Contact ☎ **403/762-1218** daily between 8am and 6pm for inquiries. There is also an online Lost Property Report available at the town's website, www.banff.ca. Outside the Town of Banff, try **Parks Canada** at ☎ **403/762-1550.**

If you lose your passport, contact your country's embassy or consulate immediately (see "Consulates & Embassies," above).

MAIL & POSTAGE Mailing a letter within Canada costs C$1.05. To the U.S., it's C$1.27. To all other international destinations, it's C$2.65. The main **post office** in Banff is at 204 Buffalo St. (www.canadapost. ca; ☎ 403/762-2586), across from Central Park. You can also buy stamps at many drugstores and convenience stores.

MONEY Canada's money is denominated the same as U.S. dollars, except its C$1 and C$2 denominations are coins rather than bills. The C$1 coin is known as a "loonie" as it has the image of a common loon on one side. The C$2 coin is known as a "toonie," for obvious comedic reasons. For exchange rates, see "Currency Exchange," p 167.

NEWSPAPERS & MAGAZINES The major newspapers in Alberta are the *Calgary Herald* (www.calgary herald.com) and the *Edmonton Journal* (www.theprovince.com), both of which publish 7 days a week.

The local weekly newspapers in Banff are the *Rocky Mountain Outlook* (www.rmoutlook.com), which publishes every Thursday, and the *Crag & Canyon* (www. thecragandcanyon.com), which hits stands on Tuesdays.

PARKING See "Getting Around: By Car," p 166.

PASSPORTS U.S. citizens traveling to Canada by any means—air, sea, car, bus, train, or on foot—will need a passport but no visa. The same applies for citizens of the United Kingdom, Australia, Ireland, and New Zealand. If you're a citizen of another country, check the **Canada Border Services Agency** website, www.cbsa-asfc.gc.ca/travel-voyage, for specific requirements.

For safety, make two photocopies of your passport before leaving home. Take one set with you as a backup (keeping it separate from the original) and leave one at home.

PERMITS Every visitor to a national park is required to have a permit (also known as a pass). You can pick one up at a park gate or information center inside the park. Permits are valid in all Canadian Rocky Mountain national parks (Banff, Jasper, Yoho, Kootenay, Waterton Lakes, and Glacier national parks). A day pass costs C$9.80 for adults, C$8.30 for seniors, and C$4.90 for children. More economical is the Annual Pass, which is a good idea if you're planning to stay for a few days and visit more than one park. It's valid for 1 year from the purchase date for unlimited entries to every one of Canada's national parks, coast to coast. Individual rates are C$68 for adults, C$58 for seniors, and C$33 for children ages 6 to 12. The pass is free for children ages 5 and under. For groups of 2 to 7, this pass costs C$136, making it the best deal for most visitors.

Permits are also required for backcountry camping and fishing inside the National Parks. For more information, visit **www.pc.gc.ca**.

PET-FRIENDLY TRAVEL While Banff has a few hotels that welcome pets, in general the Canadian Rockies aren't particularly pet-friendly. This is mainly because of the importance placed on the health of the local wildlife populations. Keep your dog on a leash at all times, especially in campgrounds and on hiking trails. To wildlife like elk, wolves, bears, and cougars, your dog may look an awful lot like dinner. Avoid any areas in the parks where the potential for wildlife encounters is high (ask at an information center), and take your dog for a walk only during daylight hours. Do not leave your dog unattended outside. Unrestrained pets have been known to harass wildlife, provoke attacks, and endanger people. And please pick up after your pooch—the "leave no trace" principle applies to pets, too.

PHARMACIES The biggest pharmacy in the Town of Banff is **Rexall Drug Store,** lower level of Cascade Plaza (317 Banff Ave.; ☎ **403/762-2245**).

POLICE Call ☎ **911** for emergencies.

SAFETY Don't drink the water from any streams, rivers, or lakes in Banff or Jasper national parks. A waterborne parasite called *Giardia lamblia* can cause an illness known in Canada as "beaver fever." It is transmitted via infected animal feces and can cause serious and prolonged gastrointestinal problems.

Also be on the lookout for **wood ticks**—small, flat-bodied, spiderlike insects that bite humans and can carry **Rocky Mountain spotted fever** and **Lyme disease** (although the latter is rare in the northern Rockies). They usually abound in dry, grassy slopes in the spring. If you're hiking through such an area, give yourself a good once-over at the end of the day. If in doubt, drop by the **Mineral Springs Hospital** in Banff to see a doctor (301 Lynx St.; ☎ **403/762-2222**). In Jasper, go to **Seton General Hospital** (518 Robson St.; ☎ **780/852-3344**). There has been no evidence of West Nile virus in the Canadian Rockies.

Hiking in the mountains is so beautiful that it may make you feel lightheaded. But lightheadedness may also be a sign of **altitude sickness.** Although elevations in the Canadian Rockies aren't as high as in the Colorado and Montana Rockies, you can still feel the altitude. People with severe heart or lung conditions should take note. Others should bring along some headache medicine and drink plenty of water.

You'll also be closer to the sun in the mountains, so wear a **sun hat** and **sunscreen.** Beyond the sun, cold and rain are the other weather factors that could hamper your holiday. Check the latest weather forecast before heading out. Always pack a rain jacket and warm clothing in your daypack. And always carry a **first-aid kit,** both in your car and in your pack. At the very least, it should include latex gloves (to prevent spreading infections), butterfly bandages, sterile gauze pads, adhesive tape, antibiotic ointment, pain relievers (for kids and adults), alcohol pads, knife, scissors, and tweezers.

Hiking in Banff involves moving through bear country and you should be prepared to encounter a bear at any time. Carry bear spray and know how to use it. Make noise while you hike, keep your dog on a leash and hike in groups. Pick up the "Hiking in Bear Country" pamphlet from Parks Canada for more information.

In terms of personal safety in the mountains, be aware that almost any slope is a potential **avalanche** chute—and even small avalanches can be deadly. Drivers should avoid stopping in places where there are signs that read NO STOPPING, AVALANCHE AREA. Anyone venturing into the backcountry—especially in winter—should know how to recognize and travel in avalanche terrain. Call ☎ **403/762-1460** in Banff or ☎ **780/852-6176** in Jasper for the latest avalanche hazard reports from Parks Canada.

There is also a risk of getting hit by falling rock and ice or slipping into a glacier crevasse, particularly in Jasper National Park. Do not ignore the signs telling you to stay back from the **Angel Glacier** at **Mt. Edith Cavell** or the **Athabasca Glacier,** both in Jasper. These can be—and have been—deadly.

Don't leave valuables in your car or unattended in public places. This also applies to hiking trail heads.

The Canadian Government website **www.safecanada.ca** has a list of safety tips in case you need something to worry about.

SENIOR TRAVELERS   Shops, hotels, attractions, and services throughout Western Canada often offer discounts for people 65 and over.

SMOKING   Smoking is prohibited in all public places in Alberta and British Columbia, including bars, clubs, and restaurants.

TAXES   All hotels, restaurants, gift shops, and services charge the 5% goods and services tax (GST) on all purchases. (*Note:* A program that allowed foreigners to receive a rebate for the GST spent during their time in Canada was cancelled in 2007.) There is no provincial sales tax in Alberta. In British Columbia, an additional provincial sales tax of 7% is charged on purchased goods.

TELEPHONES   **Dialing within Alberta** requires you to use full 10-digit phone numbers, including the area code, of which there are two in Alberta: 403 and 780. To reach the British Columbia side of the Canadian Rockies, first dial 250. **Phoning between the U.S. and Canada** requires no special trick: Just dial 1 plus the area code and local number, as you would between states in the U.S. **To dial other countries** direct from Banff, dial the international access code (011), followed by the relevant country code (61 for Australia, 353 for Ireland, 64 for New Zealand, and 44 for the U.K.) and the local number with area code, if applicable. **To call Banff from outside North America,** dial the international access code (00 from the U.K., Ireland, or New Zealand, or 0011 from Australia), the country code (1), and then the local number with area code. For information on cellphone service, see "Cellphones," p 164.

TIME ZONE   Alberta and the B.C. Rockies are located in the Mountain time zone, 7 hours behind Greenwich Mean Time (changing to the Pacific time zone between Golden and Revelstoke). The area observes daylight saving time from the second Sunday in March to the first Sunday in November.

TIPPING   Customary tipping amounts are the same in Banff and the rest of Canada as in major U.S. cities, with a target of 15% for restaurants and taxis. (Though many people round that up to 20%.) If porters help with your bags at hotels or airports, the usual tip is C$1 per bag (or C$2 if it's heavy).

TOILETS Public toilets are increasingly easy to find in Banff. In fact, there are now nine facilities dotted around the main area of town, including the Whyte Museum, the Public Library, and Central Park. You can also find facilities at the corner of Wolf Street and Banff Avenue, and in the Parks Canada Administration Building, just across the Bow River Bridge. In Lake Louise, there are facilities in the Visitor Centre, in the main parking lot at the lakeshore, and in the Fairmont Chateau Lake Louise.

TOURIST OFFICES The following on-the-ground tourist centers can help with information, maps, suggestions, and booking accommodations: **Banff Visitor Centre** is at 224 Banff Ave. (☎ **403/762-1550**), and a similar location at the **Lake Louise Visitor Centre,** in Samson Mall, 101 Lake Louise Dr. (☎ **403/522-3833**). The **Jasper National Park Information Centre** is at 500 Connaught Dr. (☎ **780/852-6716**). Just before you enter Banff National Park, you can visit the **Travel Alberta Visitor Information Centre** in Canmore at 2801 Bow Valley Parkway (☎ **800/252-3782** or 403/678-5277), which is right off the Trans-Canada Hwy. 1.

TOURS **Brewster Sightseeing** (P.O. Box 1140, Banff, AB T1L 1J3; www.banffjaspercollection.ca; ☎ **877/791-5500** or 403/762-6700) knows Banff better than any other tour operator and has a long history of guiding here to prove it. It offers many sightseeing tours in both Banff and Jasper. Taking even the 3-hour "Discover Banff with Banff Gondola" tour will teach you more than you'll ever learn on your own.

Discover Banff Tours (215 Banff Ave., P.O. Box 1566, Banff, AB T1L 1B5; www.banfftours.com; ☎ **877/565-9372** or 403/760-5007) leads small groups on interpretive tours of all the highlights in Banff National Park, including the Town of Banff, Lake Louise, and Moraine Lake, as well as the Icefields Parkway. Morning and evening wildlife-viewing tours are really nice.

TRAVELERS WITH DISABILITIES The museums and visitor centers in Banff are all wheelchair-accessible. Most hotels now have at least one wheelchair-accessible room. The **Upper Hot Springs** in Banff National Park and the Radium Hot Springs in Kootenay National Park are friendly to those with mobility restraints.

If you are planning on car camping, head for Tunnel Mountain, Johnston Canyon, Lake Louise, or Waterfowl Lakes campgrounds. In Jasper National Park, try Whistlers, Wapiti, or Wabasso.

Signs clearly mark which trails in the parks are paved. In Banff, try the asphalt-covered Sundance Trail. There is an adjustable-height viewing scope at Bow Summit. The Lakeside Trail at Lake Louise is another wheelchair-accessible trail. Wheelchair-friendly trails in Jasper include the Clifford E. Lee Trail at Lake Edith/Annette and the Maligne Lake Trail, as well as points along Maligne Canyon, at Pyramid Island, and the interpretive loop at the Pocahontas Coal Mine Trail.

WEIGHTS & MEASURES Canada uses the metric system. Remember: 1km = 0.62 miles, 1 liter = 0.26 gallons, 1 kilogram = 2.2 pounds, and Celsius temperatures are based on 0 being the freezing point (in Fahrenheit measurement it's 32).

A Brief **History**

175 MILLION YEARS AGO The Rocky Mountains are formed as the Pacific tectonic plate moves under the North American plate.

11,000 B.C. Early archaeological records date the presence of peoples like the Crees, Kootenays, and Plains Blackfoot to have lived, fished, and hunted in the vast Rocky Mountains.

1754 The first recorded visit of a European to the Rockies is made by Anthony Hendy.

1800 Legendary explorer and mapmaker David Thompson explores the Bow Valley.

1841 George Simpson, the Governor of the Hudson's Bay Company, is the first known European to visit the Town of Banff area.

1871 As part of a deal to unite British Columbia with the rest of Canada, the Canadian government forms the Canadian Pacific Railway (CPR) to construct a railway across the new nation.

1882 Tom Wilson, a CPR guide, becomes the first non-Native man to see Lake Louise, with the help of his Stoney partner.

1883 Three railway workers stumble upon a series of hot springs on the lower slopes of Sulphur Mountain.

1885 Canada's first national park is formed in Banff, preserving 26 sq. km (10 sq. miles) surrounding the hot springs. The reserve is increased to 670 sq. km (259 sq. miles) in 1887 and 7,125 sq. km (2,751 sq. miles) in 1917.

1886 Construction of the Canadian Pacific Railway is completed. Banff is named after the Scottish district "Banffshire," birthplace of two of the CPR's directors, Lord Strathcona and George Stephen.

1888 The CPR opens the elegant log-framed 250-room Banff Springs Hotel, the most expensive hotel in the world at the time.

1890 A log cabin is built on the shores of Lake Louise, soon to be replaced by a larger "chateau."

1917 The Federal Government passes the first National Parks Act in the world.

1921 A road is completed linking Banff and Lake Louise, ushering in the era of car-based tourism.

1928 A log cabin is built at the site of today's Sunshine Village as a stopover for horse trekkers.

1936 Temple Lodge is built across the Bow Valley from Lake Louise, the beginning of the Lake Louise ski resort's history.

1941 The first rope tows are installed at Sunshine Village ski resort.

1956 The Trans-Canada Hwy. 1 is completed through Banff and Yoho national parks.

1961 Paving of the Icefields Parkway is completed.

1985 Banff, Jasper, Yoho, and Kootenay national parks, along with four adjacent provincial parks, are declared a World Heritage Site by UNESCO.

1990 Thanks to a joint agreement between local citizens and the federal and provincial governments, Banff becomes a self-governing municipality within the Province of Alberta, the only incorporated municipality within a Canadian national park.

1998 The Delirium Dive area, a mecca for extreme skiers, is reopened at Sunshine Village.

1999 Parks Canada begins requiring hikers to travel in tight groups of four in high grizzly bear territory, especially around Moraine Lake during peak summer hiking season.

2007 Banff's downtown core undergoes a redevelopment to replace dated infrastructure, making it more pedestrian-friendly.

2014 Banff and nearby Canmore host the 2014 Alberta Winter Games.

Airline Websites

AIR CANADA
www.aircanada.ca
ALASKA AIRLINES
www.alaskaair.com
AMERICAN AIRLINES
www.aa.com
BRITISH AIRWAYS
www.britishairways.com

DELTA AIR LINES
www.delta.com
FRONTIER AIRLINES
www.flyfrontier.com
UNITED AIRLINES
www.united.com
WESTJET
www.westjet.com

6

Index

See also Accommodations and Restaurant indexes, below.

Notes

Photo **Credits**

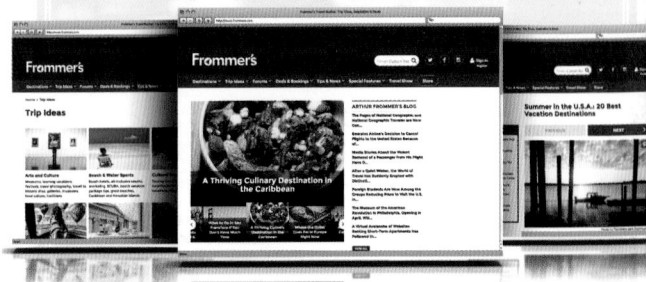